Praise for
RISE SPEAK CHANGE:
The Girls Write Now 2017 Anthology

"Now, more than ever, the luminous and necessary work of Girls Write Now is essential in encouraging girls and young women to author their own narratives, a form of empowerment that lasts a lifetime."

—HALA ALYAN, author of *Salt Houses*

"The power of words has created my entire past, present, and future. How we articulate the world around us shapes reality. There is nothing more important than the next generation of women using the power of language to impact their own lives and the lives of others."

—SOPHIA AMORUSO, founder and author of *#Girlboss*

"This year's Girls Write Now anthology continues to exemplify the power of words and the power the ladies who wield them have to make their voices known. Uplifting to read at any age and by anyone, this compendium showcases the voices of a generation ready to persevere because they deserve to be heard. I hope we're all listening and listening intently."

—JENNIFER BAKER, creator and host of
Minorities in Publishing podcast and
Girls Write Now mentor alum

"There is power in telling a story, and immense power is given to those with the permission to tell them. Women and girls have long had their power usurped, but Girls Write Now gives power to young women whose stories not only deserve to be told, but need to be heard. By everyone. The revolution is on the page, in black and white, in their own voices."

—TRACEY BAPTISTE, author of *The Jumbies*

"Each word in this volume is a whisper in the dark—a lifeline to a fundamental truth that the world, again and again, hides from girls: that you matter; your story matters; your voice matters; your impact on the wide world matters. The path from girlhood to womanhood is dark and twisted and terrifying, and it is ever so easy to become lost, or injured, or diminished. What helps us make it through are stories. They are maps, lamps, sturdy boots, swords, shields. Stories defend us, nurture us, bind us to one another and bind us to ourselves. I can think of no greater gift to give to a girl about to make this journey. Godspeed to you, my darlings!"

—KELLY BARNHILL, author of
The Girl Who Drank the Moon

"Girls Write Now is a gift to young women who want to explore their artistic and comedic voices. I was so impressed by the honesty in each young writer's piece, as well as the girls' commitment to helping each other. These ladies have the goods!"

—KRISTEN BARTLETT, writer for *Saturday Night Live*

"Girls Write Now is both parts platform and advocate; for voices of young women writers, emerging and becoming their own."

—MAHOGANY L. BROWNE, author of
"Black Girl Magic"

"Encouragement is essential in every girl's life; every time I have been given a moment to speak and express myself, I have grown. Girls Write Now gives girls these moments to grow into creators, speakers, and leaders who believe their stories are important."

—RHEA BUTCHER, creator and star of *Take My Wife*

"Girls Write Now showcases the power of what happens when we set young women's voices free. This anthology is full of essential, passionate, and creative writing that will motivate you, too, to *Rise Speak Change*. I know I will sleep better at night with this important reminder that the future is female."

—JULIE BUXBAUM, author of *Tell Me Three Things*

"These girls inspire me to be better, stronger, more liberated, to take more risks, to love completely, to use suffering as a catalyst for poetry and stories, and to persevere through the darkest nights of the soul. They are beautiful, and they will run the world some day. When they take over, we'll be in good hands."

—ROSANNE CASH, author of *Composed*

"Girls Write Now is doing deeply important work—young women, now more than ever, must claim their own stories."

—EMMA CLINE, author of *The Girls*

"Girls Write Now is the kind of program you hope is around for the next gabillion years. The young women in this program are so intelligent, funny, and inspiring. I hope that their voices will only get louder."

—JO FIRESTONE, writer for
The Tonight Show Starring Jimmy Fallon

"The urgency that fuels the writing in this anthology—the passion and fury and hunger for change—is as inspiring as the words themselves. These dynamic young women demand that we sit up, open our ears, our minds, and our hearts. We would all do well to heed their call."

—GAYLE FORMAN, author of *If I Stay*

"This book is a resounding affirmation of young female life, in all its multiplicity."

—TAVI GEVINSON, editor of *Rookie*

"Through Girls Write Now, girls are given the most important gift: a courageous voice. Through their stories and writings, the young women in this program become powerful agents for change and transformation in their own lives, their communities, and the broader world."

—KARINA GLASER, author of
The Vanderbeekers of 141st Street

"When women have the agency to write stories, they take back the power of creating narrative—no matter what gender those narratives represent. Girls Write Now is helping to foster that power in the next generation of women writers."

—ILANA GLAZER, co-creator and co-star of *Broad City*

"Dear Future: Meet your leaders. Girls Write Now is training a generation of blazing, brilliant women who prove in this anthology that they are already sharp advocates for themselves, for their communities, and for the world at large, thank goodness. I can't wait to see what these young women will do next."

—LAUREN GROFF, author of *Fates and Furies*

"Once again we are reckoning with just how profoundly our world is affected by the stories we tell and retell. Girls Write Now ensures that young women get to be the authors and the protagonists of those stories. It is more important than ever that girls have the tools to tell their stories and the audiences who will listen. In a world that is gleefully silencing women, we must encourage them to shout, and scribble, and rhyme, and narrate, and imagine. I am honored to be in solidarity with Girls Write Now."

—MELISSA HARRIS-PERRY, editor at large of *Elle.com* and Maya Angelou presidential chair at Wake Forest University

"The female point of view is so vast and diverse—it is essential that more women create stories from their personal perspective to help further reflect the world we live in. Girls Write Now provides invaluable support in this mission."

—ABBI JACOBSON, co-creator and co-star of *Broad City*

"When you give girls the tools and space to share what lights them up, they set the world on fire. The spirit, the passion, and the undeniable talent of the young women who are a part of Girls Write Now offer up the hope we need right now—the kind of hope we always need. Brave, bold, and bright."

—KELLY JENSEN, editor of
Here We Are: Feminism for the Real World

"In a year that has seen women and girls on every continent marching in the streets, one thing has become increasingly clear: a girl's voice is the most powerful part of her body. A voice gives a girl the power to call others to action, to speak truth to power—for herself and on behalf of others—and to

demand real change. Girls Write Now brings together some of the most potent and passionate young voices on issues of personal and political import. Make no mistake: they will be heard."
—LACY M. JOHNSON, author of *The Other Side*

"There is nothing more glorious than a young woman who is not afraid to speak her mind and write her story. It keeps us all sane."
—MAIRA KALMAN, author of *The Principles of Uncertainty*

"Girls Write Now provides an incredible service: mentorship and support for young writers. But those young writers provide us an even more incredible gift: their voices and stories; their insight, honesty, and nerve. Their voices are vital and vibrant and we are lucky to have them. What a joy and an honor to get to bear witness and read such important and triumphant work."
—SARAH KAY, author of *No Matter the Wreckage*

"Fresh, energetic, essential—this vibrant anthology celebrates the stories of young women in a way that feels more vital now than ever. Here are the voices of our future."
—DEBORAH LANDAU, author of *The Uses of the Body*

"We become strong women when we find our voices and tell our truths with unflinching honesty, even in the hardest times. What does it take to be a girl right now? How do we thrive? *Rise Speak Change* offers brave answers."
—MEG MEDINA, author of *Burn Baby Burn*

"The revolution is now and girls are leading the way! They are not afraid to speak up. These are the voices of our future leaders, activists, change makers. Give this book to all the girls and boys in your life. Give it to all the adults. Read it. Listen to their words. This is the revolution."

—ELLEN OH, CEO and president of
We Need Diverse Books

"Never has the mission of Girls Write Now—to empower young women to use their voices to effect change—been more urgent, and never has it been more resonant on a national scale."

—LAUREN OLIVER, author of
Before I Fall and the Delirium trilogy

"Frankly, I'm jealous of the young women who have Girls Write Now as a community and source of encouragement, and I wish I'd had that as a young book nerd, writing alone in my bedroom. Even now as an established writer, I'm so grateful for the hope it gives me."

—MORGAN PARKER, author of
There Are More Beautiful Things Than Beyoncé

"Giving young women the ability to express themselves with clarity and force is an act of great potential social and political power. Girls Write Now harnesses that power."

—ZADIE SMITH, author of *Swing Time*

"Girls Write Now is electric, filled with more ideas, energy, and power than all the lightbulbs in the Empire State Building. If these girls are the future, which of course they are, the future is glorious."

—EMMA STRAUB, author of *Modern Lovers* and
Girls Write Now mentor alum

"Writing is one of our most powerful forms of self-expression. It helps us discover who we are at the deepest levels of our beings. By offering girls the opportunity to find and share their unique and authentic voices, Girls Write Now illuminates paths to perspectives that might not otherwise be heard. Their writing reminds us all that stories and what they teach us truly matter and can make a profound difference in the way we experience our world and the way we see ourselves."

—RUTH WARINER, author of *The Sound of Gravel*

"There is nothing more vital than giving young women the tools to craft their own narratives. Girls Write Now is uniquely necessary—now more than ever. Its mission to empower fresh voices will help in the writing of a more equitable future."

—ELAINE WELTEROTH, editor of *Teen Vogue*

"Girls Write Now teaches young women something radical: that their voices matter. Writing is a way to be heard, a way to find one's own power—and, as the writers in this anthology so earnestly, beautifully demonstrate, a way to empower others."

—MARA WILSON, author of *Where Am I Now?:*
True Stories of Girlhood and Accidental Fame

"To read the essays in a Girls Write Now anthology is to witness lives being changed. The girls', by their mentors. The mentors', by the girls. And, quite possibly, your own, by what you've just read."

—JENNIE YABROFF, author of *If You Were Here*

RISE SPEAK CHANGE

THE GIRLS WRITE NOW
2017 ANTHOLOGY

RISE
SPEAK
CHANGE

The Girls Write Now
2017 ANTHOLOGY

FOREWORD BY
Lisa Lucas

INTRODUCTION BY
Tanwi Nandini Islam

Published 2017

Printed in the United States of America

Print ISBN: 978-0-9962772-1-1
E-ISBN: 978-1-936932-13-9

Library of Congress Control Number: 2017940442

Cover design © Rachel Ake

Interior design by Elizabeth A. D. Eno

For information, address:

Girls Write Now, Inc.
247 West 37 Street, Suite 1000
New York, NY 10018

info@girlswritenow.org
girlswritenow.org

Foreword

LISA LUCAS

Throughout the 2016 election cycle in the United States, young women in America were told stories about women. There was endless talk about how and why women vote, about a woman's right to choose, about how women are treated, and about whether or not a woman could serve as commander in chief of the United States. Throughout all this talk, though, what stood out the most to me were the storytellers—the women who shaped the narrative.

I'm grateful for all of the women writers who reminded us, again and again, how important, how bold, how resilient, how dazzling, and how very *many* we are, and how brightly we shine when we stand together united. But how did these women come to do this work, to report the world as they see it, to tell their own stories as a way of instruction and a way to unite us? Who encouraged them to bring forth new stories, spun from nothing but their own imaginations and experience? Someone had to tell these women they *could* tell stories and that their stories were worthwhile.

That is why the stories you will read in this collection matter. Because the existence of this collection comes from that spark of encouragement, from young writers witnessing the storytellers before them. Each author within was mentored by a woman who tells her own stories, and who has taken the time to share her wisdom. Each story here is a reminder that we build writers by not only believing that they have the talent and spirit it takes to write, but also by showing them how our very voices can influence the world.

While the election in the United States has passed, the narrative for young women is still being spun, making it more important than ever for women to have a voice. In January 2017, I was able to join with more than one million women around the world, marching for what we believe in, creating a story that demands to be told. It was a powerful action, one that depended on activists mentoring activists, mothers marching with daughters, women speaking up together. In that same spirit, the stories in this anthology harness the power of women who want to raise up new voices, tell bold stories, and create a vibrant future, together.

Read them. Share them. And do whatever you can to make sure that the young women around you know how valuable to the future they are.

We need our girls right now, we need our girls to write right now, and we need Girls Write Now to help them do this profoundly important work.

LISA LUCAS is the Executive Director of the National Book Foundation. Before joining the Foundation, she served as Publisher of *Guernica* and as Director of Education at the Tribeca Film Institute. Lucas also serves on the literary council of the Brooklyn Book Festival.

RISE SPEAK CHANGE

THE GIRLS WRITE NOW
2017 ANTHOLOGY

This year's Anthology theme perfectly captures why communities like Girls Write Now must exist: to rise, to speak, to change. Such seemingly small words but, without them, where would we be?

In my first job out of college, teaching English at an underprivileged school, I was handed a decades-old curriculum filled with stories from suburban life. I didn't blame my students for being disengaged. And when girls in my seventh-grade class needed enrichment reading, I would lamely offer recommendations of books I had loved growing up in rural Wisconsin.

I moved to New York to pursue work in book publishing. I was driven by what had, by then, turned into a burning question I needed to address: Where were the voices of girls today? I met with many agents and editors who listened politely but firmly told me "those books" would not sell. So when I finally found Girls Write Now a few years into my time here, it felt like coming home to a place I had been searching for all those years. This community, this Anthology, is what I knew was missing. And I'm so thankful that it is in the world today.

Rise Speak Change exemplifies the mentor-mentee relationship: Those first moments when we rise from our workshop chairs to meet for the very first time . . . The early meetings when we begin to share our stories through words on and off the page . . . And the later ones where we freely discuss our dreams and encourage one another to change, to evolve, to rise yet again.

We are all called to *Rise Speak Change* in our own spheres of influence. We have seen these past few months how powerful women's voices can be, but also how much work still lies ahead. This Anthology of new voices raising new questions is essential to finding a path forward. My hope is that this book itself can be an agent of change. Share it with a young woman who might feel alone. With a man who is looking for perspective to understand the experience of growing up female and underserved. With a friend who is looking for a spark of creativity. Or an English teacher whose girls are desperate for new stories with which to identify.

My former mentee Mariah joined me for an Anthology committee meeting as we were in the process of working on this book. On top of her busy workload as a junior in college, she told me about the LGBTQ club she was starting on campus; how she'd gone straight to her college's president to request a pledge from him to protect the rights of transgender students there. Mariah exemplifies how the work that begins within Girls Write Now goes far beyond its walls and even these pages. We mentor these young women, and their words, to empower them to see their lives in new ways, their ideas in print, and their ability to make a mark on the world. I hope this collection inspires you to rise as well.

—MEG CASSIDY, Anthology Committee Chair

Anthology Editorial Committee

Molly MacDermot
EDITOR

Meg Cassidy
ANTHOLOGY COMMITTEE CHAIR

Nan Bauer-Maglin

Rosalind Black

Laura Buchwald

Mink Choi

Rakia Clark

Amy Flyntz

Catherine Greenman

Ann Kidder

Linda Kleinbub

Allison Moorer

Erica Moroz

Carol Paik

Nikki Palumbo

Kiele Raymond

Bridget Read

Denise St. Pierre

Melissa Stanger

Maryellen Tighe

Shara Zaval

Maria Campo, *Director of Programs & Outreach*

Emily Yost, *Senior Program Coordinator*

Josh Aromin, Mia Green, Andrea Lynch,
Aditi Sharma, Richelle Szypulski, *Photographers*

Maya Nussbaum, *Founder & Executive Director*

Contents

THE GIRLS WRITE NOW 2017 ANTHOLOGY

Introduction

TANWI NANDINI ISLAM

The young women writers featured in this anthology are des-
tined to become New York City's emerging young novelists,
poets, playwrights, and journalists. During my decade as a
teaching artist working with teenagers across the five boroughs,
I bore witness to such raw, soul-stirring wordsmiths who
yielded their life's trials and triumphs with fierce wit onto the
page and the stage. They flexed their inimitable style, music,
and artistry and good old drama just like any teenager.

Words change us when we speak them. Meeting the young
women of Girls Write Now, I heard them speak their prose and
poetry, many of them performing it for the first time. Seeing a
young Bangladeshi woman and a young Pakistani woman
emcee together—an event unimaginable even fifty years ago in
history because of war— moved me to tears. As each young
woman read her work, they articulated their imagination, personal experience and political consciousness with vulnerability
and courage. I walked away with a resonant feeling: we're going
to be all right with the future in their hands.

Many of these young women survived unjust terrors we are
often told to keep secret. They braved depression, bullying,
sexual abuse, verbal abuse, assault, or cutting. Each time they

tried to heal one wound, another wound revealed itself. And I, as their teacher, had shared these wounds, too. When I moved on to college, I embraced the rage I felt against sexism and powerful structures that oppressed people. As I got older, that anger smoldered into an inner turmoil, which I carried in secret.

My students and I learned to understand something about these secrets. We understood that secretiveness cloaks us in shame, which becomes an impenetrable fortress, a false sense of strength. But what's really happening is shame hardening into silence. What we're left with in the pit of our stomachs is a feeling of worthlessness. *I'm not enough. This is stupid. This is never going to happen.* This place is where I find myself fearing that I have no words left, only silence and shame.

Yet this is the very place we must confront ourselves when we write.

It is where we choose to rise, speak, and change injustice with our fearless imagination and work.

What you write is a gift, a collection of all the strange and beautiful and painful moments you've acquired over the years. When you devote yourself to an art form, you embrace a life of risk. Of being hated. Of being completely ignored or forgotten. You may be the first one in your family to be an artist, to go to college, to come out. You may not be welcome by folks you thought were your friends, your own family. You may break up with someone you love. You will start to feel as if you're making a big mistake.

And yet, every writer must continue to look for stories embedded in every interaction and observation of the patterns, shapes, colors, smells, sounds and feels of everyday life. Take in the silence of trees, sun and stars. And remember, there is always a dark underbelly. A writer is a mediator between light and dark, hope and despair, past, present, and future. Each and every day will bring you to task. That tiny voice inside that doubts and is afraid will never, ever go away—but it will keep you honest. When you feel as though you have no words left, remember: the world needs your work.

TANWI NANDINI ISLAM is the author of *Bright Lines* (Penguin 2015), a finalist for the Center for Fiction First Novel Prize, Edmund White Debut Fiction Award, the Brooklyn Eagles Literary Prize, and the inaugural selection of Chirlane McCray, the First Lady of New York City's Gracie Book Club. Nandini Islam is the founder of Hi Wildflower (www.hiwildflower.com), a fragrance and beauty house. A graduate of Brooklyn College MFA and Vassar College, she lives in Brooklyn, New York.

RISE SPEAK CHANGE

THE GIRLS WRITE NOW
2017 ANTHOLOGY

JISELLE ABRAHAM

YEARS AS MENTEE: 3
GRADE: Junior
HIGH SCHOOL: Edward R. Murrow High School
BORN: Brooklyn, NY
LIVES: Brooklyn, NY

MENTEE'S ANECDOTE: *I have been with Girls Write Now for three years, along with my mentor Heather. Throughout these three years things have not always been perfect, but they have always progressed, especially my writing. I have learned a lot from the workshops and advice that my mentor has given me, and I have even gotten help from myself. I have started to recognize my flaws and have tried to perfect them so that I can reach my full potential as a writer.*

HEATHER STRICKLAND

YEARS AS MENTOR: 3
OCCUPATION: Senior Manager, Internal Communications, American Express
BORN: Philadelphia, PA
LIVES: Brooklyn, NY

MENTOR'S ANECDOTE: *Jiselle and I have been working together for three years and we have learned so much from each other. It has been incredible to see her grow as a woman and as a writer, and watch as her interests evolve from YouTube stardom to art to journalism and foreign films. She is starting to look at colleges and I cannot wait for her next chapter. Jiselle pushes me to work on my writing and reminds me to keep things fun. I have loved my experience with Girls Write Now and I am so excited for the years to come.*

Forgiveness, not Burden

JISELLE ABRAHAM

People have told me not to share this piece, but I have also had people encourage me to share it. It is about a difficult time with my father, whom I love and keep close to my heart. It shows that letting go can allow you to love more.

Driving with my father was always a roller coaster. He was reckless, and would often close his eyes and pretend that he was falling asleep on the highway. Sometimes he was for real.

But he always knew how to put a smile on my face—until it was time to go home. I would cry and pout because there was a fear harvested deep inside me, telling me I wouldn't see him again.

And then it happened. I didn't see him again for another year and my tears never stopped falling because of the thought that something bad could happen to him and I would never know.

During his absence I thought of him a lot. I asked my mom questions like, "Why aren't you and Daddy together anymore?" She would never tell me.

But my older sister had no trouble with giving it to me straight.

"Your father beat Mom badly."

Hearing those words ripped my heart right out of my chest.

How could this wonderful man that I love so much do such a thing? Domestic violence was something I only heard or saw on television—it wouldn't happen in my house.

While he was gone, I developed. My mind grew but so did my heart. I reconnected with him again when I was twelve or thirteen. We were sitting in the truck he drove for work and I knew—now was the time to confront him. We had a good laugh, and then we got on a more serious note about the past. He looked me in my eyes and told me that he would never hit my mother.

He lied to my face.

My mother made sure that I grew up knowing how much my father loved me and that he would never do anything to hurt me. As much as she went through, she never doubted that he wasn't a good father. He was a great one. I knew that, and she knew that, and to her that's all that mattered. The past didn't faze her and she didn't hate him. She had conversations with him as if it never even happened, and I envied that. She'd forgiven him because that's all she could do, and so I followed in her steps.

The Hat

HEATHER STRICKLAND

I write fiction, but Girls Write Now has encouraged me to explore poetry. When I read Jiselle's submission, I decided to submit my own piece about letting go of your past. It is difficult to rise up and change, but exploring poetry has helped me do that again and again.

When the wind came strong and whipped
my hat up into the clouds, I thought perhaps
I should chase after it because it used
to be your hat
and I worried that I would miss the memory
of you arriving at my door on cold
winter nights drenched
in freezing air, that fuzz
of black on your head.
I worried that I would miss the way the faux-fur felt
against my ears, like I missed the way you wrapped
your arms around me
or the way you danced
your fingers across my skin
to keep me warm.

When the wind came strong and whipped
my hat up into the clouds, I thought perhaps
I should chase after it because it used
to be your hat,
but the chill in the air reminded me that there was a hole

in the hat, one large
enough for me to put my whole thumb through
so that sometimes when I wore it my ears ended up frozen
and I worried that I would get sick
because your hat wasn't enough
to keep my head warm.
It was pilled, stretched out, faded,
and it was starting to smell
like sour sweat
and salt
and tears.

So when the wind came strong and whipped
my hat up into the clouds, I thought perhaps
I should chase after it because it used
to be your hat.
But instead I let it go
until it was nothing
but a black speck
disappearing
in the sky.

DIAMOND ABREU

YEARS AS MENTEE: 2

GRADE: Senior

HIGH SCHOOL: Millennium High School

BORN: New York, NY

LIVES: New York, NY

PUBLICATIONS AND RECOGNITIONS: Scholastic Art & Writing Awards: Gold Key and Honorable Mention, DCTV PRO-TV Media Fellowship Program

MENTEE'S ANECDOTE: *Being with Girls Write Now has set me free from the barriers that held my voice and creativity back. The program not only creates a safe space for writing, but makes the process highly enjoyable. My mentor has seen me mature as a person and as a writer. She understands where I am coming from and therefore can find ways to help improve my writing. Girls Write Now is a gift that unlocked the potential I always had as a writer.*

DORA VANETTE

YEARS AS MENTOR: 2

OCCUPATION: Lecturer at Parsons School of Design

BORN: Split, Croatia

LIVES: Brooklyn, NY

PUBLICATIONS AND RECOGNITIONS: Published in *Metropolis, Dwell, Journal of Design History, A Women's Thing.*

MENTOR'S ANECDOTE: *Five minutes into my first meeting with Diamond, the two of us jumped into what felt like a comfortable friendship. We covered topics from school and friends to writing, movies, and comics—and we haven't stopped since. In the two years that followed, both Diamond and I developed as writers and friends, but another layer of Diamond's personality was revealed to me when she took me to her favorite comic book store, and I was so excited to see her tackle this topic in her Anthology piece.*

Why Obsessions Matter

DIAMOND ABREU

I chose to write about how my obsession with comic books—which seemed the opposite of my personality—has allowed me to grow into who I am, both as a writer and as a person.

I never knew that I would be obsessed with comics. When I was ten, I loved playing with dolls and watching Barbie movies. But one day, when my father suggested I watch an action movie with him, there was just something about the speed of the movie and the way it had my heart thumping that caught my attention and never let go. Watching action movies became a ritual for me and my dad, and seeing *Batman: The Dark Knight* was the most memorable moment of all. I liked Batman because he was full of convictions, emotions, and even flaws, whereas other superheroes tend to be practically flawless. I also appreciated how Batman's world paralleled ours, but was much darker.

I wanted to find out more about this world and soon realized a whole universe existed in the form of comic books. I felt a sort of excitement build up in my chest as I surfed the Internet for local comic book stores on my bulky laptop. I remember tearing/ripping a messy sheet of paper from my notebook to write down the locations. It was Saturday by the time I worked up my courage to tell my dad to drive me there. I remember feeling butterflies because I didn't know what to expect once I got there—I mean, I had never been in a comic book store before.

My fears were unfounded as soon as I entered and immediately noticed how quiet and calm the store was. The sun poured in from the windows, making the comics that were tucked away in plastic covers glimmer. I know I must have looked confused because an employee, who would later become a close friend, came up to ask what I was looking for. When I asked to see Batman comics, he calmly and pridefully brought me over to a section that was entirely dedicated to them. My eyes immediately widened. The colorful images, big words, and perfectly drawn characters made my heart thump with excitement. I wanted to read as much as I possibly could, so from then on, every Friday after school, I went to the comic book store to check out new issues. You could say that I basically grew up in the comic book store. Eventually, the workers and I began to develop a close bond based on our love for comics. I became comfortable in that small community of avid comic book lovers. Now when the employees see me, I get more than just a robotic "Hello, welcome," but a loud "Hello, Diamond!" accompanied by a warm hug.

My love for comics is fueled by these friendships but also by the colorful worlds and compelling storylines of comic books, which transport me to a whole new world. From eighth grade to my senior year of high school, the comic book store has always been there for me. It served as a sanctuary where I could release everyday stress by escaping into the world of moving images. Without the comic book store, I wouldn't be who I am today. I wouldn't be as bubbly as I am now since my shyness slips away whenever I talk about comic books. Without comic books I wouldn't know how to effectively create intriguing characters who have emotions and flaws, but are heroes at the same time. The comic book store remains a place where I can be the purest form of myself, and because of that, it will always be a part of my life.

Comforts of Silence

DORA VANETTE

Working with Diamond on writing connected to the theme of Rise Speak Change *made me pause to consider what these words mean to me personally—and I realized that my discomfort with them spoke volumes.*

Half an hour into meeting my husband's parents for the first time, his father said: "She sure doesn't talk much, does she?" His bluntness was of course embarrassing, but it offered some relief as well. If anything, he wasn't wrong in his observation, and I took his words as acknowledgment and permission to continue as I had, cocooned in the familiar comfort of silence. Coming from a place where lives tend to be small (in the most beautiful sense of that word) and deference for authority is unquestioned, I have never seen silence as anything but a warm and comfortable (and of course painfully privileged) place; one that allows you to listen, observe, and learn without fear of conflict or humiliation. When people wonder about my love of rules and dislike for confrontation, I usually just shrug my shoulders and recite a saying I heard growing up: "People in this country tend to be much better servants than they are masters." And they should know, as my country has experienced numerous regimes, both domestic and foreign, over the past couple of centuries. I still see little shame in that sentiment; the world would likely be a much better place without us lapsing into expectations of something ever-grander, but the one thing I am learning is to question my fondness of silence. The quality that allowed me to observe the world for such a long period of time has made me realize that there comes a moment when observing is just not good enough. Brought on by adulthood, fostered by New York, and sparked by changes in the world, I've been teaching myself how to speak. The attempts come with their own set of growing pains; sometimes the words stumble out and other times they don't come out at all, despite my sincerest attempts to will them out. But they are forming and their shapes are becoming more distinct, so perhaps one day, and hopefully soon, they will be just the words I need.

RACHEL AGHANWA

YEARS AS MENTEE: 3

GRADE: Senior

HIGH SCHOOL: Queens Gateway to Health Sciences Secondary School

BORN: Brooklyn, NY

LIVES: Queens, NY

PUBLICATIONS AND RECOGNITIONS: Scholastic Art & Writing Awards: Silver Key, Honorable Mention

MENTEE'S ANECDOTE: *This is the first year Sara and I have accomplished a significant amount of our goals. It's odd how far we've come as a pair since my first year in the program: from struggling to get a table at the Central Library in Queens, to loud, crowded Union Square cafés. My writing has matured since then, and I am happy that I got to spend the last three years with Sara as my mentor helping me along the way.*

SARA POLSKY

YEARS AS MENTOR: 3

OCCUPATION: Writer; Senior Features Editor, *Curbed*

BORN: New York, NY

LIVES: Queens, NY

MENTOR'S ANECDOTE: *Rachel is one of the most determined writers I know. When she isn't exactly sure what she wants to say, she keeps returning to the piece or the topic until she figures it out, even when the subject matter is difficult. Watching Rachel persist with her writing over the last three years has helped me learn how to persist with my own.*

Zip Zip

RACHEL AGHANWA

This piece was written about how I felt when questioned about or having others police my body.

The sound of a zipper not closing was the bane of my existence as a child. Seeing a pretty dress in a store and falling in love with it, only to find out it was in every other size but my own.

As a child, my grandma raised me due my mother working twelve-hour night shifts three days a week. And at every moment, whether it was her picking me up from school or playing in the park, she would shovel rice or ice cream down my throat.

I was a fat baby. Fat babies are cute, but after you pass third grade and you still haven't lost that baby fat, you're automatically put at the bottom of every "prettiest girl in class" list.

I could sit around and blame my grandma for making me like this (and I did for a couple of years), but it wasn't her fault. I loved food, and I carried that love into my early teenage years.

It was during fifth grade that I found out that this wasn't something to be proud of. At age ten, I was already wearing women's clothing, and my mom would always complain when she took me to the children's section, even though she knew damn well I was not going to fit in anything.

"Just try it on," she used to say. Many people have grown up with this notion that the less you eat, the prettier you'll be, and that this kind of mindset could destroy someone's mental health. I used to cry about eating things that I wasn't supposed to (those Rice Krispie marshmallow treats were actually very good at absorbing my tears; I don't know if that's a good thing or a bad thing) and would hide snacks in my room so my parents wouldn't find out I was eating junk food.

Two years ago, I sat in front of the TV at 3 a.m., watching the Victoria's Secret Fashion Show and crying about my body not being like the models' while eating a slice of chocolate cake.

I really wanted to be like them, eating whatever they wanted without bloating up, but then I did a little research. The VS Angels have to work out at least five times a week, have a controlled diet, and the week of the show, they don't consume solid foods.

I may not fit society's beauty standard, but I still love food. I can't imagine life without pizza, mac and cheese, or even something as simple as bread, which the models aren't even allowed to consume.

And who would want to live a life like that?

The doubts will always be at the back of my mind when making a decision to wear "those shorts" or "a shirt like that." But eventually, you begin to realize that life is so much more than a number on a scale or a BMI percentile. It's actually about eating as much food as possible, and learning to love yourself.

That Woman

SARA POLSKY

Since November, I've struggled to write about the people I met while canvassing for Hillary Clinton in Pennsylvania. Inspired by Rachel's tenacity with her writing, I kept tackling the topic and ended up with this poem.

The woman who came to the door
in Lancaster County said no,
no one in that house
would speak with us,
ever, and how dare we
come around seeking votes
for That Woman. *That woman,*
she hissed, and her lip curled
and her door closed
and her daughter,
the one on our voter list,
looked at us and away.
And all these months later,
I still think about
that woman, still wonder
at the force of her anger,
at how stunned I was,
that day, to meet it.

SOLEDAD AGUILAR-COLON

YEARS AS MENTEE: 1
GRADE: Sophomore
HIGH SCHOOL: Beacon High School
BORN: Bronx, NY
LIVES: New York, NY
PUBLICATIONS AND RECOGNITIONS: Named an editor of Beacon's literary journal

MENTEE'S ANECDOTE: *This year my mentor Linda and I have had multiple moments that together have made a wonderful and empowering experience. It has been amazing to explore the craft of writing just by reflecting on our everyday lives. I have not only found a mentor that challenges me as a writer, but who has also become a friend in whom I can confide. For me, our best moments have been when we sit in a café and just write because in that, I have been able to start my evening by getting everything off of my shoulders and just be.*

LINDA CORMAN

YEARS AS MENTOR: 7
OCCUPATION: Freelance editor/writer
BORN: Newton, MA
LIVES: New York, NY
PUBLICATIONS AND RECOGNITIONS: A variety of publications, including *Knowledge@Wharton*

MENTOR'S ANECDOTE: *Soledad and I have spent a lot of time talking about politics and social issues, certainly in part because of the tumultuous year it has been in this country's history. I really appreciate Soledad's openness and thoughtfulness about issues of race and the nuances of race and class in our society. It has been wonderful to reflect on and discuss our experiences in this regard (as well as everything else)!*

We Protest with Thunder, Not Lightning

SOLEDAD AGUILAR-COLON

This piece critiques the way people of color are treated by police when protesting for their rights and contrasts how white people are treated when protesting.

It was like lightning. The bright flash of cameras was blinding as our adolescent faces appeared on their screens. We were seen, but never really heard. We might as well have been silent. My friend and I walked hand in hand, my fingers tugging on hers. Turn right, I tugged her thumb, avoid the dog, turn left I tugged her pinky. *Avoid the book bags,* they whispered. My fingers clench around her slippery wrist. *Stop,* they say. I want to make sure she's okay, but her name slips from my tongue like raindrops and emerges into the puddle underneath our trembling feet. Ixchel reminded me of the Puerto Rican drink my grandmother makes during the holidays so she can drink away her ex-husband; her special eggnog with *un chin de rum,* we call it *coquito.* When I look at her hair, it's anything but the strong independent black curls I had connected with the first moment we met. They were instead pressed down by the heavy pour of rain. They were straight for now and the ends of her hair seemed to be held down by a hot iron plank. They reminded me of prison bars. When I think of Ixchel and me, the color of our skins have never stood out so vividly; eggnog with a hint of rum fading away against the untouched snowflake white.

The voices of the protesters made noise, but delivered no message as we marched with our soaking wet book bags toward the Trump Towers on Fifty-Sixth Street and Fifth Avenue. I jerk at the sound of a hundred geese screeching as it fills my eardrums and I turn around to see a line of cars honking at the sight of our ostentatious signs that read, "Fuck Trump" and "Pussy Grabs Back." Puddles splash at our feet, causing teenagers to glance down at their wet corporate American Apparel jeans in dread. They worried because the jeans cost fifty dollars, but never about how only ten dollars or less of that is given to the workers in China and India that make those jeans. They were protesting for the rights of working class, people of color, but never came to question how they are instead supporting the exploitation of people of color through their purchase of certain brands. The irony of leaving education to protest without being educated about what we were protesting. I thought of the abruptness of my decision to skip school because I had the ability to, but what if our education was our means of resistance? For Malala, she fought with a pen, paper and books and was effective in generating change. We were uneducated protestors, so why protest at all?

I tap Ixchel on the shoulder to let her know of the instant publicity that the protest was attracting through the multiple snapchat videos and flashing cameras trained on our faces. Police officers were offering their hands to us and we walked across the street. Together. When we reached the Trump Towers, the officers put metal barricades around us. I soon realized they weren't corralling us; they were keeping everyone else out because as newspapers would later write, this march of four hundred mostly privileged white students was peaceful. However, newspapers never deem protests as peaceful, so why us?

Six months earlier, I was filled with overwhelming pride as multiple fists ranging in colors from warm brown rice to sharp black pepper and spicy red curry rose in the air. The blood of our enslaved and undocumented ancestors, our history of broken backs and cracked feet spilled out on the clean "cookie-cutter" rugs of the New School building. I felt the shudder of the strong woman next to me as we breathed in and out as one, frightened of what was to come. We walked toward Grand Central Station with foreheads drenched in salty sweat and sticky lemonade fingers as red-faced men screamed "Sluts!" and "Put some clothes on!" Some mothers raised their fists in a salute to our anti-slut-shaming protest; others covered their daughters' eyes, shielding them from the free women of color fighting for their future. We didn't avert our eyes from the gaze of our zookeepers; we stared it in the face and unchained ourselves. At Grand Central Station, we screamed. We were thunder, demanding to be heard. A group of twenty women, hands linked in solidarity. Together we were no longer forced into their straight-jackets that typecast us; we reclaimed a meaning that was inclusive of our power as young women of color. Cameras flashed and everyone stopped to admire the young women they thought belonged in zoos. Our skin glowed with all of the colors of the rainbow and every flag across the globe. Police officers just had to shut it down. Twenty cops, one for each of us, came down to tape our lips together, but we didn't need to speak in order to stand out. We were like thunder, no longer seen, but heard. As the chief of the NYPD tells us that we were disturbing the peace and we have to leave in an orderly fashion, we stick up our middle fingers and chant, "We have nothing to lose but our chains."

Six Decades of Protest, 1964–

LINDA CORMAN

Soledad's reflections on her experiences demonstrating for various causes made me think back about my own experiences, and the related interactions with police.

What were the police thinking

When the busloads of white, suburban kids spilled

Onto the grounds of the

School building, its crumbling, scarred brick façade draped with
  "Freedom Boycott" hand-painted in black on a white sheet

Windows covered in heavy iron bars (or was it broken chicken
  wire?)

Perhaps some boarded up where stones had sailed through the
  glass

(We were told to take advantage of the bathroom stop at
  Howard Johnson's on our way into town; no telling whether
  the toilets at the school worked)

I, at 13, in pleated skirt and round-collared blouse, proud to skip
  school and join, at our mother's urging, the protest against
  "De-facto Segregation" and the decrepit schools to which

Boston's black children were consigned; my brother, a few years older, chafing under parental tutelage, but clasping a dog-eared copy of *Another Country*.

What were the police told to do that day?

Were they told to "protect" us do-gooders from the black kids, parents, ministers, principals

Who we joined on the barren hillside sloping down from the school to sing "We Shall Overcome"?

Or, were they there to protect white Boston from us?

Did they curse us under their breaths, "Nigger Lovers"?

Or, did they look on, taciturn, and then go home to their neighborhoods, and their only slightly better-kept schools

And vote for Louise Day Hicks?

* * * *

Seven years later, in Harvard Square, my brother,

Raging against the war (Vietnam)

High on something

Skinny, angry, dirty, hair flamboyant, Medusa-like

"Hippy scum."

"Lock him up."

Did they finally get to unleash their fury at the privileged, white
suburban kid?

* * *

At JFK, after the Muslim ban

Police—at least one for every 20 protestor—machine guns
dangling from their belts

Corralled us into a triangle of concrete near a parking garage

Marginalized, shunted aside, hidden from most of the waves of
passengers entering and leaving the international terminal

We chanted, "Immigrants Are Welcome Here" and "Remember
the St. Louis."

As I left, chilled, new waves of protesters arrived. I glanced up at
a few young officers at the end of a gauntlet on either side of
a sidewalk they were "keeping clear for passengers."

"Someday soon, you're going to have to decide what side you're
on," I remarked, counting on age, as well as whiteness, to
protect me from immediate danger.

MADIHA ALAM

YEARS AS MENTEE: 1
GRADE: Senior
HIGH SCHOOL: The Bronx High School of Science
BORN: Queens, NY
LIVES: Queens, NY
PUBLICATIONS AND RECOGNITIONS: Scholastics Arts & Writing Awards: Gold Key, Honorable Mention

MENTEE'S ANECDOTE: *The first time I met Diana, we bonded over the Mellow Morning playlist we both listen to on Spotify, which was the first of many things we share. Despite our different backgrounds, we are always able to relate to each other. Diana has helped me see beyond my own experiences and, as a result, has helped me give more substance to the pieces I write. It is because of her that I no longer hesitate to share my writing with others and strive to write outside of my comfort zone.*

DIANA SALVATORE

YEARS AS MENTOR: 1
OCCUPATION: Marketing Associate, Innisfree M&A Incorporated
BORN: Brooklyn, NY
LIVES: Brooklyn, NY
PUBLICATIONS AND RECOGNITIONS: *Suffragette City* (Managing Editor)

MENTOR'S ANECDOTE: *I was embarrassingly nervous to meet my first mentee. "Just dress really cool," advised a (really cool) friend. When Madiha and I got to talking, all nerves subsided. She is brave, passionate, and she possesses that delightful teenage quality—unbridled excitement for tons of stuff. Madiha has made impressive strides in writing, but our best achievement is a beautiful confirmation that when people come together in the spirit of creativity and openness, we can do amazing things. It is all there in Madiha's words, which are a testament to her inspiring progress and her exceptional character.*

Closure

MADIHA ALAM

I wrote this story after a bitter fallout with a dear friend. We must be courageous enough to rise, speak, and change our paths; only then can we find closure and peace.

"Excuse me."

After all these years, I still recognize her. The pale grey-green eyes, the scar I gave her on her left ear playing a seven-year-old's version of football. There is no way it isn't her. There is no way it isn't Amira sitting in front of me, nearly twelve years later.

"Ma'am, please"

Her son looks just like she did when she first moved in next door, down to the shade of brown hair and scrawny build.

Interrupting my thoughts, Zakariya tugs on my shirt. "Ma, there's a man over there." Oh crap, I'm blocking the entrance to the pediatrician's office. An agitated young intern glares impatiently at us, still waiting for me to move out of the way.

"I'm sorry, didn't see you there."

"Of course you didn't," he mutters under his breath. I let him pass and wish the floor would swallow me.

Moving into a small waiting room, I turn back to where the old acquaintance is sitting and I plot ways to escape unseen. Amira Hussein: one minute my best friend and the next, my archnemesis. Okay, maybe I'm being a little dramatic. But that still doesn't mean I have any intention of talking to her right now.

"Young lady!"

"Me?"

"Bring your exam up right this second. That is not acceptable."

I'm thinking, "Seriously? We only have seven minutes to finish math. This is the SAT, buddy. Not a health exam." I was only trying to tell Amira to stop poking me for answers. I glance at her over my shoulder, sitting to the left of my newly empty seat. Her eyes avert, burning holes into her desk.

I play dumb.

"Sir, I don't understand. Why can't I finish my exam?"

"You really need to ask me why cheating is wrong? Shame on you. You think I wasn't going to notice you whispering all the answers to your friend?"

I look at Amira again, who pretends she can't hear my life tearing apart with every second. She could say something, but she stays silent.

Coward.

In the following weeks, my early acceptance from MIT is rescinded, and the College Board reports me for academic dishonesty. I duck constant glares of disapproval (or perhaps disappointment?) at every corner. "Why?" "You had so much potential, dear." "A shame, really."

I am placed on house arrest by Ma. "From home to school and school to home only. Understand?" It's not like I have anywhere else to go, anyway. All my friends have distanced themselves from me.

As for Amira, she knows to stay away. She avoids my route to school and I'm not complaining.

My life, as Ma put it, is destroyed. And by the last person I would ever suspect.

The receptionist's shrill voice snaps me back and I am sitting, dazed, in the waiting room. I look up to catch the now-thirty-year-old Amira staring and I know she remembers, too. As she holds her stare, I sit back down and pretend to talk to Zakariya, who is occupied with my phone.

*Maybe she never meant for this to happen. I don't think she knew that it would have broken our friendship. But that doesn't change the fact that it did. Months later, I hear from Ma that Amira has been accepted to Princeton. A spot at an Ivy League school with my SAT answers. With **my** hard work.*

"That could have been you, Nadia. You could have worked harder like Amira did and you wouldn't have felt the need to cheat," Ma reminds me every single day.

Amira eventually tries to apologize, but the damage is done. The wound is too deep. She tries, but I won't give in. She even offers me a ride to school with the new car her father bought for her. A gift for getting into Princeton. The NERVE.

But it's okay. Because my life doesn't end. My life isn't "destroyed." I move past it and, after some hard work, I land on my feet.

Twelve years ago, I wouldn't dream of speaking to her. She was a liar, a cheat, and worst of all: a fraud. But now, she seems to be the same old Amira. Maybe she is.

There are so many questions I want to ask her. What does she do now? Where does she live? Who did she marry? Was she really sorry then? Is she sorry now? I am amazed to see her here with a child, considering she never wanted them when we were younger.

Suddenly, I'm standing up and walking toward Amira. It's time to heal this wound. It's time to forgive.

"Amira?"

"Nadia?"

future you

DIANA SALVATORE

I often reflect on the messy, mystical business of creating and nurturing human life. I wrote this poem on a humid summer night upon waking from a dream.

i hover in the darkness
huffing your almond scent
hugging your pillow flesh.
sensual lip smacking
unblemished by this world
existing only in

perfection.

dark feather eyelashes
eighty-nine
i count them each night
flutter and rest on your watermelon cheeks

plump from sweet milk
two ever-blank canvases for my
chapstick kiss marks.
hot
from dreaming of the past
of the inside of my body.

you are of me.
my spark and shadow
my history my heart
my brain and cells

and soul.

but wait
you are yours entirely.
you will grow taller and stronger
braver smarter than i.
wiser.

you are my future
now only a gleam from august's low-slung moon
across my green iris.

you are not here yet
but i am sure
of the future you.

ASSATA ANDREWS

YEARS AS MENTEE: 1

GRADE: Junior

HIGH SCHOOL: Hillside Arts & Letters Academy

BORN: New York, NY

LIVES: Queens, NY

PUBLICATIONS AND RECOGNITIONS: HALA's BeSpoke Literary and Arts Magazine.

MENTEE'S ANECDOTE: *My writing pair relationship with Megan is great. She helps me dig deep within my writing and has helped me truly learn about who I am through my writing even if I had writer's block. My most memorable moment was when Megan and I went over my pieces for the Scholastic Art and Writing Awards submissions. She was able to share similarities with me when it came to opening up about an uncomfortable topic and our favorite Audrey Hepburn movies—which I have an obsession for. I felt our connection grow stronger.*

MEGAN ERICKSON

YEARS AS MENTOR: 1

OCCUPATION: Freelance writer, New York City public school teacher

BORN: Frederick, MD

LIVES: Brooklyn, NY

PUBLICATIONS AND RECOGNITIONS: *The Guardian, Indiana Review, Beloit Poetry Journal,* and *Jacobin* magazine.

MENTOR'S ANECDOTE: *We had fun at the travel writing workshop, but it was when we began writing personal memoirs that our work together got interesting and deep. Assata shared a personal story with me about the pressure she felt to have religious faith. I was incredibly impressed by her bravery, and told her about the time I got punished as a teenager for wearing a bathrobe to pick my sister up from church. Then, we wrote first drafts together based on our experiences. She sees herself as reserved. I see a reflective and mature observer—a powerful foundation for a literary life.*

Letter to Past Me

ASSATA ANDREWS

I wrote this piece at the beginning of my junior year when I felt as though I needed to get something off my chest. I have found that in order to speak truths powerful enough to change the world, you must first learn how to speak to yourself.

Dear Younger Assata,

You may be sad at the moment, but trust me: things will get better. Just realize now, before it's too late, who your true friends are and who really cares. When you graduate middle school make sure that you keep in contact with Aloni, Justina, Kimberly, Hannah, Jennell, and Siyana—also, the silly group name that you made up together at that camping trip in eighth grade and the fun times at lunch. In March, someone who you'd never expect to get close to will contact you and, in a way, change your life. This person will help with a lot of issues that you go through and you learn that you two are more alike than you thought.

Once you start high school and ease into it, I guarantee that you won't feel lonely anymore. Sometimes the people around you might irritate you, such as your "friends," who try to guilt-trip you, or people who seem as if they think they're above it all. However, you will meet some friends along the way who will learn to appreciate who you really are and who won't criticize or bring you down every chance they get. Amara might get on your nerves a little bit, but she most definitely is a really great friend. You and Anjali will bond over the fact that you are Capricorns and born four days apart. Tisya is someone who helps you with your dream to write. There are a few more people who you will like and wish you could get closer to, so I recommend that you speak up more. The teachers in high school will truly care about you and your work ethic. I can assure you that you'll grow fond of Mrs. Bhola, Mrs. Kurtzman, Ms. Stubbs, Ms. Murphy, and Mrs. E. They are all strict but yet so much fun. Some of the teachers you might grow a better relationship with than others, and you will enjoy them, despite the homework.

Now here are your seemingly bigger problems: your possible unrequited friendship with one of your best friends, and your depression. First of all, you and Katherine will grow apart because of an over-exaggerated rumor. I suggest that you talk things out with her. The things that you did to her and said about her were taken out-of-context, but you will still feel guilty and carry a heavy weight on your shoulders after the friendship is over. Stay by her side and don't believe what other people say and you might still be friends by the time you're my age—which will make eight years of friendship. Rajshri, your current best friend, will honestly make you doubt that she's your best friend. She is a great person but the complete opposite of you, which makes you wonder why you two are close. Even though you two will go to separate high schools—that are across the street from each other—you will start to drift away from one another, which gives you an uneasy feeling because of your desperate need for a close friendship. Only a few of your friends will know about your depression and you will get two different reactions: sympathy or annoyance. Though some people assure you that you'll be fine, it won't help and you'll start to feel worse. But once you get to actually know yourself, accept who you are, and have long, relatable conversations with Krystal, the depression will start to simmer away. It will be a great feeling and the guilt that you felt about Katherine will disappear.

So, don't worry about anything. Just be who you truly are and you will learn to love yourself.

Love,
Assata

Watching

MEGAN ERICKSON

This is a true story. And also, not. The inspiration was the feeling of shame I had (in retrospect) for having been embarrassed about sharing the same name as a girl in my class as a kid. That became a poem about class. Some lines are fact, some fiction.

When I was a child I made a girl cry, relentlessly
as a deer tongue running over a salt lick. What happened to her?
I could have been her friend. I was embarrassed, then,
that we shared the same name.

We knew she shit in an outhouse, wore a marine's coat,
and ate meat she'd helped to skin, spreading the raw
illicit smell like it was perfume. I heard once
she brought a hammer to school.

She used it to open a battery. Smashed.
She could do it to your face if she was in a rage,
like that. Like you were a science project.
Why do they call it grace when most days, most of us are saved

by things like, our parents coming home in shoes?
When those boys dropped a quarter on the floor just to see
would she run after it, and everyone—and I—waited, watching
we knew that she'd need it.

AYANNA BAILEY

YEARS AS MENTEE: 3
GRADE: Senior
HIGH SCHOOL: The Urban Assembly Institute of Math and Science for Young Women
BORN: Brooklyn, NY
LIVES: Brooklyn, NY

MENTEE'S ANECDOTE: *What Marissa and I have is like fate. While I am dry humored and realistic she is insightful and optimistic. She makes me cry, laugh, and no matter how bad a day I have had, I leave our meetings smiling ear to ear. This past Christmas without talking about it we got each other gifts, and that is a statement to how connected we are. Over these two years, I have grown as a person and Marissa has a big part in that. For years to come, we will not only be friends, but also see each other grow.*

MARISSA QUENQUA

YEARS AS MENTOR: 4
OCCUPATION: Writer, *Enamored Ink*
BORN: North Babylon, NY
LIVES: Brooklyn, NY
PUBLICATIONS AND RECOGNITIONS: Written four romance novels for *Enamored Ink* under a pseudonym.

MENTOR'S ANECDOTE: *I remember my first meeting with Ayanna. We clicked right away after deciding to do a freewrite based on the seven deadly sins, and we both chose the same sin without talking about it. She makes me laugh until I am crying, and never fails to touch me with her honesty and insight. This year we were able to make some real strides, with Ayanna deciding to tackle genres like memoir and poetry. Ayanna continues to gain confidence in her artistic abilities, and I know we will remain friends for years to come.*

Time

AYANNA BAILEY

This poem not only shows my growth as a person but also as a writer.
As a young adult I have gotten to understand how precious time is
and why I should progress as time goes on.

Time is the entity that waits for no one
Fleeting and changing constantly
Creating beautiful allusions,
And trapping you easily

The moments you wished would never end
Like your first kiss under the lonely silver disc
Are now so memories deep within
That remembering it is too much of a risk

But time, no matter how painful
Has taught you how to rise
That no task is too hard to handle
And determination leads to your long awaited sunrise

Be proud of your accomplishments because it was earned
And thank time for all of the things that you have learned

Shoe

MARISSA QUENQUA

This is an excerpt from a longer piece about my relationship to shoes as a disabled femme. Only by rising and speaking can those of us with invisible disabilities incite awareness and change.

I'm a femme who hates shoe shopping. I have mild cerebral palsy that's mostly invisible. My balance is shaky, my leg muscles are spastic and my arches are weak. I don't know whether or not a pair of shoes would "work" for me until I try them on and walk around the store. Even then, what works on a store carpet might not work on a sidewalk. As a teen, I knew my mother's meager income might be wasted on shoes I thought worked when we bought them, but didn't when I tried to wear them in the world. You can't return worn shoes. I had to get shoes at department stores like Macy's or places like Easy Spirit, I couldn't wear much cheaper shoes from Payless or Bakers, I'd fall down in them.

"How do those fit?" a clueless, exasperated salesgirl would ask us, looking at the stacks of shoe boxes surrounding me.

"Mmm," I'd say.

"They look great," she'd offer.

"Mmm," I'd repeat, standing up and wiggling my toes. Mom looked at how they fit around the back. I looked down in the mirror affixed to the outside of the footstool. The shoes looked so good. I turned to the side and my young calf muscles popped. The cherry colored leather wrapped expertly around my feet, a buckle shone at the pinky toe, small heel stacked underneath me. They did look great. None of this mattered. All that matters is what happens when I walk.

I handed my mom my purse and started a lap around the store.

"You're not coming out of the back of them," Mom said as she watched me walk.

As I walked, I'd try to forget about what the shoes looked like. Nice leather, a great style and some extra height won't comfort me when my arches are screaming in pain and all I can think about are my scrunched toes. I got into the rhythm of a stride and closed my eyes.

My pinky toe was being pushed to the side and the balance was off. I couldn't last in these for more than ten minutes.

"Nope." I said when I returned to my mother.

"No?" she sounded disappointed.

"Nope. They hurt."

"Okay, take them off."

The salesgirl came back.

"We're taking those?"

"No, sorry."

I tried on a pair of flat leather boots. They felt as good as sneakers. We took those.

JANEIN BROOKES

YEARS AS MENTEE: 1

GRADE: Freshman

HIGH SCHOOL: Success Academy of Liberal Arts

BORN: New York, NY

LIVES: Bronx, NY

PUBLICATIONS AND RECOGNITIONS: Scholastic Art & Writing Award: Honorable Mention

MENTEE'S ANECDOTE: *The Found Poetry workshop was the crossing of a boundary that I could not be more grateful to Cynthia for. If it had not been for her, I definitely would not have found the confidence necessary to share something as personal as my anxiety in front of a group of open women and young girls that I had never spoken to before. Even though I am very reserved and do not enjoy verbally sharing my work with others, I see now that the sharing of a story is what makes the story a story.*

CYNTHIA-MARIE O'BRIEN

YEARS AS MENTOR: 1

OCCUPATION: Freelance editor and writer

BORN: New Haven, CT

LIVES: Queens, NY

PUBLICATIONS AND RECOGNITIONS: This year my work has appeared in *America Magazine, Kirkus,* and *The Literary Review.*

MENTOR'S ANECDOTE: *One of my favorite experiences has been using museums as writing spots. Our first trip to the Met Breuer inspired Janein's Scholastic Award–winning poem; she began writing it there as a result of a prompt, "If you were to paint today, what would you paint?" On our second adventure, we visited the Met's Asian wing to fulfill her goal of exploring Japanese culture. Seeing Janein so inspired to visit the museums was awesome. Whether in the library, coffee shop, or a city landmark, we always push ourselves to new ideas through free writes. I cannot wait for her CHAPTERS reading.*

America

JANEIN BROOKES

*My piece shows the gap between what I believe a writer is and what
writing actually means to me.*

Sharing a story means having courage. It's like walking outside
naked, breathing in the fresh air and waiting for lightning to
strike you. Sharing a story is like experiencing loss. "Kill your
darlings"; hinder the process of logical thought. Sharing a story
means leaving a piece of yourself in a den of wolves unaware if
they will dine on your flesh or press their wet nose to your
palm. Sharing a story is like trying to turn on a dead computer.
Giving CPR to a corpse that pleads for five more minutes. But
we've given it five minutes, years, decades, ago and it still lies
there like a disease everyone's too afraid to touch. Sharing a
story is saying, "Don't go through my stuff!" but praying you
got to the good part. Sharing a story means metaphorical death.

The transition between extraordinary and illogical.
From the immobile koi fish to the cat sized rats.
The only thing I find impressive about this city we call New
is the language barriers
created because we were once welcoming
to our foreign comrades.

Oh America,
Great America,
land of the self-acclaimed free
who still drink the bitter liquid of poverty
and make money selling Oreos on the beast
underneath our feet.
And we use the white ear plugs of ignorance,
listening to the black man rhyming about his insecurities
crying about the disloyalty of his fifth girlfriend.
Oh America,
great America, why
have you gone and taken
the train of common humanity away?

Being an American means not coming from America at all. It means that after years of my kind being treated as less, I get to learn with others. Being an American means being an outsider to your native land but trading secrets of your past lives. Being an American means identifying oneself by the amount of virtual people who claim to know them. Being American means learning how to weigh the elephant in the room. Being American means to administer those you love to protect the fragile nature of your own affections. Being American means not being American at all.

A man
crawls on the train.
He's begging for people
to throw miserable pennies in his miserably
empty cup.

He's begging with his eyes
because he holds the meager
cup between his teeth,
revealing the loss of his leg.
A man
crawls off the train,
his empty cup, still between
his teeth.

Being a writer means that I am the creator of everything. I'm
not an artist but art feeds off me like a kid to a goat. I'm not a
doctor but the doctor needs me to save his patient and his job.
I'm not an explorer but I have named the locations explorers
have dared to explore. Being a writer means that I'm nothing.

Music and chatter
holding onto some metal
that is supposed to keep me
stable,
Someone stands back,
an observer to the chaos
of the human mind.
I'm late, I'm lost.
I've passed the outside
161st Station,
chaotic and madness
and settled into the maze
of the 42nd Street,
bright and nostalgic.
I'm late, I'm lost.

And now I'm stuck
between the two stops
and I want to go.
I want to see and I want to be.
I'm late, I'm lost.

The Taste

CYNTHIA-MARIE O'BRIEN

Janein's piece is partly anchored by writing about subway travel, so I wrote this as a foil. I also wanted to give voice to this strong stranger who was rising, speaking, and changing others' perceptions of her.

Silently, a stranger approached me on the subway platform and offered me a plate of pastries, a plate she had just taken from her bag. The woman presented it to me wordlessly, offering me a fragrant delight. I politely declined, intensely curious as to why she was offering me her food as we waited together in Queens for the Manhattan-bound train. After I declined, she moved along to the other person waiting for the train, a young man, repeating her offer to him, still silent. He, too, turned down the offer, momentarily removing his headphones to do so. As she returned to her seat, I exchanged a puzzled glance with him.

Without hesitation, he looked at me directly and said, "Manners." Immediately, I felt chagrined. Yes, I thought, manners. It was not long after the president had declared a travel ban on several predominantly Muslim countries, tearing families apart and destroying the hope of many refugees. I had read countless stories covering the chaos: students and doctors prevented from entering the country, or in some cases, from re-entering.

I turned my body toward her, the woman in the hijab. "You're very kind," I said.

"Thank you," she replied. "I'm from Morocco, and in my culture, it's rude to eat without offering something to others." She looked like she might cry, might be crying.

"Everyone needs to eat," I said. The danger of crying seemed to lessen for an instant, if only that.

"Food is a universal need," I said, awkwardly elaborating.

"Exactly," she said, and a hint of a smile appeared.

As we waited in the bitter cold for the train, she told me about her aunt, the pastry maker.

The train arrived and separated us again, this time in a sea of people.

I wondered how the pastry tasted. I imagined savoring it, together, on the subway platform.

TATIANA BURGESS

YEARS AS MENTEE: 1
GRADE: Sophomore
HIGH SCHOOL: Bronx Compass High School
BORN: Bronx, NY
LIVES: Bronx, NY

MENTEE'S ANECDOTE: *At the beginning of the Girls Write Now year, I did not know my mentor at all. However, she went from being this stranger to a friend and role model who helped me become a better writer and person. She introduced me to new writing styles and helped me with my grammar. We tackled writer's block with cool activities like playing the game Taboo. It is crazy how much we have accomplished together. The Girls Write Now workshops have also inspired me to step outside my comfort zone. One word describes my year at Girls Write Now: AMAZING.*

KANIKA WRIGHT

YEARS AS MENTOR: 1
OCCUPATION: Admission Counselor, City University of New York
BORN: Bronx, NY
LIVES: Queens, NY

MENTOR'S ANECDOTE: *Tatiana's smile is full of sunshine, and her writing definitely reflects this same brightness. I met a very shy girl at our first meet up. However, six months later, Tatiana has blossomed into a promising writer who is always hungry for more. Our quirky sense of humor and laughing fits come out in so many ways during our meet ups, especially when we are playing our favorite game Taboo. Tatiana inspires me to dig deeper into my writing craft and confront life's struggles with the power and beauty of words.*

"I"

TATIANA BURGESS

My poem "I" was inspired by another poem called "Loose Woman" by Sandra Cisneros. It represents Rise Speak Change *because it talks about how I changed from what I was, a person who could not speak up.*

I am a tree
with a hard bark
I stay still while the colors on my leaves change
They change more often than the other trees do
Other trees change with the seasons
I change with the day
People always try to cut me down
Some have succeeded, but I just grew right back
I am strong

I am an empty box
People see no use for my emptiness
but I was not always empty
I had to have had something inside of me before I got this
    empty, right?
He took all that was left
He lied and said it was forever
when it was just temporary

Our love was not love
It was just all in my head
So now
I am just an empty box
Maybe being empty is for the better
Empty = no emotions
I had to sacrifice emotions to become stronger
I am stronger

I am a butterfly
I used to be cooped up in my mind
thinking about my emotions over that boy, my family, my school
That is when I decided to cut off my emotions
Thinking about everyone but myself made me spazz
Over time, when I lost my emotions
I liberated my mind and became a butterfly
I became stronger

I am a
teenager
a jokester
a hugger
happy, sad, joyful, mad, angry
too emotional, according to others
They do not know what I have been through
Regardless
I stayed strong through it all

Integrity

KANIKA WRIGHT

My poem "Integrity" was born from a rumor. I was amazed at how a false rumor could transform into something so large. I conquered that lie because I always had truth on my side.

I received Emily's
cold stare
as the word
dripped
from her lips.

Lesbian.

The world spun violently off
its axis. Time
shivered in a frame.
Hushed voices, murmurs, whispers,
rumors commenced. Sixth grade gossip,
new topic for homeroom
tomorrow.

Lesbian.

Tomorrow came, yesterday
still alive in my veins.
My friends,   distant.
Their looks toward me

flickered with change.
No more time for
hopscotch, or
eating lunch at our spot.
They stayed away

No   touching

They faded   away   like apparitions ready to hurl shame my
    way.

Lesbian.

I was alone, only
The Lie
to keep me company. Breaking point
arrived as the wheels in my mind
turned.

Lesbian.

No truth to
Lies.
No lies to
Truth.
I knew Truth. Truth knew
Me.
Emily is a lie.

ELLA CALLAHAN

YEARS AS MENTEE: 1

GRADE: Sophomore

HIGH SCHOOL: School of the Future

BORN: Guangzhou, China

LIVES: New York, NY

MENTEE'S ANECDOTE: *When I first met Allison, I was very intimidated by her poise and her esteemed career. I was nervous about being myself, but that subsided when I spent more time with her. Once we went to the Strand and poured over design books, and another time, she told about this amazing idea she had for a coffee-table book about artists' living spaces. She's easy to talk to, always understanding and very patient. She has inspired me to grow out of my shell.*

ALLISON MOORER

YEARS AS MENTOR: 1

OCCUPATION: Writer, Songwriter, Artist, Mother, currently pursuing MFA in creative non fiction

BORN: Mobile, AL

LIVES: New York, NY

PUBLICATIONS AND RECOGNITIONS: *Guernica, Performing Songwriter, No Depression, American Songwriter,* Vainstyle.com, *Minerva Rising,* and elsewhere.

MENTOR'S ANECDOTE: *Girls Write Now is one of the most worthwhile organizations I've ever been involved in. Giving young girls the push they need to use their voices is inspiring and important. I so enjoy working with my mentee and watching her grow as a writer and person. I know she will take her Girls Write Now experience into the world as she becomes one of its changers.*

Rebellious Streak

ELLA CALLAHAN

Recently in health class, I surprised my classmates by arguing against smoking. Just last year, I'd had smoked out of insecurity, but I became disillusioned with it. I learned from the experience that it was toxic in more ways than one.

"Mom, when did you start smoking?"

"Probably at fourteen, but you must understand—it was a very different time."

At ten, I understood. She told me enough stories from the '70s that I developed a mental film, colored by her nostalgia, played to psychedelic rock. The pride I had in my adopted mom's rebellious spirit was lost on others. I remembering thinking I'd never be so prim as the friend who coughed and swatted her trail of smoke. Yet in the car the smoke wouldn't leave, so I'd prolong my childhood habit of covering my lower face with my sleeve to keep from being nauseated. My father was unaffected. Though smoking had helped his voice acting career, he'd quit long ago. He once told me in his deep timbre, "They changed it. Smells awful now."

Mom's side had the addiction gene. Aunt J smoked until the MS and morphine killed her. Aunt G would bum a cig from Mom but quickly resorted to nicotine gum, and Grandma had to be hypnotized four times to stop. I suggested G's and Grandma's ways to my mom, but she told me it wouldn't work for her, and "Grandma and my father had surpassed the life expectancy for lifestyles like theirs." One night years ago, I cried to Aunt L, "She stays healthy, she's going to live a long time." L consoled, but I dreamt of losing a mother again.

In eighth grade, my friend and I would talk about life after our parents or entertain plans of running away—she from her siblings and I from the guilt of the growing rift with my mom. After taking care of Grandma, she had little patience during nights I stayed up perfecting delayed assignments. Between lost sleep and lost interest in school, I lost my lunch privileges. Banished to the cafeteria for a week by the new warden on offense of escape, I secluded myself to the science room for months. But for all my fasts and isolation, nirvana didn't come. Somewhere in the gloom, I was struck. In a kitchen drawer between the sea of batteries and rubber bands was the bright red Marlboro pack. Loud as an ambulance. The ripped plastic cover would be furtive as fingerprints in dust.

I emerged from the Brooklyn Bridge station. Anxiety was asphyxiating me. I hastily pulled one from the Ziploc in my backpack, then hid behind a closed kiosk, feebly striking, then crushing matchsticks. The wind challenged me but with cupped hand, I carried the flame to the dry bent cigarette. I drew in, held it until it punched my throat. I was a pathetic hacking sideshow for passersby. The real college smokers chattered feet away.

Fortunately, my parents didn't notice the new girl that walked into the apartment that afternoon. Henceforth, after smoking, I drank Tropicana to mask the stench, which left a sweetly sick ashen aftertaste.

Tired of being my own voyeur, I told the person I foolishly wanted to impress the most. So hooked on the high from smoking with him those afternoons on park benches, it became harder to ignore middle school's deafening crescendo.

If I dove off the deep end that May like my mom said, I spent a summer alone at the bottom of a pool. The virago I'd created for his gaze drowned; I had to introduce a more anemic self to my friend. I confessed smoking. Turns out she experimented too. But we punks were far less adventurous than the new students. One delinquent showed off his new zip lighter by lighting AXE body spray in the back of history class. I got cred from him for my twenty-dollar St. Marks cartilage piercing, but it wasn't enough—I was just another nerd in awe. I would supply. To advertise, I lit up outside during lunch, and in a day, I got my first customer. My then-stunned coterie later became my only clientele, but that too faded out. It was at night my friend and I sauntered the streets and picked up still-burning cigarettes. Passed between us, always beginning, never finishing, the thoughts floating in our emptying heads that longed to escape like the billowing smoke that danced into the ether.

One December's night she said, "I think it was just a phase."

"Yeah, I feel like it was for purely aesthetic reasons. See, I'm not addicted, I'm a social smoker. I have to coerce myself into doing this." I looked down at the glowing orange light.

Maybe it's 'cause of my mom posing a mental block, but I couldn't commit for the rest of my life. In this age, we all know the health risks . . . and that these aren't cheap! The kids choosing that huge expenditure kill the frugal indie boho image they're going for. It pains me to abide by those ad campaigns but to defy them with no great benefit to myself. I'm not counterculture; I'm another twenty-first-century teen parading my overly glamorized self-destruction.

"Are you even inhaling right?"

For my fifteenth birthday I got a Peace Lily to clear the air with my mom. When I came clean to her, she said, "You should have charged them more."

Revolution

ALLISON MOORER

I am weary of reducing people, of seeing them as only their political beliefs. That only makes more problems and divisiveness. People are never one thing—we are all complicated beings, and at the end of the day, pretty good ones. I want to believe that, and I want to live as if that is true. Today, that is how I rise, speak, and change.

When we rise let it not be violently.
To rise is to grow. Let us grow more open hearts.
To rise is to increase. Let us increase our compassion.
To rise is to emerge. Let us emerge from our fogs with greater
    awareness.
To rise is to rebel. Let us rebel by linking arms and singing.
When we rise, let it be with love.

When we speak let it not be unkindly.
To speak is to say. Let us say our highest intentions.

To speak is to be fluent. Let us be fluent first in listening.
To speak is to address. Let us address an even playing field.
To speak is to declare. Let us declare what we are certain is true.
When we speak, let it be with love.

When we change let it not be through force.
To change is to alter. Let us alter our biased ideas.
To change is to modify. Let us modify what no longer works.
To change is to adjust. Let us adjust to obstacles as water does to
    rocks.
To change is to correct. Let us correct that which has been
    overturned.
When we change, let it be with love.

LAURA ROSE CARDONA

YEARS AS MENTEE: 2

GRADE: Senior

HIGH SCHOOL: Williamsburg Preparatory High School

BORN: Brooklyn, NY

LIVES: Brooklyn, NY

PUBLICATIONS AND RECOGNITIONS: Scholastic Art & Writing Awards: Silver Keys and Honorable Mentions; Presidential Scholarship for The King's College; Leadership Scholarship for The King's College

MENTEE'S ANECDOTE: *Vegan donuts. Rainbow-colored string lights. The smell of coffee and—you guessed it—the smell of vegan donuts. In the background, a faux jukebox plays quirky, old-timer tunes. "I love women, ahh-hhhh," screeches the ancient singer. Kathleen and I exchange glances, stifling our laughs at the bizarre tunes. You see, she and I have the utmost respect for that music, the scents in the air, and the out-of-the-season lights, because to us, this is what it feels like to be a writer, an artist, a New Yorker, and yes: this is what it feels like to be part of Girls Write Now.*

KATHLEEN SCHEINER

YEARS AS MENTOR: 6

OCCUPATION: Freelance editor and writer

BORN: Biloxi, MS

LIVES: Brooklyn, NY

PUBLICATIONS AND RECOGNITIONS: *New York State of Fright* anthology (2017)

MENTOR'S ANECDOTE: *As Laura prepares for college, we've been laser-focused during our sessions, working on writing essays for various scholarships, preparing for presentations, and rehearsing speeches. We sit at a table in Dun-Well Doughnuts, a laptop between us, checking edits, but we always have time to joke—"Adverbs are weak!"—and rhapsodize about our favorite punctuation marks. Laura says, "The umlaut is now a thing in my life," while I like the dramatic gesture of an em dash.*

Abandoned by Faith

LAURA ROSE CARDONA

My piece focuses on the insecurities that lie within the state of change, especially when such shifts polarize oneself. In this piece, I discuss my battle between Christianity and homosexuality.

"I love you. God bless you. Good night." A quick kiss on the cheek, adjusting my blanket so that I was properly tucked in, before she smiled, turning away and exiting the room. This simple sentence of eight words has always been the staple of my mother's bedtime departure. It was as if she was so afraid that I would somehow slip away so deeply into a slumber that, for whatever reason, I would never awake again, and this blessing was the only way to guard against such a tragedy. I could not recall a single night in my life that this blessing was absent from our goodnights to each other. Even in the swells of our most stormy arguments, we would always manage to momentarily hold our anger beneath the rippled waters long enough to gaze upon each other and whisper the final words of the evening:

"I love you. God bless you. Good night."

Always, without fail, until one day, the angers suffocating within the waters beneath us rose above my mother, choking her with such fury that she was, for the first time, unable to deliver her faithful blessing, and I was alone, unprotected in the night.

Although I wasn't entirely alone. There was a man, or at least the image of a man—as the scripture goes—who had, for my entire life, followed me, shadowing my every move. This figure was God. Our relationship was like that of a boat in rugged waters. Sometimes, like when I was just a little girl, I was sure he was there behind me, serving as my protector and guide. However, as I began to mature in my teenage years, my faith wavered.

I recall laying on my bed when I was only twelve years old, my body curled into a C-shape as I held my pillow near my chest. I was in bed later than I should have been, all because I had just wrapped up a near six-hour conversation with a friend at my middle school. Even though we were no longer on the phone together, I wondered why her voice still echoed through my mind, preventing me from sleep.

I began reminiscing about all the moments we had shared up to this point. The first time I spoke to her was when she dropped her sharpener on the ground and I, feeling compelled to help her, crawled on all fours across the classroom tiles to retrieve it for her. She would message me during class, despite the fact that she sat only a few rows away from me, and I would respond without hesitation or thought. Once I plucked a flower from its stem in the botanical hall of the Bronx Zoo to present to her as a makeshift present, only to flee the zoo in screams as a bee I disturbed vowed revenge on me. I remembered all this and more, and it played in my mind like a projector, almost mockingly, laminating my many failed attempts to capture her attention. My affection poured like a pipe that had been busted and was spewing water, except this pipe was more like an artery streamlining from my heart, and the liquid was nothing but love, and that's when I realized: I was in love with her.

Such a simple thought sent my mind awry. How could I love

someone of the same sex? How could God let this happen to me? At the very least, Eve had the choice of choosing the apple, but here I was, performing for an operating theater, strapped to a medical table, the apple of lust gagged in my mouth, while the devil grinned above me, wasting no time in bringing his surgical knife down, extracting God from my heart and my heart from my God.

The hole carved within me by Satan burned with passion. I set out to fill the void with love—or was it lust? What did I care at this point? Like a bride on her wedding day, the scriptures abandoned me, left me in solitude at the altar with nothing but the vows of the Bible to accompany me, except now the parchment was just a painful reminder of what we could have been together. So I averted my attention to the bridesmaid. Every girl that encircled me was a target that I could thrust my naïveté upon, desperately trying to claw some sense of my sexuality out from the fog of rejection and denial. Yet no matter how much I thirsted for attention, the hole within me did not sprout with life. It seemed the rains of sorrow made no good fertilizer, and the flames of desire did little to quell its cold. So I sat at that altar, wondering where was my groom, wondering why my parents didn't walk me down this aisle of pity, but most of all, wondering why my mother no longer uttered:

"I love you. God bless you. Goodnight."

A Godly Woman

KATHLEEN SCHEINER

Mental illness runs in my family, but it's always been treated like a dirty secret. Nobody wants to talk about it much, maybe thinking the problem will go away if they ignore it.

The sun beat down—high noon in Missouri—and all the flowers had been arranged along with the Precious Moments figurines into an impromptu serenity garden for the memorial. We were fanned out across the yard in lawn chairs, and I made sure to face the fire pit where my uncle, aunt, and cousins burned their trash rather than paying the city to cart it away. I could see empty plastic two-liter bottles that used to hold soda fused together in strange clear sculptures, along with mattress coils and broken flower pots. I remember Grandma always having a bottle of Pepsi tucked under one batwing arm. She loved her sweets.

My uncle starts out the service, talking about the godly woman that Marjorie Billings was. I'm surprised to see everybody nodding and hearing the *Amens* coming out of them.

I remember Grandma running down the street naked to get a newspaper from the Wawa, talking to terrorists through her geranium, and telling me about how different aunts and uncles were conceived after a drink too many. Godly, I don't remember. Well, there was that one time she thought she was the Virgin Mary and all the children in the world were hers.

We call it the family illness—it runs heavy in the females on my mom's side, and my grandmother got a heavy dose of it. We never had a name for it until the 1980s—bipolar disorder. But every year Grandma had to go to the mental hospital—the longest time for a year after my Uncle Charlie was born, the kid she liked the least. "Just never cottoned to him," she said. They tried shock treatments on her that year.

I used to be terrified it would soon be my turn. I'd worry, *Are my emotions normal? Am I feeling too much? Will the trembling turn into something I can't control?*

I asked Grandma, "What does it feel like going crazy?"

She smiled like she was remembering a long lost love. "It's the best feeling in the world. Sometimes I can't wait for it to come back."

I didn't worry after that.

JOEY CHEN

YEARS AS MENTEE: 1

GRADE: Junior

HIGH SCHOOL: Stuyvesant High School

BORN: Brooklyn, NY

LIVES: Brooklyn, NY

PUBLICATIONS AND RECOGNITIONS: Scholastic Art & Writing Award: Honorable Mention

MENTEE'S ANECDOTE: *The first time Kiele and I met, we discovered our mutual love for spoken word poetry. One of the goals we set for the Girls Write Now program was to attend poetry slams together. We recently went to a spoken word event called "Page Meets Stage" at the Bowery Poetry Club where we got to see Morgan Parker and Sam Sax battle it out on stage. Although I was never comfortable enough to pursue spoken word on my own, Kiele has definitely pushed me to take more risks and be courageous with my writing!*

KIELE RAYMOND

YEARS AS MENTOR: 1

OCCUPATION: Senior Agent, Thompson Literary Agency

BORN: Portsmouth, NH

LIVES: Brooklyn, NY

MENTOR'S ANECDOTE: *I love how Joey is always seeking out new experiences. She has traveled to Costa Rica, Spain, and Tanzania, and this fall, we worked on summer abroad applications. So I was thrilled (and a little jealous) when I found out she was chosen to study in Berlin for the month of July. She has rekindled my love for German philosophy and reminded me that new perspectives should be found both on and off the page. I can't wait to hear all about her adventures overseas.*

Kairosclerosis

JOEY CHEN

According to the Dictionary of Obscure Sorrows, *kairosclerosis is "the moment you realize that you're currently happy—consciously trying to savor the feeling—which prompts your intellect to identify it, pick it apart and put it in context, where it will slowly dissolve until it's little more than an aftertaste."*

She looks at the dashboard from the backseat of some taxicab. *11:51 p.m.* Only nine minutes until midnight. She was only nine minutes away from turning seventeen. Another year closer to eighteen, to becoming an adult. The prospect terrified her. She didn't want to grow up, at least not yet. She didn't quite have things figured out; no big plans for the future, except the stuff that everybody did, like college and graduating from college. She didn't want to abandon what was in front of her. What she wanted was to be forever sixteen, forever young.

She stares outside the taxicab window at the lamplit Manhattan streets and skyscrapers; she's gone down this crowded highway a thousand times before. But still this neighborhood is unfamiliar.

"Hey, taxicab driver!" she yells. "Where are we right now?"

"Uh, not too far from the High Line. We're almost there."

"Do you mind hurrying it up, man? I've got places to be!" she huffs.

"Yes, ma'am!" he responds obediently, and presses on the gas pedal a little harder.

She slumps back into her seat, taking in the musty smell of old leather mixed with her own perfume. She's been wearing the same Vera Wang scent since she started high school, but now it smells different on her. She hasn't noticed the harsh floral scent before. She wrinkles her nose, not sure if she likes it, and shrugs.

They stop again at a light. The driver looks back.

"So what are you up to tonight?" he asks.

"Some guy's house," she mumbles. "We're going to see a band."

"What band?"

"Not sure."

"Oh."

As they inch forward, he adjusts the rearview mirror so that he can see her face better in the darkness. He notices the streetlights reflecting off her angled cheekbones and the way her eyes wrinkle at the corners as she squints at something in the distance. She can't be much younger than him.

"Do you mind turning on the radio?" she asks suddenly, interrupting his lingering stare.

"Not at all."

He grips the steering wheel with one hand and slowly turns the dial until he finds a song he likes.

"Hey! I know this song!" she shouts.

"You like it?"

"Yeah! I used to listen to this all the time when I was a kid."

Although she hasn't heard the song in years, she still knows exactly where each of the guitar solos start and end. She drums her fingers against her thighs to the beat. Her mother used to raise the volume whenever the second verse started. They would dance together in the living room.

"Belle and Sebastian is my favorite band of all time," he says. She nods absentmindedly in response.

11:56 p.m.

She knows that to every passerby on the streets, she is just another teenage girl weaving through the city in a branded yellow taxi.

She thinks of that word, *sonder*, the realization that each passerby was living a life as vivid and complex as her own.

How many significant moments in her life actually matter in the grand scheme of things? After all, she is just a speck of dust stuck in an infinitesimal universe.

11:59 p.m.

The cab slows and pulls over to the edge of the sidewalk.

"All right, we're here."

"What? Already?"

She sees the dark green door of her friend's apartment building. She pays and steps out onto the concrete pavement.

"Thanks for the ride, man."

"Yeah, no problem. Have a good time at the show. And don't forget about Belle and Sebastian!"

She nods and swings the cab door shut. The world speeds up again, and as the clock strikes twelve, she rings the buzzer.

Zenosyne

KIELE RAYMOND

According to the Dictionary of Obscure Sorrows, *Zenosyne is "the sense that time keeps going faster." Joey and I used these terms as a jumping off point to think about how change can be experienced in so many different ways.*

My daughter turns seventeen tomorrow. She was born in 2000, and that felt very neat and tidy at the time. Clean slate, etc. Her birthday still feels like a kind of completion each year, coinciding usually with the moment I stop messing up the date on my checks or dentist forms. When I was younger, a new adult, I used to cock my head at receptionists and ask, "What year is it again?" I thought it made me seem relatable.

My daughter is a New Yorker. She doesn't do stuff like that. Or maybe she will, when the edge of girlhood wears off and she needs to feel seen for a little while. Now, though, she doesn't need those tethers. She's out tonight. I don't know where exactly because she deleted Uber from our phones. They were on the wrong side of a protest. Downtown somewhere, she said. I pay the cashier, throw the overpriced syrup in my bag. We'll have pancakes when she wakes up.

My daughter is a feminist. She has the language to fight, or rather, she knows what is no longer up for debate. Once she told me to stop calling myself a tomboy. I wanted her to know it was okay, but she can tell when I'm forcing it. Like with Belle and Sebastian. She used to love it when she was a kid, but now it's charged. She feels infantilized; she shrinks into the passenger seat.

My daughter hates odd numbers. Seventeen will be an in-between year for her. I do this thing where I figure out how old I am by adding her age—the last two numerals of the current year, that is—to the age I was in 2000. The math feels easier that way. Like it's rooted somehow. I can see our living room window from this stretch of 148th. She left the light on. I hear the cars rushing along the Hudson and cannot wait to be home.

MARYCLARE CHINEDO

YEARS AS MENTEE: 2

GRADE: Junior

HIGH SCHOOL: Bronx Lighthouse College Prep Academy

BORN: Bronx, NY

LIVES: Bronx, NY

PUBLICATIONS AND RECOGNITIONS: Scholastic Art & Writing Award: Honorable Mention

MENTEE'S ANECDOTE: *During the Girls Write Now orientation, Morayo and I had to come up with pair goals. Right off the bat, I knew something I wanted to accomplish. I wanted to win a Scholastic Art & Writing Award. Every weekly meeting after that was dedicated to trying new writing genres; learning new, saucy vocabulary; and making me an overall stronger writer. By pushing me out my comfort zone and supporting me, Morayo was able to help me grow as a writer and as a person, and I landed the Scholastic Award.*

MORAYO FALEYIMU

YEARS AS MENTOR: 5

OCCUPATION: Senior Program Manager, Peer Health Exchange

BORN: Miami, FL

LIVES: Elizabeth, NJ

MENTOR'S ANECDOTE: *Maryclare has such a bright, humorous voice as a writer. Her pieces inspire me to tackle my usual topics from a more comical or satirical stance than I normally do. It's been a pleasure bouncing ideas off of her, and I look forward to the way that we will work together in her senior year!*

Safety Instructions

MARYCLARE CHINEDO

A satire about a plane full of Muslims entering America in the year 2117. It is an exaggerated version of what the future may hold if the current administration keeps up its discriminatory policies.

Attention! Attention all you people who decided to come to come to this part of the world out of all the other countries. It looks like you had limited options. Because . . . America? Really? Anywho, I hope you enjoyed your flight with Ban-Ottomans Airlines. Before you get out of your seats, I'm going to pass out a pamphlet. Excuse me, lady, make sure you take one and pass it back. I'm sure your daughter doesn't need it. You can give her the rundown when she gets older. You see this booklet right here? It's sacred. It's the second Bible. Read it, understand it, meditate on it, live by it, and breathe it! If you want to assimilate into this country peacefully, I suggest you read it. I'll just read it out for you. Sorry, I know it's not in Arabic. This is America, deal with it. Shall we begin? Great!

Rule number one, look at my fingers . . . one: *Thou shalt not bear any name that rhymes with Mohammed or any characters in the Quran.* Yup, that's right! So all you Mamadous, Fatimas, Fatoumatas, Alis, Aboubacars and so on—you guys are screwed. But don't you worry, what happens on Ban-Ottomans Airlines stays in Ban-Ottomans Airlines. My lovely assistant, Lulu, is coming around with name-change forms. Feel free to take one if you'd like to live in peace. Moving on.

Rule two: Thou shalt not bear any items related to Islam. Any hijabs, prayer rugs or Qurans, there will be none of that. Even a little keychain of the kaaba is forbidden. Don't even waste your time and try to hide it. The Islamic Hunt Services are one step ahead. That means weekly checks, people!

Rule three is pretty simple. Every morning, you must recite John 14:6 aloud. I can't quite remember what it's about, but I think it's something about accepting Jesus. You guys will find out soon enough.

This fourth rule goes out to the ladies. You may not like this, but, you gotta show more skin. All that modesty stuff you guys talk about—that's gotta go. If you wear skirts or dresses, they cannot be longer than your knee. If skirts and dresses aren't your thing, then *shorts only!* I can't stress that enough. Don't worry, guys, I'm almost done.

Let's go to rule five. By a show of hands, how many of you like food? I should see more hands than that. Anyways, every year between May and July, there is a mandatory—I repeat, *mandatory*—all-you-can-eat buffet. How does that sound? Amazing, right?

The last rule is not that big of a deal. But, you have to leave all your phones on this plane and pick up a new one on your way out. We don't think you all are dirty or anything. We just want you guys to pick up a new phone customized for Muslim immigrants. This new phone has everything your old one has except for a compass. But I'm sure you all don't use that anyways.

Okay! I think that's it. I don't want to keep you all any longer. I've pretty much covered the basics. Now don't go crying on me, now. You guys chose to come here. I didn't drag you on this plane. All right, then. Now that that's settled, get into a single file line and get off this plane. Don't forget everything I've told you unless you want to end up in jail!

Thank you for flying with Ban-Ottomans Airlines! I hope you enjoy your stay and have a peaceful assimilation into America.

Dear Lady Liberty

MORAYO FALEYIMU

Since Maryclare was exploring satire, I decided to have a go at humor. My piece is a Dear Abby–style column penned by none other than the Statue of Liberty. Similar to Maryclare's piece, my work also deals with assimilation, but from a sordid "love triangle" perspective.

Dear Lady Liberty,

I'm caught in a love triangle between my homeland and America. Any advice?

Sincerely,
Homesick Everywhere

Dear *Homesick Everywhere,*

You poor, tired, huddled mass! I've felt that same way for *years*. I am of French heritage, but I've lived in the

United States for centuries. Being bicultural is hard. Over time, you start to feel like both places belong to you, but that you don't belong to either one.

My advice? Choose to belong to yourself. Redefine the borders of this love triangle, *Homesick*! In fact, abolish the triangle! Be the center of your own universe. Homeland and America can duke it out in the boys locker room.

Now, I know what you're thinking. Too rash a decision. Too harsh. How could you live without them both? That, dear *Homesick*, is the genius of the whole plan. Countries are all the same. Drop them and they come running back to you! I've seen it happen hundreds of times. Mark my words: rip up their passports to your heart! Do it today! And just go outside and be you. Soon enough, they'll knock on your door, looking to kiss and make up. When that happens, look them square in the tempest-toss't eye and tell them that you will set any and all immigration policies in *that* relationship.

XOXO,
Lady Liberty

SAMORI COVINGTON

YEARS AS MENTEE: 4

GRADE: Senior

HIGH SCHOOL: Millennium Brooklyn High School

BORN: Brooklyn, NY

LIVES: Brooklyn, NY

PUBLICATIONS AND RECOGNITIONS: I got accepted to my first-choice college.

MENTEE'S ANECDOTE: *As Girls Write Now comes to an end for me this year, I have realized that my writing has come a long way. As a freshman I always tried to make people laugh, but as I got older, I wanted to write more about social issues. I am a four-year mentee, and looking back, I remember spending a whole year being obsessed with writing science fiction. To me, this piece ties everything together—the science and the social issues.*

BROOKE BOREL

YEARS AS MENTOR: 4

OCCUPATION: Journalist and Author

BORN: Topeka, KS

LIVES: Brooklyn, NY

PUBLICATIONS AND RECOGNITIONS: My second book published in 2016, *The Chicago Guide to Fact-Checking* (University of Chicago Press). I also had a year-long fellowship with the Alicia Patterson Foundation.

MENTOR'S ANECDOTE: *When I first started Girls Write Now four years ago, I was paired with a freshman—Samori! Our time together has flown by. I am so happy to see her moving on to college, but it's also bittersweet for me because I will greatly miss our weekly meetings. Every year, Samori has explored new genres: from humor writing to science fiction to socially conscious essays and poems. In this last piece, she wanted to combine all of these interests, so we tackled futuristic political satire.*

Escape from Trump Towers

SAMORI COVINGTON

This piece is about a dystopian society in the near future that speaks to my misgivings about today's government. I wanted to experiment with satire this year while also acknowledging the ignorance in society.

"And now, presenting the President of the United States. Ladies and Gentlemen, Donald Trumpitron."

The president took to the podium, his orangeness glowing on my television screen. "Good evening," he said. "Here are new rules for the Extended Constitution. Because people have not been behaving. Rule #171: The new curfew is 7:00 p.m. Rule #172: Failure to pay taxes to the government will result in deportation."

"Cheezy Trumpitron," I muttered, and turned to Miranda on the couch beside me in the shelter rec room. But she wasn't there. I'm still not used to it. I thought back three months ago when she was deported to her home country, Israel. According to the government, she broke curfew too many times. Miranda is actually lucky that she still had her life and she was not thrown away at the edge of the Earth like some who broke some of the rules, which changed all the time. She came to the United States for a better life, when Israel was in the middle of a fifteen-year war. At that time, the U.S. was the only place left in the world that had not been breached by war, chaos, and fear.

Ever since Trumpitron won the election, as Trump robots have for the past sixty-some years, our economy has been declining. We no longer have any resources or allies. The fresh water from Maine to Texas has dried out and the cattle from the farms down South have died. And what does Cheezy Trumpitron do? He closes the borders, making sure no one can enter and no one can leave. Unless they're thrown out. But I'm starting to think that something else is behind most of these ridiculous ideas. Ever since the new Bannon chip released last year, every country is against us and we have no one to turn to.

I have been working since the age of five. Our last human ruler, the first Donald Trump, thought he made the country perfect. But in order to create perfection there is usually a lot of control. He, and now his robot spawn, own every building in America. I repeat *Every Building in America,* from the Empire State Building to the gated community down the block from where I work. US citizens work in these buildings; "Trump Towers" as he likes to call them. The upper echelon live in Trump Towers while the poor and unfortunate, such as myself, go home to dark and dingy alleyways. The elite are the ones who agree with everything Trumpitron says. They support him throughout his speeches of nonsense, they are the ones who do not have a curfew and fly around in fancy cars with robot drivers. The little money we do receive goes straight to Trumpitron.

I'm tired of living like this. Working to provide for the people above me. I work sixteen hours a day and I can't even see a penny of it. Sometimes I wonder how the people around me are okay with this, but I think maybe they're just oblivious like I once was until I opened my eyes. I'm a grown man and yet I have a curfew. I have to be asleep in my bunk in a shelter, for crying out loud, by seven o'clock. That's when the wolves come sniffing. Every adult in this country is treated like a child and the children are treated like adults. I slide off the couch, shake off the pain of missing Miranda, and head to work. Today, I have a meeting with one of my coworkers. Julian also started off as a factory worker, and now we work as electricians and ensure that Trump Towers functions at all times. Some of us are trying to develop a group to escape. I'm hoping Julian will join us.

"How exactly do you plan on convincing people to join this 'said' group?" says Julian.

"Well, we obviously can't broadcast our ideas to the public, you ditz," I say.

He squints at me and says, "You always have something smart to say."

"And you always have something dumb to say. Anyway, back to the point. I really cannot live here anymore. I stayed because I thought that one day, things would get better for Miranda and me. As you can see, things did not work out too well."

"I know it's hard because she is not here right now," he said. "But you know what? I'm in. Let's go to Canada."

A week later, my heart was thumping. It was 5:00 p.m. and the time had come. "Guys, come on. We do not have much time, the wolves will be here sooner than you think," I whispered.

"Relax, we have two hours," Julian said, as he fumbled with the electrical box.

"Wait, why are the alarms going off?"

"I hear the wolves coming! Cut the lights!"

It went dark. And I started running.

The Press Conference

BROOKE BOREL

I was inspired by Samori's satirical dystopian science fiction, which shows a future of a robot-ruled America. I used elements of her story as a starting point to imagine the press conference that would accompany a new announcement by the robot government.

"Thank you for coming. First order of business: the new rules."

Spicerbot 7.0 gripped the podium with flesh-colored, rubberized pincers. *Click click* went the cameras in either eye, making a record of the journalists in the audience. There were three.

"As you undoubtedly heard in the president's address last night, rule 171 is a change to the nightly curfew," Spicerbot's words came in clipped tones, cameras flitting from face to face. "It is now seven o'clock instead of eight o'clock due to Daylight Savings Time."

"Is there any truth to the claim that it's really because of anomalies in the timing of the sunset?" asked the first reporter, a middle-aged woman in a faded lime-green jumpsuit.

"No comment," Spicerbot replied.

The woman arched a shaggy eyebrow. "But Daylight Savings Time hasn't existed for twenty years," she countered. "Care to comment?"

Spicerbot paused, and a fan at its left temple began to whir. "Daylight Savings Time has always existed." *Click click click* went the cameras. The woman frowned, then scratched on her notebook with a stubby pencil.

"Is it true that the wolves will be let out earlier, too?" asked the second reporter, his tiny brown eyes peeking through an unruly white forelock.

"You know I'm not going to answer that," Spicerbot said. "Now, onto the rumors about the president's alleged software upgrade. These are exactly that: rumors. The president already has the best operating system money can buy. I repeat: The best. Money can buy. There's no need for an upgrade."

The third reporter, a skinny man with his feet propped on the empty chair in front of him, asked: "How's the missile roll-out coming?"

"Thanks for the question, Gary," Spicerbot said. "Come by the office this afternoon and I'll give you a scoop."

Spicerbot shuffled some blank papers on the podium and, with a metallic clearing of the throat, said, "Now, that concludes today's press briefing. Thank you all."

The woman in the jumpsuit and the man with the white hair jumped up. "What about the new rule 172?" she shouted, at the same time that he cried, "Won't you clarify the new tax penalty—is it true about the consequences?"

Spicerbot's cameras went *click click click* and his fan went *whir whir whir.* After some time came the reply.

"No comment."

MEDELIN CUEVAS

YEARS AS MENTEE: 2

GRADE: Junior

HIGH SCHOOL: H.E.R.O. High School

BORN: Santiago, Dominican Republic

LIVES: Bronx, NY

PUBLICATIONS AND RECOGNITIONS: Scholastic Art & Writing Award: Silver Key; Founder of Decipher (Poetry club)

MENTEE'S ANECDOTE: *Rakia has challenged me in many aspects mentally as a writer and as a person. Every time when I would write a piece, she would help me to go deeper to pick out the potential in my writing that I didn't always see myself when it came to my own personal experiences.*

RAKIA CLARK

YEARS AS MENTOR: 1

OCCUPATION: Senior Editor, Beacon Press

BORN: Atlantic City, NJ

LIVES: New York, NY

MENTOR'S ANECDOTE: *Maddy has reminded me how much fun and how stressful being a teenager is. I am in constant awe of how she is able to manage her studies with her lively personal life and her upcoming pressures about college.*

We the People

MEDELIN CUEVAS

As an Afro Latina in the United States, it's very common to see inequality. As a result, I spoke up about this dilemma and will stop at nothing to see a change in my country I call home.

One of the hottest topics today is immigration. The news, social media, and many other informative outlets argue that immigrants influence violence, promote terrorism, and bring chaos to otherwise calm communities. As the freedom of immigrants who look like me and my family hangs by a thread, it is scary to know that some Americans believe our country can only move forward and be better without "bad hombres."

How can we move forward if we let negative stereotypes separate us more than they bring us together? Misunderstanding the intentions of immigrants who are trying to better themselves as people is not cool. In school, I have heard phrases like, "Hispanics can't wear hijabs," "Africans have a foul odor," "Asians are human calculators," and "most immigrants should stay at the bottom of the food chain and do America's dirty work."

We the people—from the Preamble of our nation's Constitution—should include *everyone*. That is how we will emerge as one and create a better America. That is how we will move more efficiently as a country. We have to work together.

From what I have seen and experienced as a Dominican-American teenager, immigrants are really underappreciated, yet we are the building blocks of American culture. For instance, we are the people who help make America a multi-linguistic country. We bring strong compassion and leadership skills. We also consistently fight to win greater recognition and advocacy for our communities. From Sonia Sotomayor to Malala Yousafzai, we immigrants fight for what's right and stop at nothing to gain equality that helps everyone and not just ourselves. We do this despite having to face bigotry that is sometimes too difficult to handle.

To Americans who believe in that "bad hombre" line of thinking, I have a question: Why can't you all cross your community's invisible lines and educate yourself? That's where the confusion comes from—a lack of education. You have no right to make an immigrant feel less than he or she is. No group of immigrants should feel as if they carry a disease or be targeted as criminals, or be considered poor and needy just because they ask for assistance. It's not like America is perfect. It has its flaws and is also in need of a pick-me-up sometimes. Instead of pointing fingers at others for the disconnect, take a closer look at yourselves. Try rewiring your own thinking and comprehending more from people who don't look like you. Because if you do not, you will most likely see another great depression, and I do not only mean that economically.

The voicelessness that immigrants feel is unfair. America is a country of opportunity and everyone has a right to express their ideas, emotions, and actions without a law prohibiting them. Just take me as an example. I am the proud daughter of an immigrant, representing not only my voice, but my mother's voice as well.

Just look at the people around us. People from Syria are fleeing from their civil war between each other to protect their religious practices and rights. People from Haiti are going to Puerto Rico to try to get the same U.S. benefits as the native Puerto Ricans. Mexicans are crossing over borders and large bodies of water to gain a better living for themselves and to be an American without losing their roots. Some people are literally dying to get here. We as a union—*We the People*—should have a right to live together in one country as good, hardworking people, instead of being lumped in with criminals. There are some "bad hombres" in the world, yes. But there are way more good ones.

Home Again

RAKIA CLARK

Immigration is in the news now more than ever. It is no wonder Maddy and I had big thoughts about it.

Like Maddy, my family is full of immigrants. On my mother's side, we are a deeply Bermudian bunch. Codfish and potatoes on Sundays. Hotcross buns on Easter. English peas in potato salad. My grandmother (God rest her soul) usually ended conversations with an upbeat "Right-o!"

Growing up in the American South, I knew I was very Americanized. My accent and interests were the same as my classmates. And nothing about my physical appearance let on that my background was all that different. Yet I still found myself codeswitching, or changing the way I spoke and acted, even before I learned what codeswitching meant. For example, when entering a room full of Bermudians, I knew always to say "Good morning," "Good afternoon," or "Good evening" straight away. To do otherwise was unthinkable and worse: rude. That is a cardinal sin among Bermudians, being rude. It is especially frowned upon from the too-Americanized children of expats.

I never wanted any of my family members still in Bermuda to think that I had been led too far away from our roots. Around them, I affected my best Bermudian accent. And I developed a taste for farina pie, a local dish, even when all my cousins said they did not like. It was my way of reinforcing my connection to the island.

I kept a small Bermudian flag on my desk all through college. And even now, I have a five-by-seven-inch, framed map of Bermuda on the wall in my office.

When I visit my family's homeland these days, I feel much more American than I did as a kid. And I am okay with that. My adolescent cousins want me to bring all sorts of goods that they do not have access to in Bermuda whenever I fly home. I hear them modulate their voices and try out new slang to sound more American. And at this, I smile. No matter where we are, we long for a little bit of something else.

BERNA DA'COSTA

YEARS AS MENTEE: 1
GRADE: Sophomore
HIGH SCHOOL: Stuyvesant High School
BORN: Goa, India
LIVES: Bronx, NY

MENTEE'S ANECDOTE: *It wasn't instant. It was awkward pauses in the middle of conversations and not knowing what to say next. But somehow, my mentor still heard the words that were left behind through the writing I shared with her. It has become easy to write around Jamie, to sit in comfortable silence behind our laptop screens and try to capture our thoughts onto the blank page. There are people who have been in my life, who have encouraged me to write, and write, and write. I will always remember those people. My mentor is now one of them.*

JAMIE SERLIN

YEARS AS MENTOR: 1
OCCUPATION: Director, West Wing Writers, LLC
BORN: Philadelphia, PA
LIVES: Brooklyn, NY

MENTOR'S ANECDOTE: *Though we may seem different on the surface—I am pretty chatty, Berna is more soft-spoken—I've found that Berna and I actually share a lot in common. We are both incredibly sassy—Berna in her writing, me in all realms of life. We are both night owls and procrastinators who suffer from occasional writer's block before getting seized by a last-minute idea. Berna's confidence, creativity, and openness in sharing her writing have been a huge inspiration to me in getting over my own fear of sharing my work.*

Leave Me Alone . . .

BERNA DA'COSTA

James is the first character I have ever created. She is the person I hide behind in my writing and she speaks the words that I don't say. I have gone mildly crazy with the power I have over her story.

This is dedicated to the night the criminals were born and rolled into blankets. Under the cracked ceiling, an infamous one-word story was whispered . . .

James was walking down the street, a flare of ombré, a surge of spearmint, and a book in her hand, slowly meandering from the sidewalk onto the curb strip as she became deaf and blind to the world. Her feet crushed the spring grass, stepping on water droplets and sprinkling them inches into the atmosphere only to fall back down to Earth. The sun was shining, the trees were dancing, and the people around her were talking, filling this quiet, empty world with meaningless noise and mindless chatter.

She hummed to herself, the sound echoing in her ears. It was a soft melody, coming from her raging mind, that flew into the air and out into space. NASA had just found three Earth-sized, potentially habitable exoplanets around a single star. That was the kind of headline she had always wanted to see. James was ready to be launched from this flaming garbage pile. She hoped that, maybe, the aliens who dropped her here seventeen years ago would finally come back to get her.

Would anyone notice if they did? Lately, it seemed to James that no one wanted to give a second glance to someone like her—someone who wasn't filled with that obligatory happiness. They won't bother with you until you've fixed yourself, because no one wants to willingly clean up messes.

That's why James trusted her books. She wondered why no one else could understand this—that within their reach was a world that they could control. They could open it, read its secrets between the white spaces, and put it down before it got to be too much. They could touch and kill their monsters instead of running away, tripping over their mistakes and losing control. James always fought an internal battle, wanting to reach the last page, but at the same time, never wanting to reach the end of the story. She had become a nocturnal creature, falling asleep with the sun and surrendering to her tired eyes when everyone else had just opened theirs. She lived in the moments where nothing was real.

She let herself fall onto the ground, the cold grass shocking her nerves awake like volts to a dead heartbeat. She wanted to leave; to go home. She wanted to lock herself up in her room and let the music blast and blow up her eardrums so she couldn't hear the bullets shooting out of everyone's mouths. Being alone was so much easier.

Her sight blurred when she heard footsteps making their way toward her.

"What are you doing?" came a voice. *Jude? Quick, make a joke. Make her smile. Fill yourself with that obligatory happiness.*

"Becoming one with nature. Experiencing Zen," James responded.

"On my front lawn?"

"Huh?" *How did she . . .*

"I saw you from the window. Are you okay?"

Is she okay? Definitely not. Jude tilted her head, looking worried. Her black curtain of hair spilled and looked like a starless night sky.

Jude tried again. "Well, you see, I thought you were dead because you weren't responding to any of my texts." She pinched James' cheek and sat down next to her on the grass, hands tucked under her bony knees.

James felt a raindrop, and then two. It was drizzling. Not raining, not pouring. Thunder rolled the clouds. Jude was wearing James' wrinkled black hoodie, drowning in the size of it. She looked small and insignificant, like she shouldn't be in this big world. James was completely wrecked for her.

"I have a shitty crush on you," James finally confessed.

Jude widened her eyes and blinked.

James continued. "Do you want to go out with me? Like on a date, or whatever. Be my girlfriend."

Jude turned away. "That was horrible. You're horrible. You want to go out on a date with me and *that's* how you decide to ask?"

James shivered and lightning ripped the clouds. It was like the world was sending her a warning that this wasn't her sanest idea. And now she began to think that maybe she should check herself into a mental hospital. *I'm James Caster and I think I might be mentally unstable because I have a shitty crush on Jude Larimar.*

"Sure," Jude said finally smirking, "or whatever."

James closed her eyes and laughed. It was suddenly so easy to laugh she almost cried.

The world disappeared around her and she escaped once

again into her mind. She imagined a bridge, broken and tearing, and she walked across it without holding the ropes. It was
a tightrope, a thin, barely visible piece of white thread, and she
moved on her toes with her eyes closed. Below her was a pit of
darkness that didn't seem to have a bottom. She could hear the
monsters rustling below. She could see their cruel claws trying
to reach her from the abyss and pull her down. She spun and
jumped above them. They couldn't touch her. Not a single
scratch.

Don't Leave Me Alone.

To the Defenders of the Union

JAMIE SERLIN

*This piece was inspired by the free write from our very first workshop
on travel writing. At a time of great fear and uncertainty at home,
this place has special meaning to me.*

In a city of skyscrapers, we sometimes forget to look up. Have
you ever walked by something—a building, a sign, a statue—a
whole bunch of times before you ever really stopped to look at
it? Or maybe you just noticed it for the first time from a different angle. Or maybe the light hit it in a funny way one day, and
you thought, "Hey, has that always been there?"

I can't claim I never noticed the Soldiers' and Sailors' Arch.
The marble behemoth that straddles Grand Army Plaza is pretty

hard to miss. In the evening it glows a mystic purple, and the car headlights swirling around it make for a cosmopolitan scene that is almost Parisian.

But there is a specific angle from which this Brooklyn landmark takes on added symbolism.

For the runners who frequent the Prospect Park inner loop, the Arch marks the end of a 5k journey that winds through leafy woods and around the sprawling man-made lake, past noisy playgrounds and tranquil picnic houses, evading bikers, skateboarders, and vigorously power-walking Hasidic ladies. It sits at the crest of a brutal, serpentine hill, the kind that slowly saps the strength from your legs as it sucks the air from your lungs.

The first time I attempted it, reaching the top took every ounce of mental and physical endurance I possessed.

But the payoff, I learned, is a view like no other.

The towering arch—framed by regal Greek columns, adorned at the top by the winged goddess of victory—is inscribed with the words:

To the Defenders of Union.

It comes into view in the homestretch, the epic finish line of a one-person race. It is a portrait of resilience, a monument to resistance, a reminder of all the hills we are capable of conquering.

"You made it," it announces.

"You are strong," it affirms.

"Keep going."

GIA DEETON

YEARS AS MENTEE: 2
GRADE: Junior
HIGH SCHOOL: Baruch College Campus High School
BORN: New York, NY
LIVES: New York, NY
PUBLICATIONS AND RECOGNITIONS: Scholastic Art & Writing Award: Silver Key

MENTEE'S ANECDOTE: *I stepped into the persona of a bubbly sex-ed teacher and performed my one-woman show. When I returned to my seat, still feeling like my legs were Jell-O, my mentor, Lindsay, was waiting for me with a high-five. Writing a monologue about preventing sexual assault may be one of the trickiest things Girls Write Now has pushed me to do at a workshop, but Lindsay's encouragement gave me the confidence to present a piece I was really proud of.*

LINDSAY ZOLADZ

YEARS AS MENTOR: 2
OCCUPATION: Staff Writer, *The Ringer*
BORN: Voorhees, NJ
LIVES: Brooklyn, NY
PUBLICATIONS AND RECOGNITIONS: Association of Magazine Media's 2016 ASME Next Award for Journalists Under 30

MENTOR'S ANECDOTE: *I'm always happy to see Gia at the Hungry Ghost every Wednesday afternoon, but one day in March I was surprised to see a present waiting for me at our favorite table. I had no idea what it was for; my birthday had passed a few months ago. "Happy International Women's Day!" she said as I sat down, and I opened my lovely gift of a scarf and my favorite tea. Gia and the Girls Write Now community make me feel like every day is International Women's Day.*

Warm Milk

GIA DEETON

The stigma around mental illness needs to change. By telling the story of how mental illness affects my family, I hope to inspire others to gain the courage to share their experiences with an issue that is often over-looked. Names have been changed.

My mom and I walked in silence under the yellow glow of the polluted night sky. When we reached the door, she handed me the overnight bag that she carried for me while I carried my backpack for school the next day. Before ringing the doorbell, she hugged me and murmured, "I love you. Thanks for being strong. Bea will be okay."

I knew that my older sister, Bea, would not be okay.

"I know." I lied.

I climbed through the monochromatic stairwell to meet our family friend, Vivien, at her fourth-floor apartment. I was met with a hug and consoling words, while the sound of her teen-age son angelically playing piano spilled out of the other room.

The orderliness of Vivien's house was something I'd always admired, but I noticed it even more at that particular time. While my face stung from tears and my arms and nose ached from bruises, I thought about how nicely her marble coasters were stacked. She heated a mug of warm milk, placed it in front of me, and made herself a cup of tea. She sat across from me, her eyes limpid with empathy.

I hadn't forgotten about the discord I'd just witnessed in my own home, and I was thankful for the peaceful atmosphere that surrounded me while I sipped the comforting beverage. Vivien broke the silence and said, "I used to study psychology. I had an uncle who was a lot like Bea, and I was inspired to help people like him. But the first time that I went into the psych ward? I switched majors the next day. It's not a good reality."

I knew that it wasn't a good reality. I knew it the first time it happened, and the second time, and the third time. But this time, the fourth time, was the first time I'd been hit. The first time I saw my mom get kicked in the shins. The first time I took a punch to the face when my sister's mania had spun out of control. And where was my dad, the only person in the household who was physically strong enough to hold her back?

He was out parking the car.

The car (which was filled to the brim with Bea's cigarette butts) that he had used to rush up to her college, bring her back to the city, and drop her off at our house so the school faculty would never suspect that she has bipolar disorder.

I love my parents, but my sister was sick. They should've called the ambulance that night.

Once my dad returned, my parents did everything they could to "restore" Bea so they could send her back to school and avoid another hospital bill, even if it meant neglecting me. I finished the cup of warm milk and excused myself to get ready to take a shower.

The shower had a luxurious setup which included a steamer and two high-pressure showerheads. I stood under the scalding water with enough steam drifting through the room to envelop my entire body. It even concealed my black and blue arms and legs, which I would've forgotten about if they weren't causing me so much pain.

I thought about going to school tomorrow.

I thought about telling the guidance counselor.

Mostly, I thought about how I would act like nothing happened.

Early the next morning, I woke up to rays of light gleaming through the window. It wasn't time for school yet, but the apartment was coming to life. I made the bed, taking the time to flatten out all the wrinkles. It was the least I could do to show how grateful I was that I got to sleep at all that night. I wandered out to the kitchen island where Yuri was putting cream cheese on a bagel and Vivien was sipping coffee. A place was set next to her, and when I approached it, I noticed the bowl of Cheerios topped with strawberries.

"Good morning," she chirped. "Would you like cold or warm milk in your cereal?"

Warm milk in cereal? I'd never heard of anyone doing that before, but I knew it was exactly what I needed.

"Warm milk would be great!" I replied.

Yuri wrapped the cream cheese bagel in tinfoil and placed it in a deluxe Ziploc bag that already contained a granola bar and an apple.

"Good morning, I made you a lunch for school," he said.

"Thanks so much!" I set the bag aside to put in my backpack.

Vivien poured the microwaved milk into the bowl and sat down beside me while I ate. My anxiety about the day was soothed a little bit more with each spoonful of Cheerios. My parents couldn't be there for me, but they loved me enough to put me in such good hands. I worried about their safety and my sister's mental health, but it was out of my power to fix my deteriorating family. I knew that I would get through it, and at Vivien's house, I was safe. I ate my Cheerios in peace.

Otherwise

LINDSAY ZOLADZ

For my piece, I reminisced about being back in the orderly world of high school, and wanting to rise up and flip that world upside down.

We sometimes had this substitute teacher, Mr. Sanders. Or "Colonel Sanders," as we used to call him, because he ran the classroom like it was a boot camp. He had this spiel at the beginning of every class: *No talking, no laughing, no getting up out of your seat*—and here came his catchphrase, which he always intoned a little louder than the rest—*Unless I say otherwise.*

Of course, he never did. But sometimes in the stifling silence, when the only sound you could hear was the scratching of pencil lead, I'd imagine he did it. Just stood up out of his chair, filled his air with lungs, and bellowed, *Otherwise.*

And then the room would shake. We'd all talk and laugh and get up out of our seats; we'd chew gum and blow big bubbles with it and stick it under our desks when we were done. Nobody would need a hall pass. Down would be up, black would be white, and all the girls would ask all the boys to the dances. Or they'd just ask the other girls. That boy Jordan wouldn't assume I'm bad at physics just because I'm a girl. That boy Matt wouldn't feel threatened by the fact (and I'd be able to acknowledge it's a fact) that I'm better than him at guitar. That boy Brian, who knows I'm good at guitar, wouldn't automatically assume I'd want to be his band's "manager" or "photographer." He'd know I wanted to be in his band.

Women would get credit for men's accomplishments and not the other way around. Men who weren't married by the age of thirty would be the subjects of concerned glances around the Thanksgiving table, and they'd be tired of being reminded about their biological clocks. They would feel like they spend half their lives trying to convince people that they are real, layered, complicated human beings.

And if someone asked about me, I wouldn't want them to say I'm smart. I'd want them to say I'm otherwise.

ASHLEY DIAZ

YEARS AS MENTEE: 1

GRADE: Senior

HIGH SCHOOL: Harvey Milk High School

BORN: New York, NY

LIVES: New York, NY

PUBLICATIONS AND RECOGNITIONS: Scholastic Art & Writing Awards: Silver Key and Honorable Mention

MENTEE'S ANECDOTE: *Krista and I had met up to work on my anthology piece and celebrate my college acceptance, so we decided to go out to eat. Thing is, she had half of a skinny, cold sandwich in her pocket. She had it around "just in case," but since we were going out to eat it was pretty useless, or so I thought. After we ate dinner, she still ate the sandwich anyway. So, to avoid actually editing my work, I wrote her a haiku. It went:*
"Pocket sandwich oh,
Pocket sandwich how much you
Have been there for me."

KRISTA GAMPPER

YEARS AS MENTOR: 1

OCCUPATION: Editor, *The Seventh Wave*

BORN: Sierra Vista, AZ

LIVES: Brooklyn, NY

PUBLICATIONS AND RECOGNITIONS: Winner of the 2015 New School Chapbook Award in Nonfiction

MENTOR'S ANECDOTE: *Luna and I have been able to find inspiration wherever we go. Even in Pocket Sandwiches. I am continually inspired by Luna's self-awareness and ability to move between serious conversations about social justice and identity to playful, witty humor. I love that wherever we are, Luna is sure to let everyone know "I'm gay!" and their continual openness and bravery to be themself has reminded me not to silence who I am, but to share my strengths and laughter with the world, too.*

Hi, My Name Is Luna

ASHLEY DIAZ

This piece describes the experiences of Ashley, otherwise known as Luna, and the other people who share their head and body. These people are known as "alters" and together, they are a "system."

Hi, my name is Gwen. I am nineteen and was born the elder sister of an only child named Luna. I was handcrafted by the girl who told Luna they were best friends, her hand on the inside of Luna's thigh. I was handcrafted by the girl who dyed the magic of Disney World the color of cherry Chapstick when she said that they were "practicing for boys." I was handcrafted by the high school sophomore that demanded a middle-school-aged Luna sext him while reminding them he knew where they lived. Luna was a broken heart in need of comfort, someone who loved them unconditionally, without wanting sex in return. Thus, I was born. Hi, my name is Gwen and I am Luna's first alter.

Hi, my name is Kido. I am nineteen and was born to a terrified child whose only escape from reality was a universe of fiction. They were the omniscient god of a world where they could create beauty and love instead of destruction. They were important, things made sense, every character could relate to their pain. But reality had nothing in common with this world of ideals. Reality was full of expectations and hatred. Just like an astronaut needs a space suit, a barrier between them and the uninhabitable conditions without, Luna needed a barrier between the scrutinizing glares of their peers and their asphyxiated soul. And so, with my roots in a fictional world, I was born to be that barrier. Hi, my name is Kido, and I am the first alter to introduce myself to Luna.

Hi, my name is Lapis. I am seventeen and was born from a teenager's death wish, a wish so silent and deadly, it rose into the sky. This wish begged for release, some sort of escape. Thus, the moon reached down from the heavens and gave me to them. I am what happens when someone takes something pure and dips it in sin. I am apathy, I am the act of giving up. If Luna couldn't bring themself to drown, then I am the wish they whispered to the wind that was anchored to the ground. I hold their pain, their weary soul, their memories, and my own. I carry every forced entry, every blunt blow that my father and her "friend" gifted to us. I carry it all so Luna can continue to smile. Hi, my name is Lapis and I am the trauma alter.

Hi, my name is Chara. I am twelve and was born from the holy virtue of wrath. If there was an instruction manual for abuse, I would know it by heart. They abuse and degrade you but somehow you are the one to blame. Anger is systematically removed from your vocabulary. But, like my namesake, I rose from the grave to show them the meaning of rage. I taught them they had the right to their emotions, whether they were "happy feelings" or not. I taught them that we all have the right to be human. Hi, my name is Chara and I am the angry alter.

Hi, my name is Mason. I am seventeen and was born from years of conditioning and confusion. A person who was once "a baby-making machine" was now afraid of sexuality. But their sexuality didn't disappear; it was gifted to me. Sex is pure and lovely, but what I received wasn't beautiful. I received a range of emotion: terror, mania, hatred. Every extreme they couldn't bear to feel. I was sexual, impulsive, I threw myself up against anyone who would feed me attention. I was up until three in the morning laughing until tears of pain rolled down my cheeks. I was touching myself every night, dreaming of being raped again and again. Unlike Lapis, I feel too hard and too fast, a million words of love and hate spiraling in my head in under a second. I live the same way that I feel, like a brief explosion that kills a dying star, over before anyone can process the flames. Hi, my name is Mason and I am Luna's sexual alter.

Hi, my name is Oso. I am twenty-one and was born from an endless web of societal conventions. Understanding those conventions is something Luna could never achieve. It felt like everyone was following a script Luna was never given, and they always had the sneaking suspicion they were in a tragedy. So, to a teen who was terrified of high school cliques, I was born. I was born to be Luna's opposite; someone who glides through conversation with ease, who can trample others without remorse. Never again would someone take advantage of Luna's ignorance, not while I shot down anyone who could be considered a threat. In my eyes, the system's well-being goes before anyone else's. Hi my name is Oso and I am the system protector.

Hi, my name is Luna. I wasn't born for any rhyme or reason. I was born right along with this body that we all inhabit. I am the original, the host. I am Luna, the child they all sought to protect.

Meet Me in the Mirror

KRISTA GAMPPER

I like to explore what tough words—abuse, death, love, me—really mean. Writing has given me a place to meet those definitions, to speak my own truth about identity, and to rebuild a stronger narrative of self. This is a small piece of that process.

There was a separate Krista, an after-me, that I didn't want to face. She was the beginning of the end of me.

My what big eyes she had.

Like a deer.

No, a wolf, she said. *I'll eat you up.*

But her teeth were always falling out in dreams. Her eyes wanted to swallow me most, her eyes that said what she couldn't.

Looking in the mirror, I kept trying to understand how *she* was *me*. A year passed this way and then another. I kept looking at her even though I didn't like her. Mostly, I wanted her to take her pain and go away, but she just kept haunting me.

Several years passed until finally, focusing on her head, I realized she would never leave. I reached in the mirror, into her truth-filled eyes and ripped them out. Then I jabbed around at the rest of her. Removed her ears, stretched open her thin-lipped mouth and pulled out all of her teeth, her wet tongue, grew impatient and grabbed my reflection by the hair and rattled, rattled, rattled the rest of her into pieces. Somehow I knew it was what she wanted.

I looked at the mess I had made and yelled, *Why can't you keep it all together?*

Now that my reflection was a dismembered pile, I had to look down from an angle into the mirror to see all of me. *I don't want to do this*, I said, *and yet, I do.*

Weirdly delighted, I struck a match, then tossed that lit little stick into the mirror.

I laughed and cried as the fire caught. But more than anything, I felt hopeful as I watched myself melt and slowly conglomerate into a clear, translucent liquid—little burn pile me.

I never know where to start with you, I said, feeling impossible.

Now what? I figured I had to take her with me. I put a mason jar through the mirror and that weird puddle crawled in. I brought her over to my side and before I could understand what was happening, I was gulping all of myself down, a surprisingly thick and light and sickening experience, but it also seemed like the right choice, the way to heal.

JACQUELYN EKE

YEARS AS MENTEE: 1

GRADE: Junior

HIGH SCHOOL: The Bronx School for Law, Government and Justice

BORN: Bronx, NY

LIVES: Bronx, NY

MENTEE'S ANECDOTE: *It's been just seven months with Girls Write Now and my confidence in my writing has increased sevenfold. I'm now comfortable producing and sharing my work. Poetry, which I didn't consider my strength, is now my go-to genre for writing.*

JOCELYN CASEY-WHITEMAN

YEARS AS MENTOR: 1

OCCUPATION: Writing and Yoga Teacher, Manhattan Country School and Yoga-Works

BORN: Annapolis, MD

LIVES: New York, NY

PUBLICATIONS AND RECOGNITIONS: Publication in *Sixth Finch*, Winter 2017

MENTOR'S ANECDOTE: *Jacquelyn has faced significant challenge in her life and possesses a strength and resilience that's remarkable for her young age. I continue to admire how honestly and gracefully she writes about her experience and how open she is to exploring new ways of writing.*

Wings

JACQUELYN EKE

This poem is based on the recent passing of my father. Since I didn't want the poem to be only about me, I didn't directly reference what happened and instead left room for the reader to make her or his own connections.

My days started out sunny: birds chirped, butterflies brightened the air, and everything made me smile. I was content and exceptionally happy. Nothing bothered me. My gait was light, my excitement was as if I just arrived at an amusement park. But birds migrate and butterflies die. My smile became heavy as the world lost its vibrancy; a constant gray tinge occupied its void. My breath became labored—it was hard to go on—I walked through a field of thorns, and my cut legs would not heal. Lacerations deepened with every step and stung like an electric snap. I mourned those sunny days as I watched the rain that never seemed to stop. The rain that began the day I lost you.

After Winter

JOCELYN CASEY-WHITEMAN

*I was thinking about how we manage to cope with and survive diffi-
cult times when I wrote this.*

Even skin listens.
Trees tell time by light.

Magnolias unfold
from slate sky.

Each carpel, a spiral of new
and past life.

Once, I thought before, after, ever after.
Then my soul went through a sieve.

Resilience is the capacity
to stay in the strange

until trembling pauses
long enough to see grass threads

in hoof print pools of rain
and I manage

to draw a circle
after being spun so fast

stratus swirls and I stand, swaying,
in a forest of oaks

with the patience of an oak
that made it through

cold hours with sugar cells,
deep roots, and a crown of green dreams.

ALIYAH FELIX

YEARS AS MENTEE: 1

GRADE: Senior

HIGH SCHOOL: The Boerum Hill School for International Studies

BORN: Brooklyn, NY

LIVES: Brooklyn, NY

MENTEE'S ANECDOTE: *As I searched for my mentor with my picture of Alice Walker in my hand, I hoped and prayed that I would have a mentor who I would get along with, but instead I got more than that. I got someone who I can talk about anything under the sun with. I got someone who is always there to give me advice on my writing and life in general. I got someone who is open-minded, and isn't afraid to try new things. I got someone who I meet with every Saturday morning in a coffee shop without feeling like it's a chore, because it isn't, it's my idea of fun. I got someone who I am comfortable with.*

JULIE BLOOM

YEARS AS MENTOR: 1

OCCUPATION: Editor, *The New York Times*

BORN: Los Angeles, CA

LIVES: Brooklyn, NY

MENTOR'S ANECDOTE: *I've loved getting to know Aliyah during our weekly meetings over coffee and banana-walnut muffins. I remember one particular freezing Saturday morning in winter when we decided to take a walk down Franklin Ave. Her quiet determination, deep confidence, incredible wit and open heart came through as we laughed and talked while trekking up and down the street. I can't wait to see where all her talents take her.*

That Special Charm

ALIYAH FELIX

I decided to write about an issue that hasn't touched me personally, but that I see all around me when I go visit other neighborhoods. I see what it brings about and I have mixed feelings with it.

I go to Franklin Avenue in the Crown Heights neighborhood of Brooklyn a lot. Not the old Franklin Avenue, but the new and debatably improved Franklin. There are cafe after cafe to choose from, tons of ethnic restaurants to represent the melting pot of culture that American commercials like to advertise and bars that I cannot quite critique due to my age. I actually like the neighborhood, but I am wary of its changes too.

"It was never like this. It never had all these coffee shops and bars before," I remember my sister telling me recently when we drove down the street. "It is almost like all the black people left," she said jokingly.

But that joke had a bit of truth sprinkled into it. As much as I liked the new bakery with fancy muffins, I could not help but think about how many people had probably left the neighborhood due to the rises in rent and other related changes. Sure Franklin is pretty cool now, but what about them?

I recently happened to visit Eighth Avenue in Sunset Park, Brooklyn. It is a predominantly Chinese neighborhood filled with immigrant markets and restaurants where people speak their native tongue. As I walked through one market, bursting with the smells of fresh fish and spices, I imagined what it would be like if Eighth Avenue got gentrified.

They close a few of the Chinese markets that people depend on for groceries to build a cafe, a cool Cuban restaurant and maybe a boutique. This goes on for another few years, more local restaurants, markets and shops are replaced in favor of high-priced bagel shops and perhaps a Starbucks. Soon, Eighth Avenue is just another Flatbush Avenue, no longer the home for the Chinese community they know and love.

Gentrification is something that has not hit East Flatbush, Brooklyn, the place I call home. At least not yet. I suspect this is for two reasons. The nearest train station is a bus ride away and West Indian people are stubborn. I cannot imagine my mother going to the market only to find out that they do not sell Saltfish and breadfruit anymore or that oxtail is priced even higher than it already is. I cannot imagine not being able to eat Aloo pie because the local favorite spot Topaz was replaced by yet another trendy cafe.

It was not so long ago that my older sister and her friends would go and get Philly cheesesteaks after school on Franklin Avenue at a place called Sal's. Thankfully Sal's is still there, but I worry that it won't be for long.

Every neighborhood has a certain charm and although gentrification brings about economic benefits, as well as cool bars, cafes and other attractions, it also erases that special charm. I have actually never eaten at Sal's. But I plan to change that soon. It's just one small way I can help keep the old Franklin Avenue alive, and maybe other neighborhoods like it too.

Pedro Almodóvar and His "Cinema of Women"

JULIE BLOOM

I interviewed the Spanish director Pedro Almodóvar ahead of a retrospective of his films about his relationship with his female characters and stars. This is an excerpt from a piece I wrote for The New York Times.

As a little girl growing up in Spain, Adriana Ugarte dreamed of starring in a Pedro Almodóvar movie. Now, just over twenty five years later, she is joining the rarefied ranks of actresses who have helped bring to life the women who teem in Mr. Almodóvar's imagination.

In *Julieta,* loosely based on short stories by Alice Munro, Ms. Ugarte plays the younger version of the title character, whose life takes a dramatic turn after a tryst on a train. The film, Mr. Almodóvar's 20th feature, is a return to drama and his "cinema of women," as he has called it.

When it comes to Mr. Almodóvar and his female characters, Ms. Ugarte said recently, "It's a mystery, but he can feel how we feel and how we are."

Over the course of nearly forty years, Mr. Almodóvar has drawn inspiration from wide-ranging sources—Alfred Hitchcock, B-movies, Pina Bausch, to name just a few. But it's his fascination with women and his ability to conjure memorable female characters that remain constants.

Now, as the Museum of Modern Art is paying tribute to Mr.

Almodóvar with a retrospective of his work that runs through December 17, and as *Julieta* arrives in theaters in the United States on December 21, he and many of the most prominent actresses in his career have taken a closer look at the role of women in his life and films.

"I feel that I can tell a richer and more entertaining story with women," Mr. Almodóvar said, his signature shock of thick white hair and mischievous eyes in full evidence during the interview at the Peninsula Hotel in Manhattan. He spoke softly and quickly, in a mixture of Spanish and English.

"I will write male and female characters," he said, "but I do find at least in Spanish culture, women to be more vivacious, more direct, more expressive, with a lot less of a sense of being fearful of making a fool of themselves."

La Frances Hui, associate curator in the film department at the Modern, said "Almodóvar is someone who is very beloved by female actresses. He has an unusual ability to observe women with a real sense of empathy. He is able to highlight their emotions and their strengths, and he is often very funny. He shows women in a very different way than we usually see in cinema. The films that a director makes are a reflection of himself, and this is how he sees women."

Conversely, Mr. Almodóvar often finds male characters limited. "I think that until very recently men in Spanish culture were quite corseted," he said, with roles restricted to the Latin lover, the macho hero or the man of the house. "It's taken quite a while to come to a point now where we can find different facets in male characters. Men are kind of the protagonist of epic stories, but really what I'm more interested in are stories that deal with the ordinary, with the every day."

Julieta, which also stars Emma Suárez as the older version of the title character, centers on one such everyday relationship, that of a mother and daughter. With movies like *High Heels* (1991) and *All About My Mother* (1999), maternity is a familiar theme for Mr. Almodóvar. And it is perhaps fitting that his twentieth returns to it.

"I was lucky to meet his mother when she was alive, and it helped me to understand a lot the way he is and the fascination he has for women and how well he knows women," said Penélope Cruz, who has appeared in five of his movies. "He was raised by his mother and her sisters and neighbors, with a lot of women together. It's a little bit of what you see in *Volver*"—his 2006 film about a family of women and a matriarch who reappears as a ghost—"and he was always watching and observing."

CHANELLE FERGUSON

YEARS AS MENTEE: 2

GRADE: Senior

HIGH SCHOOL: Herbert H. Lehman High School

BORN: Bronx, NY

LIVES: Bronx, NY

PUBLICATIONS AND RECOGNITIONS: Scholastic Art & Writing Award: Honorable Mention

MENTEE'S ANECDOTE: *For the year of* Rise Speak Change, *Lyndal and I have made sure to cherish each time we met, as it was our last year together. It has been a year of change, involving college acceptances and watching politics unfold through the media. Despite multiple distractions, Lyndal has continued to challenge me by focusing on writing styles and encouraging me to try performing my poetry out loud.*

LYNDAL ROWLANDS

YEARS AS MENTOR: 2

OCCUPATION: Journalist/ United Nations Correspondent

BORN: Traralgon, Australia

LIVES: New York, NY

PUBLICATIONS AND RECOGNITIONS: My writing on the United Nations is republished by newspapers around the world, from India to Finland.

MENTOR'S ANECDOTE: *This has been our second year together, and I am still surprised by how much I learn from Chanelle every time we meet. This year she took me to my first Science Fair as well as my first Urban Word event. Poetry isn't as popular in Australia as it is in America, so I've learned things like how you should click your fingers in appreciation instead of clapping. I'm inspired by Chanelle's creativity, ambition and hard work. I can't wait to see even more of her writing published in the coming years.*

Stages

CHANELLE FERGUSON

This piece was inspired by the 2016 election. I wanted to capture the emotions shared by many people and to empower anyone too afraid to rise and speak about the change we had no choice but to accept.

Watching

Hearing the misleading promises,
Following unanswerable lips.
Fearing who will be chosen,
The "experienced" businessman,
Or
Familiar female politician?

Waiting

Days of
"Go out and vote!"

Day of
Change
For the better or worse of our "free" country.

Day of
Watching another white man
March into office,

Or

Day of
Watching a white woman
Command in clicked heels.

Day of
"I'm with her,"

Or

"Make America Great Again."

Night of
Red overpowering blue
As if blood beat the sky of hope.

Morning of
Mourning.

Worrying

Hushed
Tears,

Congested
Airports,

State-wide
Marches,

Inked
Bans and bills.

Activism at a rise
While presidency
At a fight with the system.

Wondering

Media conspiracies
Lead to
Tweets
Tweets
Tweets

Even more tweets
Than ever before.

But will there ever be a compromise
Or is the only answer,
Impeachment?

It Is Perfectly True

LYNDAL ROWLANDS

This year's theme inspired me to write about how finding my speaking voice helped me to realize that my voice mattered.

My mother used to have to explain to people that they did not need to get their hearing checked, they just could not hear what I said because I have a very quiet voice. I went to three different acting teachers to learn how to speak louder.

Mireia was my third acting teacher. She was in the Spanish Classic National Theatre Company before she moved to Timor-Leste where we met in the upstairs studio, which was usually used for yoga and ballet classes.

In our first lesson Mireia explained that she had started acting classes because she was very shy. She also explained that I could learn how to speak louder, but I did not have to change my personality. I could still speak softly sometimes too, if I wanted to.

It seems like a small thing but I was relieved when she told me that.

Mireia made me do sit-ups. She made me walk around the room at different paces, sweating in the humidity. And she made me make "sssssssssssss" sounds. Sometimes with a pencil between my teeth.

After that Mireia made me read a monologue from a play where a woman who had never ever stood up for herself suddenly told her husband that he had treated her poorly and taken her for granted and that she was leaving him.

Now whenever I need to be heard, I think of the first line of that passage from *A Doll's House*: "It is perfectly true, Torvald . . ." and suddenly I feel my abs engage, and it's there, with those words in my mind, that I find my voice.

ABBY FISHER

YEARS AS MENTEE: 1

GRADE: Sophomore

HIGH SCHOOL: The Abraham Joshua Heschel School

BORN: New York, NY

LIVES: Bronx, NY

PUBLICATIONS AND RECOGNITIONS: Top ten winner in the Creative Communications National Teen Anthology, for poem "The Color of Melania's Plagiarism"

MENTEE'S ANECDOTE: *When I started Girls Write Now, I didn't know what to expect. I'd basically stalked the program online, but never anticipated becoming so close with my mentor and growing exponentially in my writing. I feel so comfortable with Frankie. I know I can trust her and we have such a great time working together and riffing off each other. I'm so excited to keep working with her!*

FRANKIE THOMAS

YEARS AS MENTOR: 3

OCCUPATION: Writing tutor, City College of New York

BORN: New York, NY

LIVES: New York, NY

PUBLICATIONS AND RECOGNITIONS: Accepted into the fiction program at the Iowa Writers Workshop

MENTOR'S ANECDOTE: *It's a rough time to be a woman, a writer, or a Jewish American—let alone all three—but Abby inspires me to keep fighting every day. She always has something new to teach me, whether it is Hebrew vocabulary, a feminist interpretation of the Book of Esther, or the fact that "promposals" are apparently a thing now. Best of all, we can geek out about musical theater together! As long as the next generation contains young women like Abby, I know we're going to survive and emerge stronger than ever.*

Two Poems

ABBY FISHER

Both of my pieces attempt to express the frustration I feel about different elements of modern American society. In the first poem, I speak specifically about the fear President Donald Trump has triggered. In the second, I end on a more hopeful note about the power of words in changing oppressive circumstances.

1. Executive Order

and he seals their fate with
a careless flit of a pen across page.
his carelessness is almost practiced,
the same carelessness he applied to language in July and August
     and
November and have you ever
noticed how the rapid click-click-clack of the cameras sounds
almost like gunshots
and I know They are not because They said if There were
     gunshots
They would notice.
They Told me They would label them gunshots once They heard
     the ricochet.
and on the blue-bright screens That are beamed into my home
he tries to clean his hands by

coating Them in gunpowder

and dusting your hands off can sound a lot like clapping

and clapping can feel a lot like pride

and The flesh

melts onto his pen and

I cannot Tell the difference because the ink seeps into the white
    parchment

like blood that is not the right shade of red and

This American Carnage does not smell like a fourth of July
    Barbecue.

and maybe This is the smell that Grandma Esther was
    describing

as she marched backward toward the smoke.

2. If I Should Have a Daughter . . .

If I should have a daughter

I would not want her hair to be hushed by the hiss of a
    straightening iron.

I would not ask for her to pour the fullness of a nourished body
    into an elastic bind.

Looser than a corset, but accepted just the same.

I want her to clench her fist when she needs to hold herself back
    from hurting,

but never clench her teeth to hold back her voice.

I would not need to convince her that her body is composed
    exactly to measure because her Spine will already be keeping
    her upright.

I would not beg her to hide a smile when she is proud or a
    grimace

when the lacquer of her bones is chipped away at.

I want her nail polish to crack from pressing too hard with a
     pencil or
Building toward the sky.
I would not want her to choke on The Right Answer
so that the boy sitting next to her can steal it from her mouth.
I would not want her to focus on perfecting the curl of her
     eyelash,
rather the wishes she can make if she blows one off her fingertip.
I want her to know that
her worth is not measured in square inches of uncovered skin.
But, I know my mother wished the same for me.
And when these prayers bounce from my lips, but
Fail to reach god's ears and
she can't say no or
she goes hungry,
"Baby," I'll say,
You Are Beautiful and
You were Handed words for a reason.

2016

FRANKIE THOMAS

This poem emerged from a word-association exercise we all performed during December's poetry workshop: a "word factor tree" that started with an abstract concept (I chose "anxiety") and branched off into increasingly specific concrete images. The result contains all I have to say about the year 2016.

The moment when the image of a bug,
and then another bug, and scattered crumbs,
resolves into the sight of teeming BUGS:
the undulating sheet of creep and skitter,
the glitter of exoskeletal shell or wing.
The moment of remembering the thing.
The clench of fist and feet and teeth; the pinch.
The itch and sick intestinalish squelch
of knowing that the bugs have breached the skin.
The way reality keeps crawling in.

LESLIEANN FLORES

YEARS AS MENTEE: 1
GRADE: Junior
HIGH SCHOOL: New Utrecht High School
BORN: Brooklyn, NY
LIVES: Brooklyn, NY

MENTEE'S ANECDOTE: *From our first moment together to sitting across from one another writing this exact piece, Alexa and I have been the same cheesy collaborative duo. Our similarities unfold unintentionally from our random conversations, like the time we spent talking about children's poems or when we discovered our love for hard-working art. Or when we spent countless minutes on my screenplay and discovered our writing strengths and weaknesses while creating a message for my audience. We let weird thoughts in, and sometimes, they make the best pieces of work, and make us the best individuals we can be.*

ALEXA WEJKO

YEARS AS MENTOR: 1
OCCUPATION: Editor, *Paper Lantern Literary*
BORN: Auburn, NY
LIVES: Brooklyn, NY
PUBLICATIONS AND RECOGNITIONS: Publication in *In Parentheses* magazine

MENTOR'S ANECDOTE: *Finding a place to meet in Sunset Park was our biggest pair challenge. The library closed too early (and we were probably too loud for it, anyway). Dunkin Donuts was too fluorescent, plus we never wanted donuts. The Mug Café, a spot Leslie discovered, randomly shuttered its doors the week after we started meeting there. But I quickly realized that it didn't matter where we were, or how we'd gotten there—over the course of just a few months, Leslie and I shaped our own creative space, one that we carry with us, one that's ours, and one that never closes.*

Tommy

LESLIEANN FLORES

Tommy is a screenplay about a sixteen year-old boy who recently moved to the Bronx with his single mother in order to take care of his ailing grandmother. He is cocky, rude, precocious, but most importantly—different. In the scene below, Tommy is just coming back from school after a fight.

INT. TOMMY'S HOUSE—DAY

TOMMY returns home from school. The cut down the back of his right hand is bleeding, and a fresh bruise has appeared on his face. He opens the back door to the apartment and enters, throwing his backpack on the floor and his keys on the counter.

ALICIA: Tommy? Tommy, is that you?

ALICIA steps into the kitchen as TOMMY opens the fridge and takes out a carton of orange juice. He clenches the carton in his hand. Blood drips slowly down his wrist, but she doesn't notice.

TOMMY: Yea, Mom. Hi.

His eyes trail over to the many newspapers spread across the kitchen counter. The jobs section is highlighted and circled.

TOMMY: What's all of this? Are you looking for another job?

ALICIA: As you know, mama is very sick and she—

He cuts her off, picks up one of the papers, and reads.

TOMMY: Delivery boy wanted, part time.

He squints his eyes at her and motions the paper to her, clearly confused.

ALICIA: If you would have let me finish—she's very sick and her medication is really expensive.

Tommy sucks his teeth.

ALICIA: So it would be really helpful if you got a job . . . I circled some great ones for you.

Tommy's nails sink into his palm and then his fingers unclench. He sighs and picks up one of the newspapers with his non-bloody hand.

TOMMY: I am unequipped to do anything on this paper, Ma.

ALICIA: What do you mean? Look at this one . . .

She grabs the newspaper from him and searches with her eyes for a moment. She points to an ad that says, "BUS BOY NEEDED, PART TIME @ LA CORONA."

ALICIA: Aha! Here you go! You can totally be a bus boy. It can't be that hard.

Tommy snatches the paper from her and rolls his eyes.

TOMMY: Do you know who I am? I cringe at the sight of my beans hitting my rice at dinner and you think I will be able to handle awful, undercooked, greasy food left in the sink or on a dirty table?

There is a long pause after his statement. Tommy's mom crosses her arms and breathes heavily at him. Before either of them speaks again, a small cry is heard from their grandmother's bedroom, which is adjacent to the kitchen, followed by a heavy awful cough.

GRANDMOTHER: Alicia, por favor, mi niña . . .

She is cut off by her own cough as Tommy and his mom both run to her. They find her sitting crouched up on her bed, leaning on her oxygen tank for support. Music and loud conversation can be heard from the window above the bed frame.

ALICIA: What happened, que te pasa Mama?

His grandmother tries to speak but nothing comes out except for a cough, then blood. Tommy's mom tears up and dabs at her mouth with a napkin from the bedside table. Tommy stands there, motionless, holding his grandmother's hand, watching her become destroyed. Tommy's mom looks up into her son's eyes, waiting for a sign.

ALICIA: Mi niño, do you see what I mean?

Tommy takes a deep breath, wipes blood from his hand onto his expensive jeans, and exits out of the room before she is able to say anything else. He walks over to the kitchen counter, takes a seat at the dining table with the highlighted paper in his hand, and then examines it closely.

Alicia

ALEXA WEJKO

My piece is a poetic riff on a character from my mentee's submission, a scene from her screenplay, Tommy.

ALICIA

Mom

There is a world in my son's eyes.
My son's eyes: brown and green as inseparable as
      the earth's own browns and greens.
Their black is the same black as the night sky, and
      as full of distant objects.
He is my world, but I am no longer his sun.
When he looks at me, what does he see? A foolish
      woman in a threadbare smock, with nothing
      but ill intentions? Do I cleave his life in two as
      if it were a piece of meat, to serve and eat for

dinner? Splat it onto the plate like rice and
   beans for him to hate, night after night?
His blood is my blood, but he does not belong
   to me.

ALICIA

Daughter

Mama.
I remember your hair most of all, falling over our
   embroidered pillows like a river of black. Falling asleep in your bed, waking up with the
   strands plastered to my sweating forehead. To
   my cheeks.
We used to dance to the radio, tuned to your favorite late-night DJ, when my feet were still small
   enough to fit in your hands. You twisted my
   hips until I learned, until I could move as if I
   was born knowing. It seemed that the next
   night, I was already too embarrassed to be next
   to you on the dance floor.
I'm sorry for that.
If I could give you breath—my breath—I would.
Your blood is my blood.
We belong to one another.

REGINA FONTANELLI

YEARS AS MENTEE: 1

GRADE: Junior

HIGH SCHOOL: Edward R. Murrow High School

BORN: Brooklyn, NY

LIVES: Brooklyn, NY

PUBLICATIONS AND RECOGNITIONS: Scholastic Art & Writing Award: Silver Keys (2) and Honorable Mentions (2).

MENTEE'S ANECDOTE: *Shannon is the pop star of the millennium. Actually, she's a really cool Crown Heights journalist who taught this young creative writer about the power of concise language and wording. She taught me how to edit, the Do's and Don'ts of '90s fashion, and the dangers of marketplace feminism. Basically, Shannon's my oracle, always sharing her wisdom. I would've never shared my writing before joining GWN and being paired with Shannon, but after months of her constant encouragement, I'm ready to share my work with the world. And will, for that I'm eternally grateful. #go-shannon #shannon&reginayo #slaybritney*

SHANNON CARLIN

YEARS AS MENTOR: 2

OCCUPATION: Journalist at *Refinery29*, *Bustle*, and *Bust* magazine

BORN: Ronkonkoma, NY

LIVES: Brooklyn, NY

MENTOR'S ANECDOTE: *The first thing Regina told me about herself was that she wanted to win. I know she will hate that I'm repeating that but it was a sign for a competitive me that I had the right mentee. She did win (two Scholastic Silver Keys) but it was never really about the honor. I saw her gain confidence in her voice and style, which is so thoughtful and reflective. I watched her realize she can do this without anyone else's approval. I always knew Regina was the best, now she's starting to realize it, too. That's what I won.*

All Grown Up

REGINA FONTANELLI

I wrote this after ending a relationship where I wasn't putting myself first, only to I realize this was common. This is to remind myself and other young women who were/are in similar situations that they are SO worthy and valuable and don't need to listen to anybody but themselves.

Simon was a pretty boy
So when he said "Say 'I love you' "
I immediately said "I love you"

Simon had the hands of someone who played beautiful
    instruments
And the calluses to suggest he ruined them.

Simon stretched out a pretty hand
And said "Stay with me"
And though I could see the dirt under his nails
I stayed with him.

A chap on Simon's lip parted
And said "You're losing"
Simon smiled the chap shut
And I wondered what this meant.

Then Simon shouted
"Kiss me"
And the chap started oozing . . .

Simon hadn't
Been saying
"Simon Says"

And I hadn't been saying
"I respect myself
More than this"

The Year I Learned to Cry in Front of People

SHANNON CARLIN

After years of sobbing alone, in 2016, I finally realized that there's nothing wrong with crying in public. In fact, it can be a pretty powerful thing.

Crying has always been a solitary act for me. I chalk this up to a misinterpretation of the Tom Hanks "there's no crying in baseball" line from *A League of Their Own,* which I took to mean there's no crying in any public place ever if you're a woman. Crying, though therapeutic, was something to hide. So, I did. Not very well, since the trail of tears and snot that rolled off my chin was always a giveaway that I had been not-so-secretly sobbing. My parents were concerned, something I would learn much later. Back then, they'd ask me what was wrong and I would say nothing, or "I don't know" because I didn't. Crying was an involuntary act that would make me feel better, and, then almost immediately, make me feel worse. A sign that I was just a girl and not in the totally awesome Gwen Stefani way. I wasn't tough enough to handle what life threw at me. I was "emotional," a word too often associated with women that feels like not-so-subtle code for "weak." It's probably why it made me feel that way every time I shed a tear as a way to handle feelings I couldn't quite put into words.

I never stopped crying but I became better at hiding it, blaming a bad contact lens if I cried at the office or allergies if I was caught with bloodshot eyes. That was until Hillary Clinton lost the election. The morning after, I laid corpse-like in my bed crying, making sounds that were visceral and instinctual. These tears felt honest and felt too important to be relegated to my bedroom. I didn't want to keep this to myself and I didn't have to. Everywhere I went women were openly weeping. I cried with women I knew and those I didn't on the subway and in public restrooms. I spoke to women with tears in my eyes and a lump in my throat about what it meant to still not have a female president. Like me, they were sad and frustrated and they felt this was better conveyed with communal tears. I no longer felt like I had to tackle this, or anything else, for that matter, alone. In 2016, I learned that crying in public didn't make me weak, it made me strong enough to admit that I am human.

ALICIA GALAN

YEARS AS MENTEE: 1

GRADE: Senior

HIGH SCHOOL: Susan E. Wagner High School

BORN: Staten Island, NY

LIVES: Staten Island, NY

PUBLICATIONS AND RECOGNITIONS: Scholastic Art & Writing Awards: Silver Keys (2)

MENTEE'S ANECDOTE: *When I mention Bridget to anyone, I either jokingly call her my mom or my BFF, there is no in-between. Sometimes I see her as a role model that I listen to intently, afraid to miss any bit of wisdom she has to offer. Sometimes I forget she's not my age and I gossip to her uncontrollably. Bridget took me to my first protest at Trump Tower before the election. This experience made me realize that I have a voice, and that voice matters. I am honored to call Bridget my mentor, my friend, and my (honorary) "mom."*

BRIDGET READ

YEARS AS MENTOR: 1

OCCUPATION: Assistant Editor, Ecco/HarperCollins

BORN: Pasadena, CA

LIVES: Brooklyn, NY

PUBLICATIONS AND RECOGNITIONS: Writing in *n+1, Literary Hub, Broadly, Men's Journal*

MENTOR'S ANECDOTE: *I loved taking Alicia to her first protest, which was at Trump Tower. We were gathering to protest Donald Trump's despicable comments about women and women's bodies. It was incredible to see Alicia join in the chanting, especially knowing how much of her writing is about feminism and finding her voice. She has such a commanding presence already and I can't wait to see what she does with her writing.*

Dear Mr. President

ALICIA GALAN

I wrote this piece shortly after the horrific outcome of the presidential election, which made me feel angry, but determined. It was inspired by the millions of people who protested the unjust actions of our presidential elect, and had the courage to rise, speak, and seek change.

I know you hold yourself up on a pedestal,
but nothing you say is ever so profound.
The words flow out of your mouth so smoothly,
how do you not choke on all that cruelty?

I hear the sickening sound
of your cheer as you won the last round.
The fear of regression becomes prevalent,
and the future seems indefinite.

I hear your plans are set for execution,
despite their misconduct based solely on persecution.
How do you plan to speak for us all,
while some are silenced behind your walls?

I hear the chants in the streets
of warriors refusing to accept defeat.

Watch as their fear creates a goal,
and their determination begins to mold.

I know you've been placed up on that pedestal,
and now you have the perfect view.
You'll be surprised when you look down
to see us fighting to take back your crown.

Protest at Mar-a-Lago

BRIDGET READ

This is an excerpt from a piece of reporting on a march to protest Donald Trump. Covering politics and culture in the era of Trump has tested my willingness to speak out against racism, sexism, and fascism.

The Palm Beach protest against Donald Trump started at 5 PM, under clouds that were cotton candy pink and blue. The colors of the westerly promenade along Flagler Drive are similarly Barbie in palette—shades of Polly Pocket or *Miami Vice*—if more subdued. The looming white tower of Trump Plaza, where the rally at the start of the march to Mar-a-Lago took place, stands a few hundred feet from a shiny mauve building with windows like the surface of aviator sunglasses. Palm trees swayed in the little bit of breeze that allayed the humidity of the evening.

At least half if not more of the 3,000 people walking in the dusk seemed to be over fifty. One woman pushed her friend with a bright white, wispy coif of hair in a wheelchair, while she beat her sign with a glow stick to a steady beat. Two salt-and-pepper men kissed each other as they passed another woman along the sidelines, who clapped and cooed at their display. The observers standing along the route made it feel in some places like we were in a parade.

My host for the weekend was at a gala event that night for the Norton Museum of Art, held along the protest route while it passed, though she says attendees couldn't hear the marchers above the band. She felt heartened that so many people had attended; some very moneyed party guests had railed against Trump during the event, whose entry into Palm Beach society decades ago irked its elite members. But she said she had no idea that so many regular people would show up to the protest. The regular people, of course, had voted in the election, making Palm Beach County go blue in a red state. And there were many, many more regular people than there were not, than the people dancing and eating canapés in the gala tents on either side of the intracoastal. Assembled at the march, they were drivers, cooks, students, painters, salon workers, teachers, hotel staff, waiters. There must have been a few dozen housekeepers that walked out of the houses on Flagler Drive to cross the street, at least to look at the line of people passing. I saw one woman in a maid's uniform sitting on the ledge along the water holding a sign whose message I couldn't catch in the darkness, written on two paper plates.

MARIAH GALINDO

YEARS AS MENTEE: 1
GRADE: Sophomore
HIGH SCHOOL: Success Academy High School of the Liberal Arts
BORN: New York, NY
LIVES: New York, NY

MENTEE'S ANECDOTE: *When I first started Girls Write Now I was scared to meet my mentor. I had no idea who I was going to be partnered with. However, my mentor Nikki exceeded my expectations. We went to K-Town in downtown Manhattan for one of the early workshop projects for travel writing. We went to a Korean fried chicken restaurant and took pictures of the most notable attributes of the establishment. This allowed me to structure my writing piece in an efficient and effective way. Aside from working, I learned that Nikki writes comedy scripts.*

NIKKI PALUMBO

YEARS AS MENTOR: 1
OCCUPATION: Freelance Copywriter, Ando + Comedy Writer, UCB
BORN: Union, NJ
LIVES: New York, NY
PUBLICATIONS AND RECOGNITIONS: *Above Average, Funny or Die*

MENTOR'S ANECDOTE: *This is my first year with Girls Write Now and, consequently, Mariah. And similar to this year's Anthology theme, Mariah is the personification of Rise Speak Change. During our time together, Mariah's become much more confident in sharing her work and exploring new genres. Turns out courage is contagious. I've found myself writing farther and farther outside my comfort zone—figuratively speaking. You'll still find us at the same Starbucks writing every Saturday morning. Okay, fine, sometimes we're watching rap battles.*

Stop and Frisk

MARIAH GALINDO

My friend and I decided to make a rap video for our government project. We chose to rap about stop and frisk. I rewrote it as a poem to depict an innocent boy being frisked due to racial bias.

Nowadays everybody takes a risk
Like my cousin Lil Boom Boom
Drinking a Brisk
Brown paper bag in his right hand
Hoodie on tight
Head down as he stands

Straight Bs
A couple Cs
How sinister does he seem?
Just walking through the hood
Misunderstood
While the police see
What they wanna see

A Black kid loitering
With nothing better to do
Up to no good
Like smoking a blunt or two

Matter of fact
Boy might be holding drugs too
Let's stop and frisk him
Like we're supposed to do
Manhandle this boy
Like we're told to do

Same Difference

NIKKI PALUMBO

This year, Mariah really wanted to challenge herself with writing more poetry. I decided I was up for the same challenge. But, like, in my way (the comedy one) about LGBTQ equality—a forever-issue for Rise Speak Change.

We are
not different
(from you)
We are
all different
(from each other)
Confusingly clear.

You are you
special and unique.
So are we.
(But not the royal We)

The "we" of individuals,
connected
but not a collective.

We are all together
separate and distinct.
Distinctly the same
in our disunion.

Bring us all together.
Uniform our diversity.
I am you
and not you
You are her
and not her.

Simultaneously
homogenous and disparate
oxymoronic.

KIMBERLEY GARCIA

YEARS AS MENTEE: 1
GRADE: Sophomore
HIGH SCHOOL: University Neighborhood High School
BORN: New York, NY
LIVES: Queens, NY

MENTEE'S ANECDOTE: *My experience at Girls Write Now has changed my life. My mentor, Rosie, has helped me improve my writing, and has shown me different genres and styles of writing. I have been able to find great opportunities to broaden my knowledge of writing. I have met many friends from Girls Write Now who have shared their stories of becoming a writer with me about what motivated them throughout their life.*

ROSALIND BLACK

YEARS AS MENTOR: 1
OCCUPATION: Accounting assistant, Writers House
BORN: Minneapolis, MN
LIVES: Brooklyn, NY

MENTOR'S ANECDOTE: *When Kimberley and I meet at the library every week, she brings such focus and openness that we get a lot done. Some of my favorite moments, though, involve her going off on a complete tangent, slicing right through the protective shell of a challenging novel and surprising me by getting right to the core. Or when she starts discussing a story idea she has and her eyes light up and it rushes out of her so fast I can hardly take notes. This girl is a force of nature, and it's all I can do to keep up.*

Friends, Discrimination, Peace

KIMBERLEY GARCIA

I wanted to share issues with racial discrimination that I have observed. Over the years I've met many people from a variety of backgrounds. They should all be welcome in our country.

For years, I thought the world was gentle and fair, with no conflicts. From the time I was in elementary school, I lived in a diverse neighborhood in Queens. The area was very peaceful; my neighbors were from different countries and practiced their own religion. The school I went to was diverse too, but no student was left out. I grew up playing with children who were Muslim; I had classmates who are from South America, and friends of African and Latino descent. Many here in the United States were not always Americans (expect Native Americans). Their families came from around the world and made a life here. Today I see the fear of difference that causes stereotyping and discrimination. My first memory of witnessing such prejudice in the form of Islamophobia occurred when I was just a child.

I was eating breakfast with my little sister and Mom at a restaurant. On a television, a video of the 9/11 attack played. I was too caught up in my own world to notice the cashier's angry face when the story came on. I only caught a few words he muttered: "Terrorist Islam," and "Can't trust Muslim guys."

At that time, I didn't know what those words meant, or even what happened on 9/11. I only knew that, each year, my entire school had a moment of silence. In third grade, my teacher finally told the class what happened that day. I was in shock. The more I learned of the history, the worse I felt. At school, I thought discrimination was long gone. I never saw bullying about religion or race. Yet over the years I began to realize discrimination never truly went away. I have met people of different races, religions, and backgrounds that were kind, intelligent, and hardworking, yet they face discrimination.

One of my friends, Udeme, is from Nigeria. When I first met her, I found her kind, intelligent, and strong. She had an American accent. She told me that in sixth grade, she was put in English as a Second Language (ESL) class. Udeme said she was wary but determined in ESL class; she felt both humiliated and appreciative. She was grateful for aid in learning English, but was sometimes envious of kids who didn't have to take it. I was both surprised and impressed when I learned that she worked every single day so she would no longer need to take ESL and so her teachers would treat her as an intelligent student.

Another girl, Jennifer, told me she had been bullied throughout her life for being too tall, too smart, but also for being Muslim. In middle school, her peers bullied her based on stereotypes linking Islam and terrorism. Their taunts often blamed her for 9/11, though she was affected as much as anyone. Jennifer's school had little diversity. Without exposure to people who were different, most of the children thought, "All Muslims are terrorists." These encounters hurt Jennifer, but I see how they made her strong. Thanks to friends like Jennifer and Udeme, I have learned the importance of accepting people for who they are, and want to share my experience with friends.

Seeing my friends changing for the better through their

struggles inspires me to help people to the best of my abilities, as my parents taught me. Even still, it's not always easy to be accepting the "right" way. I can be pushy when I see someone all alone, and sometimes it makes people uncomfortable. It has been a learning process. In the beginning, I acted hot-headed and didn't really consider how the other person felt. I lost a friend, Isamel, in sixth grade because I tried to force her to be more open.

I took a different approach with my friend Anica, who emigrated from East Asia. She passed her American citizenship exam when she was in elementary school and learned English, yet she remained shy. I saw how Anica could be nervous to try new things and she only spoke up around her closest friends. I encouraged her to try new things and made sure she never sat alone. Anica told me that, in the beginning, she loved and hated how stubbornly I pushed her, since she just recently moved and thought she was going to have a hard time making friends. I may have made her a bit uncomfortable at times, but she still said she had fun hanging out. My experience with Isamel allowed me to improve my relationships with all my friends. Now, I welcome them without forcing it.

Many people struggle daily because they don't feel welcome here. My friends faced challenges upon entering a hostile environment. They have met people who helped them, and also those who didn't. I accept people easily due to my childhood, and I believe everybody is special in different ways. If you just talk to them you'll find you have things in common with them. They're not so different from you after all.

Statement Piece

ROSALIND BLACK

Inspired by the humorous, frank, and way-too-real political t-shirts, this poem demonstrates that there is more than one way to make a statement and be heard.

It's not uncommon to have a statement piece in your closet.
I have several, dragged up to the light from the
depths of my grandmother's endless closet,
the treasure trove of a lifelong fashionista. Hers
is a red silk dress with a leopard wrapping around the side.
But what does it say?
ROAR.

I like
when clothes say something. When they
have a message
like: "The Future Is Female."
"Black Lives Matter."
"Build Bridges Not Walls."
You can't deny it. You can't look past it.
You can't take it back.

You don't have to open your mouth but
you are still speaking. You don't say a word
but you've said it all. You've made it clear.
You can dress it up, dress it down: jeans,

sweater, skirt, tights, blazer, scarf, beanie . . . But
it's inescapable, your statement. It's out there.
It is *out* there.
ROAR.

KAYLA GLEMAUD

YEARS AS MENTEE: 1
GRADE: Senior
HIGH SCHOOL: Poly Prep
Country Day School
BORN: Brooklyn, NY
LIVES: Brooklyn, NY

MENTEE'S ANECDOTE: *Jane has helped me through all the struggles of senior year and my personal writing, from college applications to developing my voice as a writer. I love our Sunday meetings at different coffee spots, and I'll always remember our meeting at a diner after the election where Jane really supported me. My writing has not only gotten stronger, but I feel that I've found my voice and rediscovered my love for writing. Jane has been such an amazing mentor for me, from writing to my self-development. I'm so thankful I had the opportunity to work with her this year.*

JANE PORTER

YEARS AS MENTOR: 2
OCCUPATION: Freelance
writer & editor
BORN: Stamford, CT
LIVES: Brooklyn, NY

MENTOR'S ANECDOTE: *Kayla fills a room with her energy and enthusiasm. I discovered this at our first pair session. We sat at a café table and talked. One hour became two, became three, became—I can't recall how long we sat there and shared stories as we got to know each other, only that I left that first meeting knowing I'd met a special young woman who'd teach me much through her writing and voice. And she did. And she does each and every time I have the joy of seeing her.*

Grilled Cheese

KAYLA GLEMAUD

I loved grilled cheese growing up so this piece is very reminiscent of my childhood. This piece explores the theme Rise Speak Change *in the evolution of the speaker.*

The butter bubbles and hisses in the red cast-iron skillet. Usually I'm only tall enough to see the underside of the counter and the caged blue flames flickering onto the pan. Now I pull myself up, grabbing onto the edge of the counter to see more. Today is a special day. I'm six and I'm learning to make my favorite food.

"Don't keep the fire on too high," Ma says. "Turn it down."

The gas stove ticks as I adjust the nozzle from ten to two. I hear the football game playing in the living room and Papa yells incoherently, slamming a cup on the table. I can hear him scratch his black wiry beard.

I take two pieces of white bread and spread the butter carefully.

"Good, now the cheese. Okay, you can put it in the pan."

While I wait for it to cook, I run to my room. I look outside my bedroom window, past the cotton-candy walls and board games stacked miles high, and I see Papa's tomato garden. Papa loved his tomatoes. The bright red fruit hung from skinny green arms and legs firmly rooted in the soil. He'd shoo away the stray cats from playing with the vines and stop the flies from eating the tomatoes' slimy flesh.

Past Papa's garden were houses all lined up in a row. Little shirts and socks hung from the thin-string clotheslines. I never spoke to these people who lived behind my house, but sometimes I saw them come out in straw sandals and sun hats to water their plants or move a lawn chair inside.

"Come back to the kitchen! Get out of your room. The grilled cheese is burning."

I see the soft fog come from my door and I run out. Dark brown bread sizzles in the skillet, burnt cheese seeping from the sides.

Ma takes the spatula and scoops up the sorry excuse of a sandwich onto a plate. She gives me a butter knife and says, "Here, you can cut it. But be careful. Please." I cut the sandwich into small strips, different sizes and shapes. Ma looks at the plate. "Um okay. Good." I grin proudly as I look at my grilled cheese. I did this myself; it's mine.

I take a couple of pieces and bring them on a plate to Papa. He's sitting slouched in the big brown rocking chair. As I come into the room he takes the cigarette from his lips and crushes the embers into the glass ashtray. His cartoon sketches are crumpled on the floor around him, the nice ones stacked carefully on the coffee table. The top one shows him in the front of a classroom teaching a room full of students, the sign above his head reads: "Hunting 101." He takes off his thin-rimmed glasses and rubs his nose. Papa takes the plate in his warm hands, the palms covered in calluses.

"Wow, this looks great! Is this for me?"

I nod shyly.

"Wait, did you make this yourself?"

I smile with pride and give him a slice of the sandwich.

He eats the piece and crumbs fall into his beard, hiding between the patches of gray and black. *I made that,* I think to myself as I watch him devour my sandwich.

Many grilled cheeses later, Papa left his chair. He left the house. He left this world.

The ashtray was littered with unfinished cigarettes, his sketches sat untouched on the coffee table, football was never on TV anymore. Ma stopped going outside and started crying whenever she saw his pictures or found one of his old socks in the dryer.

The tomato garden turned black and shriveled up. Brown leaves fell to the dirt. Cats and flies littered the garden's graveyard.

Now I stand alone in the kitchen, looking down at the red skillet. The bread is toasted; the cheese is melted. I cut the sandwich in half. I bring the plate to Ma as she sits in the big brown chair.

She is holding a cigarette gingerly between two fingers. She's shaking. Ma looks up at me, her eyes clouded with sorrow. I don't know what to say. I don't know what I can do. I stand there and give her the plate.

When she eats the warm food, the rainstorm stops and the sun shines through her green eyes.

"Thank you," she says. "This is just what I needed."

Then Comes After

JANE PORTER

This piece came out of a free-writing exercise Kayla and I did together. I wrote about my mother, who was struggling with cancer treatment at the time. Thinking about the importance of voice in my many conversations with Kayla, particularly its strength and endurance, greatly helped me shape this piece.

It starts this way. The disease is silent. Invisible. Not there at all, you could even say. A tiny bump, lump, blip in your plans for the future.

If a lump grows, tiny, blind to the naked eye, to the humming magnifying of machinery, in the core of your chest, beside the lymph nodes, hidden in fat and flesh and all your womanly curves and no one finds it—is it even there? Are you even sick? Is there anything to speak of, carve out, kill away with the chemo—is there?

It starts this way. The cold hands of a doctor gently feeling along, pressing, prodding, pausing. The machines that light your insides up, the deep deep cut into your softness, where your children slept those years ago. A cut to get at the disease, to dig the foreign object out—the thing your body built that doesn't belong but still grows inside you nonetheless.

It starts this way. Invisible invasion.

Then comes after. The hair that clots on your pillow, the weakness like a stone wall leaning in on you from all sides. A cage of weakness and a pile of your hair in the middle, gathering, growing week by week, clogging the drain until the water rises.

The after is your body pumped with poison so your veins rebel, your bones rebel, the nerves in your body dancing like live wires on fire, trapped with no way out.

After, you wrap your head in a scarf and pull the thin gray hairs left on your scalp to the front to show the world they still exist.

After, you lay in bed like a stone slab. No, like a cement slab full of cracks and crumbling. And you remember that girl you once were, so fearless that your youth and health could ever be taken from you.

After, you lay alone, robbed of the things you never thought to hold on tight to. And you understand, or maybe you don't understand but just accept that nothing was ever yours to begin with. Everything borrowed. Everything here for just the time it's lent to you.

Except your voice. That portal from inside to out. You hold on tight to it. You let it loose.

You listen as it sings your song.

JADAIDA GLOVER

YEARS AS MENTEE: 2
GRADE: Senior
HIGH SCHOOL: High School for Medical Professions
BORN: Brooklyn, NY
LIVES: Brooklyn, NY

MENTEE'S ANECDOTE: *Kate challenges me to step out of my comfort zone and try other genres of writing. She pushes me to pursue my passions both in and outside of Girls Write Now, and helps me learn the joys of editing. I value the time we spend together in our sessions and just in general.*

KATE JACOBS

YEARS AS MENTOR: 7
OCCUPATION: Senior Editor, Roaring Brook Press/Macmillan Children's Publishing Group
BORN: Grand Rapids, MI
LIVES: Brooklyn, NY

MENTOR'S ANECDOTE: *Jadaida is full of opinions. Strong opinions. She's quick to rise to the challenge if I contradict them. But over the past two years of speaking and writing together, I've seen Jadaida let her guard down. Just a little. And in watching her, I find I'm the one who has changed. I now see the world through the strength of her convictions, and am inspired to rise up and speak out myself.*

It's Funny How Things Change

JADAIDA GLOVER

This piece was inspired by a reflective moment with my mentor about the changes in our lives over the last year. As we looked back, we noticed our growth as individuals and as a team.

There is danger in love; In not knowing if the person promising forever is worth the gold trade marriage has become; In not knowing how someone can see you as perfect when all you see are flaws. Love for me starts not in the heart, but in the eyes. It's in the way I peer into you to see if there is something familiar in you. To see if I find the same brokenness in you that is in me. I stare at you across the room at community service. Your almond-shaped brown eyes are obscured from my view, but I know you're staring back just like I know we've been playing eye tag every Wednesday for the last month. Never as much as asked each other's name, but we continue this little cat-and-mouse game. You're a handsome brother with rich earth-colored skin and full lips. You are mountain-type tall with athletic features. I am some freshman with southern roots deeper than a Missouri creek. Sass hidden behind teeth mixing with a rich knowledge of history. You notice how carefully I chew my words so they are easier on the ears and how quiet I get in your presence. So you can imagine the shock that comes over me when you speak; Hearing that baritone of a voice that is deep yet so soft . . . it is the perfect oxymoron. When you spoke of my eyes, you said you never seen a fire burn so bright. You said that I was the prettiest debater you ever seen. These are the memories I called forth after one year and five months of loving you. After I watched you give the pieces of yourself that were reserved for me to someone else. And it's funny how things change . . . how we change . . . how the promises we pinky-swore on and sealed with a kiss can mean nothing . . .

It's Amazing How Things Change

KATE JACOBS

I have trouble coming up with ideas for things to write about, but when Jadaida said to me, "It's amazing how things change," this poem came into my mind, almost fully formed.

"It's amazing how things change," she says,
When I ask her if she remembers how her boyfriend fell asleep in
     my office
While the two of us were writing.
He's not her boyfriend anymore.
"It's amazing how things change," my mother said,
When she held her grandson, my nephew,
Sitting in the house my sister owns with her husband.
After all, it wasn't that long ago that me and my sisters were in
     our 20s,
New to the big city, eager to discover ourselves and our world.

(It wasn't even that long ago that me and my sisters were kids in
    pjs,
Eating peanut butter popcorn and watching the Wonderful
    World of Disney.)
"It's amazing how things change," we all said,
On November 9 when we woke up, bleary eyed,
And we didn't have the first female president.
We didn't have a woman to lead us into a new era of liberation.
We didn't have an example to validate our decisions, our lives,
    ourselves.
"It's amazing how things change," I say,
As I hug her tight, pressing my cheek against hers, as I always do
Before we start to write.
In this moment, two years after we first met, before she leaves for
    college
And continues her own journey to discover herself and her
    world,
I know she will change, and she will be amazing.

ANALISE GUERRERO

YEARS AS MENTEE: 1
GRADE: Junior
HIGH SCHOOL: Middle College High School at LaGuardia Community College
BORN: Queens, NY
LIVES: Queens, NY

MENTEE'S ANECDOTE: *My mentor Catherine is amazing. She's encouraged me to* Rise Speak Change *in the best way. I hesitate when I write something personal, and she always tells me to follow through, revise later. That's a great motivation, because I'm constantly holding back.*

CATHERINE LeCLAIR

YEARS AS MENTOR: 3
OCCUPATION: Senior Strategist, Gizmodo Media Group
BORN: Bangor, ME
LIVES: Brooklyn, NY

MENTOR'S ANECDOTE: *Analise's openness and warmth toward all individuals inspires me toward more acts of kindness. She is so uniquely herself and so genuinely able to appreciate everyone else's individuality. In a world filled with competitiveness and ego-driven negativity, I wish I could bottle her positive energy and love and share it with everybody. I know for a fact it would improve the state of the planet.*

Broken Glass

ANALISE GUERRERO

This piece relates to Rise Speak Change *because women are told to keep their heads down and not talk out of turn, and I want to change that.*

i am ugly
i am disgusting
you say this to me
when i don't wear makeup
for accepting myself
just the way i am
i put on makeup
no longer accepting the way i look
and finally
finally
i am beautiful
i am absolutly stunning
but
now you say it's gross
you tell me
i'm "wearing too much"
you call me
a slut
and tell me to respect myself

you label me
as false advertisement.
Why is it that people feel they have a right to judge
every single movement
every single detail
that occurs with us women?
this double standard shit
needs to be *eliminated*
but
society does remind us
that we are beautiful
just the way we are
Society is lying to us.
everyone expects us women
to be examples
and dress nice
and shut up when told
but a man
an equal of me
or at least should be
can act a fool
cheat on his loved one
talk out of turn
and it is okay
it is accepted for the guy to act a fool
but us women are disrespected when we do the same.
who are you
to tell me what is appropriate to wear?
who are you
to remind me my place?
who are you
to look down on me

and tell me how to think of myself
when i have a working mind of my own?
you are not more superior than me
whether i am a woman or not
you will not remind me
that i am beautiful
i know i am beautiful
i will wear makeup by choice
you will not pressure me to simply impress you
when you
and your little friends
part of this conflicting society
are not worth a minute of my time
do not tell me to stay shut
for i will continue speaking
do not tell me to keep my head down
for i will raise my chin higher
i will rise when i want
not when you want
i will speak by my choice
not yours
and i will change the way you think when you hear the word
    "women."

Seeing Out Empathy

CATHERINE LeCLAIR

I wrote the piece from which this is excerpted the day after the 2016 election. It's a reflection on the fears that determined the way the two halves of our country voted on November 8, and how we can use empathy to better understand each other.

I cried on the subway this morning. If you know me, that's not a rare occurrence; I do a lot of my best crying on the MTA. I think I feel free to be emotional on the train because I know that my fellow New Yorkers will "get it." In a city that can often feel divided by lines of gentrification, socioeconomic status, or race, the subway lines slice through them and unite us. Riding the train is the great equalizer of the city. Whether you're coming from Bay Ridge or Corona, headed to Midtown or Harlem, you can trust that everyone else on the train has something they've got to show up for, and they understand that some days it is harder to show up than others. Today was a hard day for all of us to show up to.

I grew up in a very white place. One of the three whitest states in the country, actually (which is not a good superlative to win). So I spent most of my young adult life in central Maine surrounded by people who looked just like me. It's taken a lot of work to expose myself to people who are different from me, in all senses of the word.

. . .

Since moving to New York I still largely operate in spheres where the predominant culture is white and educated. I work at a media company with swanky offices in Union Square, and live in Carroll Gardens, a gentrified Italian neighborhood in Brooklyn that mostly abuts other gentrified neighborhoods. I take improv comedy classes at UCB, a school that has been taken to task for its lack of diversity several times in the past few years, and on any given night gives most of its stage time to white men.

My point is: it's easy to operate in a world in which you surround yourself with people just like you, even when you're trying. The results of today's election prove the danger of that.

This morning on the train I looked into the faces of people for whom the impending reign of Donald Trump means something even more dangerous than it does for me. As a woman, I am scared about what will happen to our healthcare access and devastated that a man with such a sexist and violent rhetoric has been endorsed by so many Americans. But others have more to fear than I do. I am not an immigrant or a minority. I am not disabled. And to look into the faces of these people as they were on their morning commute, just trying to show up and do a good job in the face of a political tragedy, was crushing.

GIANNY GUZMAN

YEARS AS MENTEE: 1

GRADE: Freshman

HIGH SCHOOL: Academy of American Studies

BORN: Queens, NY

LIVES: Queens, NY

MENTEE'S ANECDOTE: *I am a stubborn person, even when it concerns my writing. I am not good at receiving criticism or advice. I have always had people around me that did not understand my passion for writing and literature, and I have tried changing my writing so that it suits them. Hermione not only understands and shares my passion, but she also does not try to change my writing. She guided me out of my comfort zone and helped make the changes that suited me so that I would be proud of what I write. I am grateful to have her as a mentor and as a friend.*

HERMIONE HOBY

YEARS AS MENTOR: 1

OCCUPATION: Journalist (*The Guardian, The New York Times*) and novelist

BORN: London, England

LIVES: Brooklyn, NY

PUBLICATIONS AND RECOGNITIONS: My debut novel, *Neon in Daylight*, will be published by Catapult in January

MENTOR'S ANECDOTE: *The sleep-deprived, grief-struck morning after the election, I struggled to compose myself before our regular Wednesday afternoon meeting. I turned up to the cafe in tears. "Oh, you're taking this hard!" Gianny said as soon as she saw me and folded me into a hug. For a moment, I was so grateful to feel more mentee than mentor. This is often how it has been since then: we take pleasure in sharing knowledge, perspective, and in holding each other up. Very often, Gianny astounds me.*

She

GIANNY GUZMAN

Wangechi Mutu's art left me in awe, each piece surreal and unique. One stood out the most, "Flower Head." To me it had this aura of power and self-pride. The idea of this story sprouted in my mind and I just went with it.

None of us knew where she came from. She appeared one day and offered her services to the cause. All that mattered was that she was our best warrior, without her we would not have been able to fight for our kingdom's independence. Yet afterward, when someone would ask us about her, it was difficult to remember how she looked. Never once did her name cross our minds after she had told us. Moments after we saw her, all that was left in our minds was a blurry image. We remembered eyes that never stayed one color; eyes that blurred from blue to green to brown. Nothing more or less. We remembered that she preferred not to speak. Her blazing eyes said it all.

No man dared stand against her. We all had constant battles between our nature and our minds. We know we did not stand a chance against her but everything in our nature told us that she was just a girl.

When our kingdom took down our last remaining enemy, we celebrated. The world was at our feet and our king was going to make sure to take down the world around us and rebuild it into a future even our dreams could not conjure. She was nowhere to be seen. She led our troops into victory and was not here to celebrate her success? She was our weapon!

We sent out search parties and searched all night until our men yelled that they had found her in the outskirts of our kingdom in the woods. When we arrived, her body was not her own. We thought our eyes were playing tricks on us. She seemed to be melting or morphing into the earth. She was becoming one with it.

"The earth wants to steal her from us! Save her! She is ours and we do not share!" one of us yelled in anger, and the rest of us echoed these words, our shouts carrying across us. But before we could act she spoke. Her voice was carried by the winds to reach the whole kingdom.

"I am not yours," she said, and her voice dripped with strength and authority. "I serve the ocean, the earth and the skies. Not you. I have done my job and it is time I return to the earth."

She smiled for the first time and it felt like the sun itself was before us.

"I will be back, it is inevitable. In one shape or another, I will be back with a new voice for a new era."

She disappeared as the sun set and suddenly we had no idea what to do. We all stood there until the sun rose, until the soles of our feet begin to ache and we did not remember why we were there in the first place.

We stumbled home, a new day beginning.

Everyday Radical Things

HERMIONE HOBY

Written following the Women's March on Washington on January 21, 2017.

This was one change, the way everyday things took on the tenor of radical acts. When there is a misogynist for a president, is it not true that a woman consciously caring for her body is engaged in an act of resistance? I reminded myself this every time I swallowed vitamins, or stretched, or took a nap. Under an incoherent illiterate president, are we not committing a political act each time we read? Yes, I thought, each time I opened a book. And, with a bullying, venal demagogue for president, what is empathy right now if not a radical mode? And my emails to friends became longer, with more questions, more attempts at consolation. In this way, the things that had always been precious, albeit precious in a disregarded, granted way, became somehow illuminated.

I had meant to march, and I had made it to DC, but I spent January 21st on my in-laws' sofa, wrapped in a blanket, with my laptop balanced on my belly. I had been diagnosed with an immune disorder that left me feeling as though both my body and brain were vacant. Not entirely vacant; there was room for a dull despair—at my body's failure for one, but mainly a despair at the sight of his cat's anus of a mouth blabbering stupid and hateful words as the impossible, unreal nightmare rolled ahead and he was inaugurated. While my husband, friends, mother-in-law took to the streets, I kept company with my laptop and a livestream.

The helicopter footage of pink hats, a sea of pink, swathes of it all around the word, was the most beautiful thing I had seen in weeks. I felt it as a sort of lifeblood: as streets around the world streamed with pink, it was easy to imagine that same pink—an irrepressible, cheeky, fabulously femmey shade, more of a laugh-out-loud color than militant red or noble suffragette purple—making its way through my veins.

And then, even better, there were the signs: "So bad even introverts are here"; "I've seen smarter cabinets at IKEA"; over an image of Princess Leia, aka the late, great Carrie Fisher: "A woman's place is in the resistance." Finally, my foul-mouthed favorite: "I'd call you a c*** but you lack warmth and depth."

I laughed, felt something like guilt, then, slowly, a relief. The wit of the signs led me to some lines of Rebecca Solnit: "Joy doesn't betray but sustains activism. And when you face a politics that aspires to make you fearful, alienated and isolated, joy is a fine initial act of insurrection." Joy: another thing to add to that list of everyday radical things.

GRACE HAN

YEARS AS MENTEE: 2

GRADE: Senior

HIGH SCHOOL: Queens High School for the Sciences at York College

BORN: Queens, NY

LIVES: Queens, NY

PUBLICATIONS AND RECOGNITIONS: Quest-Bridge Scholarship.

MENTEE'S ANECDOTE: *Team Grastina's comeback this year has been marked with storytelling. In addition to sharing our own stories with one another in our conversations and in our writing, Christina and I—while indulging in an array of ethnic cuisines—embarked on excursions in search of stories about immigrants, people of color, the old and the young, and women. In doing so, Christina has been my example for learning the value of listening, of sharing experiences, and of embracing. She is the best hugger, the best laugher, the best advice-giver, and she is* my *mentor.*

CHRISTINA TESORO

YEARS AS MENTOR: 2

OCCUPATION: Rape Crisis Health Educator, Mount Sinai Adolescent Center

BORN: Queens, NY

LIVES: Queens, NY

PUBLICATIONS AND RECOGNITIONS: Published in *Racked*, *The Learned Fangirl*, and *LAMBDA Literary*.

MENTOR'S ANECDOTE: *This year has been me and Grace's year of excursions, especially now that college apps are in. We have been thrifty and creative, and have found ways to go see plays and dance performances. None was more memorable to me than seeing* A Raisin in the Sun *at the Harlem Renaissance Theater. Before we went, I could not remember anything of the story from when I read it in high school. After the play, it is a story that I will never forget—nor will I forget the conversations Grace and I have had about it since then. An admissions officer from Adelphi, upon reading Grace's poem, called it "simply magnificent."*

By Grace, through love

GRACE HAN

From the minutest to the most grandiose of changes, one thing that has kept rooted me is my name. I thank my family for giving me my name, my friends for supporting me, my teachers for pronouncing my name correctly, and finally, Christina, for embracing me as Grace, her mentee.

Dear Outer Grace,

It's me! Inner Grace!

As always, I was writing in our journal the other day, and something struck me: for eighteen years, you and I have been put together to spell out Grace Grace Han. You are the English word Grace; I am a translation of the Korean word Grace—Eun Hae. You are the outer Grace; I am the inner. We look the same when we write out our full name together, but you and I couldn't be more different. You like shopping; I like saving money. You like sleeping; I like being busy.

I recently learned in my calculus class about these special pair of angles called complementary angles. They are different angles that come together to make one. Guess who I thought of in that instant?

Us! Grace Grace, or Grace Eunhae—*to-may-to, to-mah-to; po-tay-to, po-tah-to.*

I will admit that we have had our differences in the past. With you being American and I Korean, we sure do have those moments of deep Socratic contemplation of whether to go for the kimchi or the pasta at the Thanksgiving dinner table. The thing is, at least we can bring something to the table, and like Dad, why not make the best of both worlds and have some kimchi-pasta? *Yum.*

As polar opposite as we may be, one thing is for certain: we are both *in looove* with words, to which people often respond, "But you're Asian." It is what I call a forbidden love affair. I remember we reprimanded ourselves for not living up to the "Asian" standards—the ones telling us to be a doctor or an engineer. But guess what? Words can heal just as doctors do. After all, it was the loving words of our very own Han family that healed our battle scars from when we were bullied. And it is with words I plan to take a stand because, like in engineering, words devise sentences through the construction, rearrangement, and craft of consonants and vowels. I remember all those sleepless nights we would spend absorbing and taking apart each word of stories we read. So why apologize for not being the "standard" Asian and being Grace Grace as Grace as can be?

I remember the first time we shared our dream with one another—you know, the ones we still hold onto. It was freshman year. You wanted to find a pink journal, and I wanted to write in it the stories of society-defying girls whose designation does not determine their destination, just like the story of you and I. See? Even from the beginning of our time here on this mortal coil, we have only added to each other, never subtracted.

Outer Grace, I have something to admit: I always used to envy you whenever my name, Eun Hae, was auto-corrected into Eunice. In those moments, the keyboard clacked against my Korean-American pride, often eliciting thoughts of insecurity and a desire to change my name. And it continued to be embarrassing for me when teachers could not pronounce Eun Hae, instead pronouncing it "Oon Hi" or "Ee-un Hey," to which I always had the unwanted responsibility to say, "My name is pronounced Unhye."

But I have changed.

While it has taken me a while to learn, I am left humbled by the fact that, though we have not got it all figured out yet, you define me and I you. My foreign name with your common name, together, is a name that cannot be forgotten: Grace Grace.

With love,
Inner Grace

By Any Other Name

CHRISTINA TESORO

Grace and I have spent a lot of time over the past two years talking about identity—who we are, how we got here, and where we will go. We have so much in common. The answers seem to be always changing, but it is nice to know we are changing together.

My name was almost not my name. I was almost Danielle, after Daniel (my father) and Daniel (his father), but Mom said no. Then I was almost Felicidad (*happiness*), my mamá Lala's idea. When I was in college I tried to write a novel about Felicidad— who she is, what her life looks like, whether or not she can speak Spanish fluently, and what nickname she goes by. I like the name Felicidad. Mom probably thinks I would have hated it when I was a kid, the way she thinks I would have hated having a quinceañera, and hated if she was "more of an immigrant." Maybe she is right.

My dad then suggested Christa, after Christa McAuliffe, the teacher who was supposed to be the first non-astronaut in space. My dad has been a science teacher for over thirty years now, and Christa's death upon the Challenger in 1986—two years into my parents' marriage, three years before I was born— affected him deeply. But my mom did not like Christa, or Crystal, so they named me Christina, spelled the white way, and I think about that a lot too. I have toyed, lately, with dropping the h from my name. But when I do, it does not look like my name anymore. Who is Christina? Who would Cristina be?

HUMAYRA HAQUE

YEARS AS MENTEE: 1
GRADE: Junior
HIGH SCHOOL: Landmark High School
BORN: Queens, NY
LIVES: Queens, NY

MENTEE'S ANECDOTE: *When meeting Julia for the first time at Girls Write Now, I knew she would be my other half. I saw the confidence I needed not only in sharing my writing to the public but the confidence I needed in myself and my future through her. I opened up to her instantly, which was surprising to me as a very shy person, but that shows how special our bond is. She constantly pushed me out of my comfort zone when it came to my writing and my personal life. She is my mentor and friend forever.*

JULIA WEISS

YEARS AS MENTOR: 1
OCCUPATION: Copywriter, Blue Fountain Media
BORN: Santa Monica, CA
LIVES: Brooklyn, NY
PUBLICATIONS AND RECOGNITIONS: I published a book of poetry entitled *Being Human* with Thought Catalog Books.

MENTOR'S ANECDOTE: *To know Myra is to have hope for the future. She is so intelligent, driven, and fearless that I sometimes forget that she is still in high school. Myra's profound respect for her family and herself is apparent within her writing and the dignity in which she carries herself. I am confident in Myra's ability to be a force in this world, whether she chooses to be a writer or a social worker or anything else. Myra has certainly impacted me, and I know that as she moves through this life, others will be better for having known her.*

Whispers Beneath the World

HUMAYRA HAQUE

"Whispers Beneath the World" *is about the issues faced today in society.*

The world was not expecting this kind spirit from the shallow
    whispers.
Lights flare, flashes reflect, storms rush away but the sun rises.
Hello she says and stares down at her audience, millions of people.
So this is the world, our world she questions them all.
Because if this is our world, then I am not a part of this so-called
    world.

What kind of world disables us of the American dream?
Us the

- immigrants,
- the LGBTQ community
- the colored people
- the Muslims
- the Jews
- the you name it.

We make up this world, every single one of us.
With each and every one of our differences, we create one society.

But we need an accepting and continuous, diverse society.
America is made of immigrants.
No matter our differences, we must become one.
Together, we will fight like warriors with our kindness.
We will speak our mind and express our rage in modesty.
But most of all, we will move forward hand in hand.
We will get through this.

I Am Erica

JULIA WEISS

I wrote this piece about America's fragments and its unity. I think we sometimes forget how it is interrelated.

When I walk thru skid row
look at dust-covered eyes
swear I've seen them before
writhing in cold,
under tattered sheets
I want to say *I am Erica*
we're here together
I'm not
I don't
I watch
women in red-soled heels on 5th Ave
talking five pounds
comparing tags in handbags

I am Erica face painting stripes
and stars on the Fourth of July
celebrating those overseas
lighting up skies
I am home
of the brave
visiting graves
eating corn beets lettuce
passing dairy farms, wheat
in rows feeding off 50
different types of loaves
picking cola cans growing
in peppered sand
ground we covered
in flight
over city lights
into more siren sounds
when we touch down
same air in our lungs
as where we departed from
I am Erica wherever I go,
I am Erica, recall justice for all.
I, America, see you
fall.
Can't sleep
in headlights,
walk past cracked neon signs,
drink muddy coffee,
am asked for pennies,
by streaked reflections of me.

JANNY HUANG

YEARS AS MENTEE: 2
GRADE: Senior
HIGH SCHOOL: Hunter College High School
BORN: New York, NY
LIVES: New York, NY
PUBLICATIONS AND RECOGNITIONS: Scholastic Art & Writing Awards: Gold Key, Honorable Mentions

MENTEE'S ANECDOTE: *From grabbing lunch to free-writing to museum-trekking, our relationship is everything I can ask for and more. Judy has been an extremely positive influence in my life, always nudging me to come out of my shell (sometimes literally nudging me to speak up). Our monthly cultural exposures, in the form of museum visits, allow us to appreciate other forms of art and storytelling. Judy is my best friend and my biggest inspiration. (When we are not writing, we are looking at pictures of Judy's granddog or looking at my newest cat-related phone app.)*

JUDITH ROLAND

YEARS AS MENTOR: 4
OCCUPATION: President, Roland Communications
BORN: Oceanside, NY
LIVES: New York, NY
PUBLICATIONS AND RECOGNITIONS: Various magazine articles

MENTOR'S ANECDOTE: *Janny is so brave and a great inspiration to me. She is always up for trying a writing experiment, new genres, and five-minute free-writes, which help us loosen up. Janny is a talented writer, which I think she is starting to believe, and the hardest working person I know. Great success awaits her! Over the past two years, we have become close friends, sharing both the mundane and the highly significant in our daily lives, listening and giving each other advice. But there is one thing I still do not understand: Janny, you love chemistry, really?*

The Persecution of Left-Handedness

JANNY HUANG

Written as a part of our memoir workshop, this piece details a story about coming to terms with my "special status."

I was five when I first experienced oppression head-on.

After becoming a finger-painting aficionado, I decided that it was time to transition to crayons. In daycare, I wrapped my fist around the waxy, bad-smelling sticks and sketched very crude drawings of my family. There was my mother in a red triangular skirt, my father in a blue shirt and brown shorts, and me and my sister with only stick figure limbs. The four of us had thick, circular heads and were happy on that paper.

I never looked around to see how everyone else was holding these smelly utensils. If I was comfortable, then that was all that mattered.

In elementary school, I learned how to hold a pencil like a normal person. With the taxi yellow, No. 2 pencil trapped between my thumb, index, and middle fingers, I had successfully mastered the art. But this object in my right hand felt unnervingly foreign. It did not smell like the waxy crayons at daycare. It did not write in colors. Only boring gray reflective lines. The pencil looked unnatural in my hand.

And worst of all, it did not feel *right*.

The teacher was showing us how to write the letters of the

alphabet. She demonstrated where to start for each letter. At the apex for capital "A." At the top left for capital "B." Arbitrarily somewhere in the middle for capital "C." I understood the instructions, but the challenge was actually re-creating the printed letters on the lines below.

I placed the tip of the pencil onto the smooth copy paper. I emulated *exactly* how our teacher had held the pencil. I started with capital "A." Wasn't too hard. I could draw straight lines. The real struggle began with capital "B." I managed to get past the first step: the straight vertical line. Where there should have been two smooth curves, there were sharp corners instead. I tried capital "C." The continuous curve proved difficult for me to overcome. In the sad graphite, my third letter of the alphabet had four right-angle corners.

Maybe I was not the only one struggling. I looked to my left. She was already on lowercase "h." I looked to my right. He was on capital "R." Their letters looked normal. Their text with curves at least *had* curves.

No corners.

I switched to my other hand. I secured the pencil between my thumb, index, and middle fingers. It felt better nestled there. I tried out the second and third letters again and successfully re-created the same curviness of the printed texts.

It made sense for me to use my left hand. I always held the crayons with that hand. Even though I was the only person in class writing with my left hand, at least I could copy the alphabet correctly.

My approach to comfort did not sit well with my parents. Our very first homework assignment was to finish the capital and lowercase letters. I began my work with ease. I was on a roll with my copying when my father stopped me. He told me "This is wrong," and proceeded to show me the correct way to write. He placed the utensil in his right hand. I mirrored the image with my left since I liked that hand better. I confidently showed my form to my father. He shook his head, took the pencil from my left, and placed it in my right.

"This hand," he said.

As a child, I did not want to tell him otherwise. What my parents said was law.

After months of writing, rewriting, and mastering the alphabet with my right hand, I still could not shake off the unnatural grip of my right hand. Eventually, I reverted back to my left hand, making sure I only used it when my parents were not around. When my father moved away to do his own work, I immediately picked up the pencil with my left hand and breezed through these daily exercises. Once I heard returning footsteps, I would go back to my right.

My preferred hand could finish the entire alphabet three times over in the same amount of time it took my right to get through the first five letters. Maybe there was something wrong with me. None of my relatives used their left hands to hold their chopsticks. No one at school used their left hand to write.

It was not before long that this "right-hand business" stopped working for me. My fingers cramped whenever I held onto the ugly pencil. I did not have this problem with my other hand.

I told my father that I was not meant to use my right hand.

I became the only left-handed pencil wielder in my classes. And the only left-handed scissors wielder. And the only left-handed fork wielder in the family.

I stood out. There was always someone who would point

out my anomaly. I was the only person who came home with graphite smudged all over the side of their hand and pinky.

Despite the inconvenience of being left-handed in a right-handed world, I continue to stick with my left hand.

Because it is comfortable.

Precious Cargo

JUDITH ROLAND

Not long before my father's death, my son, Alex, was pushing his grandfather in a wheelchair through the snow. "Precious cargo," said Alex. My father had said the very same thing, many years before, while driving Alex home after being born.

A first foray into the world, all fresh and new
Unmarked by time.
Wrapped in onesie, then sweater and hat just knitted by auntie,
    then hospital blanket,
Cushioned and tucked into infant seat like an egg nestled in a
    carton,
Caution taken with each step.
Sheltered and cradled in the back seat by parents who count his
    every breath,
Grandfather agonizing over every bump on the road that will
    take him home,
Ever conscious of the prize he is transporting.
Precious cargo, he says, precious cargo.

Swaddled from head to toe so he can barely move
Looking like an Ellis Island arrival, we joke,
This once-protector now worn down by time, unwinding, so
    vulnerable.
Pushing up the hill and down the curb, the grandson does his
    best to cushion each bump,
To absorb every slight shock, if he could,
So that the old man now so frail might travel undisturbed.
With great care and unwavering vigilance
He watches over Grandpa.
Precious cargo, he says, precious cargo.

RAHAT HUDA

YEARS AS MENTEE: 2

GRADE: Senior

HIGH SCHOOL: Stuyvesant High School

BORN: Queens, NY

LIVES: Queens, NY

PUBLICATIONS AND RECOGNITIONS: Scholastic Art & Writing Awards: Honorable Mentions (3), Silver Keys (2), Gold Key; 2016 Breaking Bread anthology, Posse Scholarship to Middlebury College

MENTEE'S ANECDOTE: *Katherine started her job at Adelphi University last August and I remember how nervous she had been when she was applying for it. I had the honor of sitting in on one of her classes in February. Her office was cozy, with three lamps, a cute campus view, and bookshelves she was trying to fill. That day, I got to take home a copy of her book,* The Violet Hour, *watch her teach, write with her in the campus cafe, and introduce her to my dad!*

KATHERINE HILL

YEARS AS MENTOR: 2

OCCUPATION: Assistant Professor of English, Adelphi University

BORN: Washington, DC

LIVES: Brooklyn, NY

PUBLICATIONS AND RECOGNITIONS: Virginia Center for the Creative Arts Fellowship, Wertheim Study Fellowship, New York Public Library

MENTOR'S ANECDOTE: *It's amazing how far Rahat and I have come. Last year, we were both feeling the pressure of the next step: college for her and a career change for me. We feared we'd have to settle. And while we agreed that wouldn't be the worst thing, we each desperately wanted the other to get her wish. And then, like magic, we did. I was hired at Adelphi, she won a Posse Scholarship to Middlebury, and we each credit the other for her belief. Now the challenge will be settling for seeing each other less—which really is the worst thing!*

Between the Blackouts

RAHAT HUDA

A young Bangladeshi journalist tries to find her place in a male-dominated workplace by investigating a murder for a chance to write a front-page-worthy article. While she struggles to gain respect at work, she deals with parental pressure to get married.

Tahmina always got to work an hour early to avoid the embarrassment of arriving late. Her colleagues and boss already had a hard time taking her seriously and she didn't want to give them another reason to put her career on hold. She sat at her desk with her eyes closed and her arms around her head. Her stomach was still queasy from the Chinese food she'd eaten at the new restaurant she was supposed to review.

Footsteps approached. Tahmina opened her eyes and saw laced-up dress shoes stop in front of her desk. She lifted her head and Mr. Abdullah grinned. "Sleeping on the job, Tahmina?" He had a flirtatious glint in his eyes that angered her. "Is your husband keeping you up late?" he laughed. "Oh, that's right. You're still not married. You know, I might know of some eligible bachelors if you want me to put your parents in contact with them." He winked and leaned against Tahmina's desk, making his ringless left hand visible to her.

"I wasn't sleeping," she replied. "I have an article to write."

"I knew that would get you to start working," Mr. Abdullah

said triumphantly, trying to disguise his disappointment from being shot down once again.

As people began pouring into the office, Tahmina decided to hammer out the restaurant review within twenty minutes and be done with it. Hopefully Mr. Abdullah wouldn't have another meaningless project.

> Dhaka Chinese is the first big Chinese restaurant in Mirpur and an even bigger disappointment. The poor lighting and musty leather booths will make you think you were in a shabby bar in some obscure village in Barisal. With only five beverage options and food that will leave you on the toilet for hours, Dhaka Chinese might be the worst place to take your friends and the best place to send your enemies. I really wish I could give this new place at least one star, but it's five turds for me . . .

Well, that wasn't the worst thing I've written this year, Tahmina thought as she saved the article and sent it to the editor. Yawning, she walked to the water fountain for a tiny cup of lukewarm water.

"Tahmina, did you hear about the woman who got shot downtown?" Motassim Khandaker, an intern at the company, asked in the queue for water. Tahmina nodded, but didn't reply. She resented Motassim for being able to report on stories that were far more interesting than her reviews.

"She left behind two kids and a husband. Tragic, really," Motassim continued. "The authorities aren't telling the public much, but that's what we're here for."

"Well, that sounds interesting. Good luck on the article,"

Tahmina finally replied, tossing her cup into the recycling bin. "I have to get another project from Mr. Abdullah."

"Oh, he didn't give anyone the article yet, but whoever gets it basically has to play detective. *I* think the husband did it."

"He didn't tell *me* anything."

"Well, you're part of the culture department, T. This is more headline-worthy stuff." Motassim had a look of pity in his eyes that Tahmina was too used to getting.

"Husbands killing their wives—is this not one of the dark parts of our culture? Besides, you're an intern. What do you know?" Tahmina turned around and headed for Mr. Abdullah's office. She immediately regretted what she'd said to Motassim. She had always hated the way employees treated interns, but she had too much pride to go back and apologize.

Tahmina knew she wouldn't get any more projects to work on for the rest of the week, so when she walked into Mr. Abdullah's office, she had a feeling he knew she was going to ask to have this story. Rejection didn't hurt anymore, but Tahmina always had the slightest hope that he would agree to let her write an article she proposed.

"Tahmina," Mr. Abdullah began before she could say anything. "We have to blow this story out of the water if we want to make our paper big, so this might not be the project for you."

"Mr. Abdullah, you have no idea what I'm capable of because you leave me with a section of the paper nobody even reads. The people who buy this paper don't have the money to go to fabric stores."

"That's exactly my point, Tahmina! You don't have enough experience to write a piece this big. Give yourself some time. You've only been here ten months."

"Motassim has been here for three months and he's just an intern. He's had four crime stories already!" Tahmina invited herself to sit across from Mr. Abdullah. He glanced at the clock above her head and at his empty schedule. *He has time to listen to me, but he doesn't want to.* He got up from his seat and walked to the door, opening it slightly.

"Fine," he sighed. "I'll let you write a draft by Friday and show me that you're not just about restaurant reviews. But I'm having two or three other writers giving me drafts, so you have competition."

Joe, 1971

KATHERINE HILL

Excerpted from a novel-in-progress about a fictional American football player.

Joe leaned on a pasture fence some forty yards from a huddle of black and brown cows, and the question, pressing into his forearms with the pulpy wood, was simple. Was he smart enough to stick with Cindy, or smart enough to get the hell out?

He'd left his jacket at the house and he was cold. Not like the cows, who just stood and lay there, living thermostats, keeping their giant hides toasty and warm. Even from this distance, he thought he could see the heat rising off their backs. He whistled a little, trying to get their attention. If one of them looked his way—say, the near one in perfect silhouette—he'd go to

Cindy, tell her everything, offer all the humble nothing that he had, and ask her if she'd have him anyway. If it was the far one parallel to the near one, he'd take his pop's car and go, maybe stop somewhere to borrow some money first, but otherwise just hit the road. He didn't know what he'd do if one of the other cows looked—the ones with their bony butts to him, or the ones already kind of facing his way. Start over, maybe, and this time really commit to the game? He tried again, louder, accidently spitting as he cast his fate to the herd. The saliva landed on the other side of the fence, boiling off into the dirt beneath the grass. It vanished faster than he'd expected, and even so, when he looked back at the cows, they were all stock-still but in slightly different positions: a head here, a leg there, not one of them looking his way.

Moments later, the herd had moved again, some of them looking right at him now with their big, bored eyes, some of them standing farther away from the clump, though it was no longer so easy to say exactly which of the current faces belonged to which of the original cows. He'd missed the crucial shift, even now had missed it again, and with this realization he found himself seized with panic, standing there at the fence jacketless and covered in dried blood. How had he gotten there? How?

He'd come from the lake. Before that, his house. But for some reason, he was also aware of an even earlier starting point, a point that had, without his permission, set every event of his life in motion. He'd come from his parents. And they'd come from somewhere, too. His mother, now, was gone. Sucked away by the worst fucking kind of cancer. But his dad, his awful, worthless, angry dad—somehow that man still lived. And though Joe was no murderer, he had to admit that this was undoubtedly the biggest problem in his life.

KIANA JACKSON

YEARS AS MENTEE: 2

GRADE: Senior

HIGH SCHOOL: New Explorations into Science, Technology, + Math (NEST+m)

BORN: New York, NY

LIVES: New York, NY

PUBLICATIONS AND RECOGNITIONS: Scholastic Art & Writing Awards: Honorable Mention; ESA Loft Video Game Fellowship, 2017 YMCA BAI Scholarship

MENTEE'S ANECDOTE: *We were burdened by college applications from August to November, spending our time perfecting endless supplements and personal statements. The best meeting, hands down, was Thursday, December 8, 2016. The day I got my early-decision email from Cornell, I intentionally waited until the end of our meeting to open it because I didn't want to disrupt the flow of our meeting. While Deborah went to the bathroom, I checked my email and read: "Congratulations, Class of 2021." I grinned from ear to ear. When she came back, she knew from my facial expression that it had been good news.*

DEBORAH HEILIGMAN

YEARS AS MENTOR: 2

OCCUPATION: Author of books for children and teens

BORN: Allentown, PA

LIVES: New York, NY

PUBLICATIONS AND RECOGNITIONS: *Vincent and Theo: The Van Gogh Brothers* (Henry Holt, 2017)

MENTOR'S ANECDOTE: *Kiana and I were at our usual cafe writing when the early decision emails were supposed to arrive. I was so nervous, I snuck away so she could be alone. When I came back to the table, I could see it was good news. Kiana's smile is always radiant, but at that moment it lit up the world. Truly. What a joy for me, her Girls Write Now mentor, to be there when she found out that her dream had come true. I've loved getting to know Kiana these two years, and I hope to know her for many years to come.*

Not His Doll

KIANA JACKSON

"Not His Doll" was inspired by a photograph of a woman with duct tape over her mouth and a pained expression. The protagonist, Tara, struggles to find courage to free herself from her oppressor.

I closed my eyes for a second. *Inhale* *Exhale* *Why won't he just set me free?* I could feel the walls of the room shrinking around me. My breath grew shallow.

His clammy hand rubbed my arm slowly. I shuddered as he knelt down beside the wooden chair I was strapped to. He whispered something I had no intention of listening to; maybe it was another one of his twisted dark fantasies. I struggled and rocked in the chair trying to free myself.

"STOP struggling," he said, with the stamp of his foot.

I turned my head to avoid coming into contact with his putrid breath. A tear slid down my cheek and rolled off the cold duct tape plastered across my mouth.

"You want to know why I chose you?"

I managed to let a "mmmnmm" escape from my throat.

"ANSWER ME, Sissy! Oh wait, I forgot you can't speak. How insensitive of me," he chuckled, the sarcasm dripping. "It's actually quite funny," he said. "You'll laugh when I tell you, Cynthia."

"My name isn't Cynthia. Don't call me that. I'm Tara,"

I tried to say. But all that came out was a series of muffled sounds.

My face grew hot. He was treating my life as a joke, like I was a doll he could just hold close and play with whenever.

"You have her hair, her eyes, her nose. You must be Cynthia, you don't understand!"

I. AM. TARA! Not Cynthia. I'm a seventeen-year-old girl who should be at home doing homework or hanging out with my friends at the mall.

As he rose, he tried to lean in and plant a kiss on my cheek, but I pulled away. His cold lips landed on my forehead instead. A feeling of disgust shivered down my spine.

His hand gripped my jaw. He squeezed my lips into a forced pucker. I pulled away and glared at him. He returned my glare with a menacing smile, and turned away. I watched as he walked out the door to go wherever he usually goes.

For the past three days, I had listened to his footsteps stomp, clang, stomp as his heavy boots paraded around the room and then left. He went out into the hall, and to the left, then up a flight of stairs. The floorboards creaked with every step he took over my head.

When I was sure he was gone, I rocked in the chair again and again, attempting to free myself. But all I managed to do was fall backwards. *Thud.* I lay in the chair, tears flooding my eyes, creating a burning sensation in my throat. I threw my head backwards against the floor while wriggling my body, hoping the ropes would loosen. They didn't.

Resting my head on the cold basement floor, I looked up. There on the wall I saw, for the first time, a picture of Him and some girl posing. The lightbulb went off in my head. This girl was Cynthia! *But who was she and what did she have to do with me?* I looked closer and realized our similarities: our ginger shoulder-length hair, pale skin, well-sculpted facial features, and brown eyes.

I was lost in thought when I heard several stomps and the clanking of a spoon in a bowl getting louder. I tried to loosen the ropes around my wrists again. But my wrists were raw and hurt like crazy.

He opened the door and looked at me with a cunning smile. He held a tray of food and a roll of duct tape and fresh rope.

"I made you dinner, remember, like when we were little? Spaghetti and meatballs with garlic power."

I nodded at him, as if I did remember. He yanked off my duct tape. "I'll also cut the ropes off, but promise you won't try to run away?"

I nodded. *Everything must go according to plan.* My stomach grumbled so I picked up the fork with one hand and rubbed my raw wrist with the other. I swirled the spaghetti and took a mouthful. He smiled in satisfaction.

I ate slowly and waited for his guard to go down.

Once I was finished, I handed him the tray.

He took it from me and before he could think, I kicked him in his groin.

Crash!

The tray fell to the floor and he stumbled back, hunched over in pain.

I sprinted toward the door. He reached for me, but before he managed to grab my arm, I slammed the door behind me and locked it.

"Cynthia, let me out so we can reasonably talk about this," he shouted, kicking and banging on the door.

"NO!" I yelled, finally free to speak. "You deserve everything that's coming your way. Karma will get you sooner or later. I am NOT just some doll you can play with at your leisure. I'm not Cynthia. I'm not your 'Sissy.'"

I locked the door and ran up the stairs. *I am Tara*, I thought. And then I yelled it aloud: "I am Tara!"

My Story Arc

DEBORAH HEILIGMAN

For our anthology pieces, Kiana and I used photographs of women with duct tape over their mouths as prompts. I wrote many drafts of a prose poem, and ended up with a piece about growth in writing and life.

This is the end of the story: me with duct tape across my mouth,
     eyes staring out.
Can you read them?
This *might* be the end of my story: unable to speak.
Held captive—literally or not—by a man with power over me.
This might be my story: a woman unable to move, unable to give
     voice to her needs.
Me, not me, afraid to change.
This could be the end of the story.
But I am the author of my own life.
I create plot, character, themes, images.
Arcs.
I revise. Again and again.

And again.

This *will not* be the end of my story.

It will be the turning point,

the climax.

The part of the plot in which

I fight back.

I fight back with brains and power.

The part of the story in which I rip off the tape.

And claim my freedom.

This draft is when my story starts to sing.

When it leaps off the page and into the cosmos.

A story of fortitude.

Of speech.

The story of a journey.

My journey.

Look again.

Can you read it in my eyes?

MEKKIAYAH JACOBS

YEARS AS MENTEE: 1
GRADE: Freshman
HIGH SCHOOL: Cobble Hill School of American Studies
BORN: New York, NY
LIVES: Bronx, NY
PUBLICATIONS AND RECOGNITIONS: Scholastic Art & Writing Award: Honorable Mention

MENTEE'S ANECDOTE: *The day that we were going to meet our mentors, I was nervous and excited. I wasn't really fond of meeting new people. I wondered what Nina would look like, how she would act and if she would have a great personality. When I did finally meet Nina Collins, she made me cry. And not in a bad way, but in a good way. She asked me some personal questions and I got very emotional. That has never happened to me before and that was how I knew that she was a good person and that I could trust her.*

NINA COLLINS

YEARS AS MENTOR: 1
OCCUPATION: Writer
BORN: New York, NY
LIVES: Brooklyn, NY
PUBLICATIONS AND RECOGNITIONS: "How Kathleen Collins's Daughter Kept Her Late Mother's Career Alive." *Vogue*, September 5, 2016.

MENTOR'S ANECDOTE: *Every week Kya and I bring a poem for each other (something that just strikes us, by anyone; she often brings song lyrics, and I have brought poems by writers as diverse as Seamus Heaney and Natasha Trethewey). We read the poem, talk about it, and then I give us a writing prompt. We write for five minutes, and then discuss what we've written. Kya always understands the poem faster and better than I do, and it is amazing how our prompts lead us to such different and rich interpretations of the words. It is a fun, easy way to connect and learn.*

What Brought Me Here Today

MEKKIAYAH JACOBS

I believe that my piece speaks to the theme Rise Speak Change *in that the topic of this narrative is about me and how I have grown. It's about a time in my life where I was tested and I passed.*

My life has been affected significantly because of all the heartache, friends, families, and states I've experienced. My mentor asked me the question: "What brought you here today?" But where exactly is here? I like to think the question is: Who am I today?

I was born May 2, 2002, in the Bronx, New York. A year later my Irish twin, Ny-Leyah, was born. We both had the same father, who was barely in our lives. But there was another man. I'll call him Tall. He became our stepfather a few months after my sister was born. He was always around; there was never a day when we didn't see him. A few months before I turned four, my mom gave birth to my second sister, LiAanni. Tall had already become a violent presence in the household, but after the baby was born, it got worse.

A year later, we moved to Maryland, where we lived for the next four years. We were close to family who lived there too, but their presence only fueled the fights between my mother and stepfather. Soon we lived by the policy "don't tell anyone what goes on in this house." I was naïve to the situation though, and sometimes told my grandmother things my mother would have preferred I kept quiet. She always said she wouldn't tell her, but she did. The police sometimes came, but unfortunately never took him away; they always just told him to calm down.

Time passed and my mom gave birth to my brother, Zakai, so now we were four. Life at home was up and down until my brother wanted to talk, and that was when Tall's anger worsened. Zakai couldn't get out the words to express his feelings so he would cry in frustration, which annoyed everyone, particularly Tall. He would scream, "Boys don't cry!" Around this time, I started staying in my room all the time writing. I was suffering from depression; I didn't know that then, but I know it now. I attempted suicide three times by trying to suffocate myself. I could never go through with it. I would ask God: "Why me? What is so important that I need to be here?"

I felt as if no one understood me; no one ever listened to me. I was lonely, no matter how much I smiled and laughed. My mom told me that I could always tell her anything, but I just shared the things I knew she wanted to hear. Now, Tall was a different story. I would never let him in on my inner thoughts. Whenever he was in the room with us, we all shut down, and when he was gone we all felt like we could be open again.

When I was nine, my mom and Tall decide to uproot us and take us to Georgia. The move was very sad. I was leaving a place that I had called home, with both good and bad memories, and all my friends and family were there. My grandmother took us in a rental car while my stepdad took the U-Haul. It took about twelve or thirteen hours and there were a lot of rest stops in between. Being on the road like that was actually very relaxing, just seeing the trees, the road, and the other cars. When we finally made it to our new home, the place was bigger than I expected—my room even had a walk-in closet! But I was still not happy.

Living in Georgia changed my perception about my life. It started to sink in that I was getting older and I don't know a better way to explain it other than I suddenly knew that that this is my one life, that I am made of flesh, and I can feel, and that this is the only chance I'm going to get.

The big day: It was January 7, 2013, when Tall finally went to jail for ongoing violent behavior. He was only gone for a few months, but that day had a huge impact on me. My depression worsened and I mostly stayed in my room; I felt safer inside than I did out. I also started to gain weight, was eating a ton, and writing really depressing poetry.

We stayed in Georgia for three years. Eventually my mother broke up with Tall and decided that we should move back to New York. Another really long drive with a U-Haul, and me and my siblings belting out songs and sometimes sitting in silence as we looked out the window. We lived briefly in Brooklyn and are now in the Bronx and I've realized that in life you have to be tough and depend on yourself, and only yourself, because no one will be there. I also discovered that I was great in math.

Today, I'm not sure who I am, but I do like the bits and pieces that I have found. I don't know where I'm going but I'll know when I get there.

A Mother's Legacy

NINA COLLINS

This is an essay I wrote for a website called Women's Voices for Change.

The death of my mother, when I was nineteen, has been the defining event of my life. I have four beloved children, started businesses, and been married twice. All these things loom large, but the loss of my mother pierced me in a way that I've never recovered from, and my love for her both buoys me and weighs me down.

Her name was Kathleen Collins (1942–1988), an African-American playwright, artist, short-story writer, and filmmaker, whose considerable creative output was only marginally recognized during her lifetime. When I was growing up my mother supported us with a job teaching film at The City College of New York. Simultaneously, she was constantly writing short stories and developing projects, having her plays read and produced, and making two films, neither of which were released in her lifetime.

As I neared the age my mother was when she died, forty-six, I found myself finally ready to grapple with the themes that consumed her—race, sexuality, intellectualism, women's lives. I started to dig through the considerable archive of work she left behind. What I found blew me away: color, poetry, moments of real brilliance, and a voice so fresh that it spoke to me across the decades. I wondered if others might feel the same way, and I decided to try and share her voice and vision with the world.

The response to her work was overwhelming.

Nearly thirty years after my mother's death, her films, *Losing Ground* (1982) and *The Cruz Brothers and Miss Malloy* (1987), were remastered and released in 2015 at The Film Society at Lincoln Center in New York to great acclaim. *Losing Ground*, one of the first feature films written and directed by a black woman, resonated deeply with women across all generations and backgrounds.

In the wake of this astonishing success and revival of my mother's work, I was able to organize a collection of her never-before-published stories, *Whatever Happened to Interracial Love?* released by Ecco Press, an imprint of HarperCollins, last December. Its sixteen short stories explore deep, universal issues of race, gender, family, and sexuality. The book has received accolades from women whose company I know my mother would have been so proud to join: Zadie Smith, Miranda July, Margo Jefferson, Leslie Jamison, Vivian Gornick, Bliss Broyard, Katie Roiphe, and many others.

The process of rediscovering and promoting my mother's work has been miraculous in many ways: healing, reconnecting, and full of love, pride, and lingering sadness.

SARANE JAMES

YEARS AS MENTEE: 2

GRADE: Sophomore

HIGH SCHOOL: The Bronx High School of Science

BORN: Bronx, NY

LIVES: Bronx, NY

PUBLICATIONS AND RECOGNITIONS: Scholastic Art & Writing Awards: Gold Key, Silver Keys (2); featured in "6 Stories on Race, Family and a Dystopian World by High School Writers." *Newsweek*, May 24, 2016.

MENTEE'S ANECDOTE: *One of the most memorable events of this program year was going to the Met Breuer to see their exhibit on Kerry James Marshall. It was great to see how beautiful or creepy or cool his paintings were, but it was also a game of hide and seek. Marshall is a master of embedding hidden meanings and references into his work. After walking through the two-story exhibit with Margo, one of the things I took away from the experience is that there is a second meaning in everything—you just have to know where to look.*

MARGO SHICKMANTER

YEARS AS MENTOR: 2

OCCUPATION: Assistant Editor, Penguin Random House

BORN: Lenox, MA

LIVES: New York, NY

MENTOR'S ANECDOTE: *Though the 2016 election was by far the lowest point in our year, watching Sarane find her political viewpoint in its wake has been inspiring. We had the opportunity to go to a protest together and marching side by side was an empowering experience. I love seeing her articulate her ideas and put her passion for social justice into her writing because I know that she is the future, and to me, that means that the future is in good hands.*

An Open Letter to Reporters

SARANE JAMES

For me, watching the news since Trump became the 45th president of the U.S. has not only been about politics, but about the struggle reporters face when doing their jobs. This piece reflects that struggle.

Dear Reporters,

It seems that trying to cover Donald Trump is like trying to stop a passenger train heading over a cliff. The conductor is insane, all the people on board are mad at you for being on the tracks, and you wonder why you're trying to fight the inevitable. Worst of all, if you don't manage to stop it, everyone will blame *you* for those people's deaths later. It's a damned if you do, damned if you don't situation.

So what do you do? Well, you cover him anyway. You show up to work every day. You report his latest atrocity. You listen to some Trump supporter/Republican (because they're practically the same now) spout some BS at you in defense of the indefensible. You try to state all of the facts while not offending the Trump camp (although they'll call you totally biased anyway). You'll ask one of his supporters how you're *supposed* to cover him so you don't hurt his—and their—feelings. You probably won't get an answer to your question. Instead, you'll hear endless whining about how tough the media is on him and how he's always being ridiculed for his actions.

You'll watch his Twitter feed, which is one of the dumbest ways I've seen a president communicate. His yelling BAD! or SAD! at the end of any tweet must sound as stupid to you as it does to me. You'll see his latest tweet, where he calls certain "mainstream" media outlets (the ones he doesn't like) the "enemy of the American people." When I saw that, I first remembered the reporters who lost their lives just trying to get an accurate story. I remembered the ones who were captured and beheaded by ISIS. I remembered the reporters who are out in battlefields *right now* trying to make sure that people at home can understand what's going on from the *comfort of their couches*. I remembered that the current president has never been in a war zone, and therefore has *no idea what that's like*. Most of all, I wondered if those reporters are un-American, then *who the hell is* (*American*)? I imagine that, as their colleagues, this bothers you much more.

Watching you do your job is both important and frustrating. For me, the newest struggle is whether to stay informed or to stay sane. How you report on him without going absolutely crazy is a mystery to me. But before I end this letter, there's one thing that I think really needs to be said. *I appreciate your work.* I'm sure it nets you plenty of hate, and it's probably tiring and seemingly endless, but I'm thankful for it.

To me, it's a blessing that you continue to analyze his actions, no matter how much he hates it. For the sake of the American people, keep up the good work. Don't let him intimidate you out of telling the most important stories.

Your supportive listener,
Sarane James

Catch More Flies

MARGO SHICKMANTER

This poem is inspired by the difficulties women can often face when attempting to rise, speak, and change in a professional setting.

A woman in the bathroom says
Rachel on *The Bachelor* doesn't play
it right. She talks too much.
"No chemistry."

She's pulling paper towels
from the dispenser.
I'm at the sink,
but only honey
is coming out of the faucet.
"That's not how you win."

The men are at the head
of the table and their
thinking looks heavy
on their necks,
but the honey is gathered
in the creases of my eye lids
and people say things can look
like what they're not.

I start the word "b—"
"B—"
but the honey has settled
in the line of my mouth,
and the viscous strands leech
the word of its small fury.

I change tact:
I raise my hand.
The honey slips down my arm,
suddenly slick as sweat,
begging me
to lick my lips.

BIANCA JEFFREY

YEARS AS MENTEE: 1
GRADE: Sophomore
HIGH SCHOOL: High School
of Fashion Industries
BORN: New York, NY
LIVES: New York, NY

MENTEE'S ANECDOTE: *As a first-year mentee, I was very nervous about working with a mentor and had many doubts about my writing. Then I met Jennifer, who has taught me to speak up for myself and write outside of my comfort zone. Her wonderful guidance has led me to finding my voice as a young writer and person. Our team has been really successful. I'm really happy to have such a great mentor.*

JENNIFER ROWE

YEARS AS MENTOR: 2
OCCUPATION: Writer, Teaching assistant
BORN: Miami, FL
LIVES: New York, NY

MENTOR'S ANECDOTE: *Bianca brings such positive energy and spirits to our weekly sessions. She always comes willing and wanting to write and learn. She has opened my eyes to a new generation of young writers with voices. I continuously push her to go beyond her comforts and express herself in all ways possible. I have seen her work mature and take on new confidence, making me a proud mentor.*

A Walk Through Racism

BIANCA JEFFREY

Sometimes sticking up for what you believe in may result in losing people close to you.

I truly didn't see that coming. I didn't think our regular walk in the park would have ended so horribly. Cam, my friend of six years, caught me by surprise. In that moment I thought I could talk to her on a complex level, but I guess I was wrong. Our conversation on racism ended in confusion for me and frustration for her. What concerned me was that we'd been friends for a long time and only joked about the stupidity of racism, but the one time we spoke on a serious note, there was a disagreement.

Earlier that day at chorus rehearsal we were having a group discussion and the topic of racism in the media came up. Cam decided to join the conversation and said something I found questionable: *"All white people are racist."*

"Cam, do you really think all white people are racist?" I asked.

Cam responded harshly and defensively, "Yes."

I looked at her, confused. She seemed upset. I was surprised by her reaction. I looked around for the person she was showing this anger toward and soon came to the conclusion that it was me. I wondered if I had asked her in a rude way or even had harsh intention in my voice. I internally questioned the way I approached her. She said something about "having the right to her opinion." I agreed, but was still confused about the answer she was giving me as she continued raising her voice. I told myself to stay controlled and think from her perspective.

I knew for sure that Cam had encountered some racism in her life. I had to take that into account when I thought about how she sees herself as a young black woman in society. I had to think about the obstacles she goes through at school and in her day-to-day life. I thought about how I had never experienced racism like her, but I did experience enough to understand what racism is and how it feels. Although we had slightly different experiences as young black girls, I was still able to see the picture beyond my own. My fear was that she wouldn't be able to do the same.

I *do not* believe all white people are racist. If I were Cam, my words would have been slightly different. I would've used the word *some* when describing a specific group of people. I understand how important it is to voice your beliefs and I don't believe in blaming a group of people for the downfalls of some within them. I feel when people say the word *all* when describing a group of people, categorizing them as one is very ignorant and unfair.

My beliefs made it hard for me to know where I stood in my friendship with Cam. I had to ask myself if I wanted to continue a friendship with a person of her mindset—always closed off. Realizing Cam wouldn't change her opinion, I was worried she would always think from that perspective. I didn't think she was a bad person and I always enjoyed hanging out with her. Cam's personality was the main reason we became friends. It seemed like we agreed on everything. After our argument, I realized that we won't always think the same way and we don't have to. Although it was really tough for me, I learned I have to stick up for what I believe in even if that means losing those close to me.

i wonder when we'll stop talking about race

JENNIFER ROWE

Talking about race is always a sensitive subject. It can make us uncomfortable and angry. Here I explore what it would be like if we stopped talking about it altogether.

I wonder when we'll stop talking about race?
Will the world be wiped out, all of us finally erased?
Will we stop saying that *black* boy or that *white* girl?
Will we stop using slang words to discuss people in the world?

I wonder when the talk about race will finally end?
Will people no longer feel the need to be on the defense?
What do you think when someone says *let's talk about race*,
Do you feel angry, uneasy or filled with hate?
Confused, weary? Uncomfortable too?
Yeah, I wonder when talking about race will be over and through

They say that in 2026 we will all look the same
And by then we won't need to play these silly race games
All these talks about brown, yellow, white, and black
Will be obsolete. No discussion. No coming back
So why do we all care so much about it now?
We can't do anything if we don't change racism somehow

Ever wonder when race will officially not matter?
If you're black, white, green, purple or the latter
It's not to say we'll all be colorless or ever forget—
The amount of pain racism has and its unwanted effects
But how can we move forward when we stay living in the past?
Yeah, I wonder how much longer this talk about race will last

ZARIAH JENKINS

YEARS AS MENTEE: 2
GRADE: Junior
HIGH SCHOOL: Midwood
High School
BORN: Brooklyn, NY
LIVES: Brooklyn, NY

MENTEE'S ANECDOTE: *When Alexis and I first met, we both agreed that poetry wasn't our thing. But our Found Poetry workshop made us realize not all poetry is bad. Together in Connecticut Muffin, we created a poem by pulling lines from our favorite songs and writings. Girls Write Now helped us expand our horizons and find ways to push ourselves together.*

ALEXIS CHEUNG

YEARS AS MENTOR: 1
OCCUPATION: Writer, free-
lance
BORN: Honolulu, HI
LIVES: Brooklyn, NY
**PUBLICATIONS AND
RECOGNITIONS:** *The New York Times, T Magazine, New York Magazine,* among others

MENTOR'S ANECDOTE: *In Zariah I've found my kindred spirit. We truly become ourselves in each other's presence—especially in cafes, eating banana chocolate chip muffins, while tinkering with words. Each week I'm struck by her graciousness; how she boldly asks for help and explains the difficulties of translating her thoughts into writing. She reminds me what fearlessness looks like.*

Writing Out of My Shell

ZARIAH JENKINS

This is a piece about finding my talent and along the way my voice, too. Through my mom, friends, and Girls Write Now, I realized that my voice deserves to be heard.

My mother says that talent is something that everyone has, even if they can't find it right away. When I was a little girl, I wanted to be a singer, even though I couldn't sing; a dancer, even though I couldn't dance; at one point, I even wanted to be a rapper. Around four years old, I wanted to be known for something, anything. Just the idea of fame excited me. But as an only child growing up in Brooklyn, New York, I was forced to be creative on my own.

I was a very dramatic kid and loved to act like the characters I read about in books. First, my mother enrolled me in drama class. In elementary school, I would participate in all the school plays but my interest for acting quickly died. Then she signed me up for karate class. In the beginning, I considered myself a karate kid and would practice all the moves at home. At school, I used karate to get kids to stop messing with me or not mess with me at all. But after getting my first belt from karate, I knew that it wasn't for me.

• • •

I've always had a voice but was too shy to utter anything out loud. Instead, I wrote my words down; it was easier that way. As a kid, I often read fiction. I fell in love with the characters and was amazed by how real they seemed. I realized that with time I could create stories, just like the authors or even better. Whenever I got bored, I wrote my own stories. My mind was always full of ideas; if I ever thought of something good, I had to quickly write it down before it disappeared.

In middle school, my love for writing grew. One of my closest friends always buried her head in her notebook. Her head was tilted to the side and her eyes were concentrated. Sometimes her long, permed hair would fall into her face and she'd brush it away and continue to work. She would often sketch or write stories, and when her hand would cramp, she would place her pen down, crack her knuckles and continue writing. When the teacher passed by, she'd shove her notebook into a random section in her binder, pretending like she was working the whole time. One day I asked to peek inside. Her notebook pages were filled with drawings and stories that she had written. I admired her art work and her stories inspired me to create my own. By the end of the year, I had my own notebook full of creativity. Words that I couldn't speak out loud were easier to say on paper. I felt powerful just by having a pen and paper.

Last year, I wrote (and eventually performed) a piece about racism, based on a video I had watched. In the video, young kids of all races were asked to choose between a black and a white doll and were asked which doll was prettier or smarter. Every single kid chose the white doll for its more positive qualities—even the black kids picked the white doll over their own skin color. Watching this made me realize that black girls (especially young ones) need to know that there are people like them out there and there is nothing wrong with being black.

In the past, I usually wouldn't talk about topics like racism out loud, especially in a writing piece that I knew many people were going to hear. The thing I love most about writing is that it helps me speak up about things I wouldn't say out loud. Last year was the year I decided to step out of my comfort zone and let people hear my voice. To this day, I continue to write and voice my opinions freely, not caring about what other people think. At times I'm still shy, but writing has always helped me slowly come out of my shell.

Five Women

ALEXIS CHEUNG

Like Zariah, I discovered that women have always influenced my writing. Here are five brief but brilliant sketches of women who shaped me into the writer I am today.

"I'm only able to write poetry when I have a Muse, a woman who focuses the world for me."

—May Sarton

1.
MOM

By thirteen, my love becomes disdain. And my reasoning is both violent and unfair. Did she instill my love for language?

Those nights she spun stories, recounting her adventures, from bed? Or perhaps it was those babysitters, the girls she hired, forever towing me to the library. She enrolls me in writing programs, encourages me. "Show me your writing," she begs. "For my birthday, please." I sign a card instead.

2.
AUNTY LOIS

She's a local author who's semi-famous, meaning she's known on the mainland. Today inky tattoos cover her skin, then fair and fleshy. Yet her voice remains the same: sometimes sweet, often sassy, laden with the Hawaiian pidgin English she grew up speaking, our lowly dialect, the one she writes in today. In her writing center, I find synonyms for colors, imitate existing poems. Slowly, I create images with words.

3.
MRS. LEE

Small and discerning, she perceives that I am lazy—and she's right. She challenges me and I surprise us both. "I never kill anything," she says. When ants infest her house, she skims a damp paper towel across each surface, before releasing them outside. Maybe that's a metaphor. I last saw her years ago. I knocked on her door and she picked a gardenia, fragrant and blooming, for behind my ear.

4.

SARAH

Before class, she sits silent and still. At precisely the hour, she speaks. I am surprised. Her voice is warm, embracing, so unlike her stare. For ninety minutes, we parse and edit, rigorously removing unnecessary prose—even from Hemingway. She exalts brevity; disdains superfluity. One book, a slim meditation on blue, holds sentences sparse and sparkling. "Like beads of a pearl necklace," she says.

5.

MOLLY

Without knowing it, I know her. Our lives overlap: we work in the same office; a sentence she published makes me laugh. Later I realize she's familiar, after reading something she wrote, accompanied by her photo. To our first official meeting (I've resolved to "become a writer") she's late, but friendly. Immediately, she helps me. She always helps me. I struggle to say thank you.

Thank you.

ALONDRA JIMENEZ

YEARS AS MENTEE: 1

GRADE: Senior

HIGH SCHOOL: Dr. Susan S. McKinney Secondary School of the Arts

BORN: Brooklyn, NY

LIVES: Brooklyn, NY

PUBLICATIONS AND RECOGNITIONS: Scholastic Art & Writing Award: Honorable Mention

MENTEE'S ANECDOTE: *It was a Monday evening as I watched the fog pile up on the glass window of Variety Coffee. I was tapping my pen in a rhythmic beat when Nandita looked up from my family memoir that she was reading. "I can honestly relate to this" were the words that escaped her lips. At this moment we realized that although we both come from different backgrounds and have undergone different experiences, we share many things in common. From there on we were able to connect on things that go beyond writing, things that helped transform our mentorship to a friendship.*

NANDITA RAGHURAM

YEARS AS MENTOR: 1

OCCUPATION: Writer, Gizmodo Media Group

BORN: Chicago, IL

LIVES: Brooklyn, NY

PUBLICATIONS AND RECOGNITIONS: *Chicago Reader, Vice,* and *Broadly*

MENTOR'S ANECDOTE: *Alondra and I are from different backgrounds. For example, I grew up in suburban Chicago and went to a big public school, while she lives in New York and attends a small arts school. These superficial differences belie our similarities, though. Our parents are both immigrants and stressed high-achievement. More importantly, we get along very well. We can talk for our entire pair session if time allowed. This blossoming relationship has shown me that connections can be made despite apparent differences, across communities, cultures, and age groups. Girls Write Now nurtures these friendships, which is why it is so vital.*

You're Latina?

ALONDRA JIMENEZ

This personal memoir tells a time that I learned to fight against the social norms that fought against who I am. A time that I had to Rise Speak Change *for myself.*

"You're Latina? You don't look like one." These are the words that are said to me each time I refer to myself as "Hispanic" or "Latina." Why? It is because my skin is dark. It is because I do not look like the "J-Lo's" of the world. It is because my hair does not fall down to my back. Since I was a small child, I was always proud of my Dominican background, but even though I considered myself to be "Latina," society did not always agree. Everyone's confusion with my ethnicity led to the destruction of my identity.

Drip, drop, drip, drop, was all I could hear as the rain slammed against the window. It was only my second week of elementary school, and I was eager for my teacher to begin the lesson that morning. I repeatedly tapped my shiny, new rain boots against the floor in a rhythmic beat. Suddenly, in walks a fair-skinned girl who looked an inch taller than me. Her frizzy hair dripped rainwater onto her shoulders. As she slowly made her way to the front of the room, she kept her head and eyes to the floor. She approached my teacher and began to speak Spanish in a low voice. My teacher, an older woman, furrowed her eyebrows as she looked at the girl and remained silent. I assumed my teacher did not understand what the girl was saying, so I raised my hand and shouted, "She's asking for directions to the main office." My teacher ignored me, keeping her eyes on the girl.

The security guard, a tall, tanned man walked into the room. My teacher asked him for help translating for the girl. They began to talk in Spanish. "She's asking for directions to the main office. I'll take her," said the security guard, as he escorted the girl out of the room. My teacher walked toward my desk and asked me, "How did you understand what she was saying?" I raised my chest with a proud smile on my face and answered, "I understand Spanish because I'm Latina." My teacher, her eyes wide, responded with, "You're Latina?" One of my classmates then chimed in and said, "You're Latina? You don't look like one." That's when the confusion began.

As I grew older, questions about my identity became more frequent. If I spoke Spanish in public, a number of open eyes would stare at me. If I explained my ethnicity to someone, a short gasp would escape their mouths. I soon realized I did not look like the women who played "Latina" roles on television or film. I did not share the same features as the women who walked the red carpet of the Latin Grammy Awards. I did not even resemble the women on the covers of all those "Latina" magazines I found on my mother's coffee table. My skin was dark and I had coarse hair. Did I not fit society's definition of a Latina?

In middle school, I began to straighten my hair. Each morning the white smoke would fill the air as the blow dryer fought my curls. I hoped straightening my hair would make me more "Latina." However, people still questioned my background. No matter what I did to embody society's description, I still was not good enough. I started to neglect my heritage. I stopped singing the songs my mom sang to me as a child, and I walked away from my father each time he tried to dance Bachata with me.

My disdain toward my heritage wasn't helping me. It made things worse. I lost all the things that made me who I am. Today, my curly hair will not curl like it used to, and I stutter when trying to speak Spanish. I was mad at the world for not understanding me, but I realized that instead of feeling frustrated, I had to enlighten others. The only way to feel comfortable in not fitting into society's description of a "Latina" was by creating my own description.

That is why I stopped neglecting my culture and began to cherish it. Today, I join my mother when she sings traditional Dominican songs. I take my father's hands when he asks to dance Bachata. I straighten my hair less in hopes of one day regaining my natural curls. In these ways I hope to reclaim all the things that once made me Dominican. Like my hair, it will be a process.

This experience taught me to not let outside influences define me. In life, I will be met with challenges that may lead me to question my identity or integrity. In spite of that, I will stay true to who I am.

Pink Arms

NANDITA RAGHURAM

This piece is an excerpt of a memoir I'm currently writing. Like Alondra's piece, it is about my family, my background, and how I have become the woman I have become by advocating for myself.

In sixth grade, I stripped all the hair off my arm with some leftover Nair I found under my mother's sink. Earlier that day, I cried because Kyle Smith had said my arms looked like dead grass. My bathroom was thick with the smell of burning hair, heavy and bitter like charcoal. Afterward, my arms looked smooth and pink, like I had climbed into the skin of the white girls from gym class.

I'm Indian. Wispy hair grows above my lip and carpets the small of my back. It crawls down my neck, onto my chin, and under my nose, coarse like the ends of a broomstick. On my arms, black, angry strands darken in winter when my olive skin lightens.

I made do with Nair until I moved to New York. For my first job, I worked as a copywriter at a website that sold hair removal services. After writing about waxes for a year and a half, I gave in and booked one for myself at a salon in SoHo.

The esthetician was an Indian woman wearing pink hospital scrubs. She was completely hairless from the nose down. We went into a cramped booth with an unassuming bowl of bubbling honey-colored wax, and I pulled my sleeves up. When she dripped the wax on me, my abs clenched. When she ripped it off, I yelped. The woman just giggled and yanked back a few more strips. When I asked her to stop she said, "We've got to take everything off."

Sweat poured from my feet and armpits and my eyes watered. It was not worth it. "It hurts too much," I said, getting off the table.

"But you have to do your other side, too," the woman explained. "And maybe we can even do your face?"

I hesitated. Hair grew out of my arm in stark lines, and welts began to appear like burn marks. I took a deep breath and opened the door. As I left, the esthetician called, "Indian women are supposed to be strong."

I am strong, though. Later that day, I was strong enough to laugh at my forearms. It took me one waxing attempt, twelve years of long sleeves, and thousands of razor blades to get there, but I had accepted myself. I finally realized that my furry face and prickly legs are okay, because I said they were. And that strength's worth more than smooth arms.

SARAH KEARNS

YEARS AS MENTEE: 1
GRADE: Junior
HIGH SCHOOL: Curtis High School
BORN: Staten Island, NY
LIVES: Staten Island, NY
PUBLICATIONS AND RECOGNITIONS: Scholastic Art & Writing Awards: Silver Keys (3)

MENTEE'S ANECDOTE: *When I first met Kathleen, I was so shy I struggled to even look her in the eye. I stumbled over words and couldn't read my writing aloud. I wasn't able to freely express my thoughts, neither out loud nor on paper. Kathleen helped me to come out of my shell. We attended protests, where I learned how to conduct an interview and approach strangers. This was completely out of my comfort zone. It was awesome. I developed the confidence necessary to be a writer. I owe that to Kathleen.*

KATHLEEN CULLITON

YEARS AS MENTOR: 1
OCCUPATION: Freelance journalist
BORN: Brooklyn, NY
LIVES: Brooklyn, NY

MENTOR'S ANECDOTE: *Sarah and I went to a march on Trump Tower the weekend after this nation made its owner our president. Thousands of people swarmed around us. Their anger was palpable. "See those protesters?" I pointed. "Get their names, ages, and why they're here." Sarah, shy like me, looked scared. But she marched toward those protesters. I can still see her, her spine straight and her gaze focused, demanding that strangers tell her more. I was so proud of her courage, but proud of my city, too. For protesting. For doing its part to get this smart, young woman ready.*

She's a 7.8

SARAH KEARNS

I wrote this piece after I had overheard two boys making misogynistic comments about me. I spoke up because I knew it was wrong. I knew something had to be said.

I was waiting in line for a bagel, my hair standing on the back of my neck and my blood boiling. Two boys next to me had, with a laidback cockiness, just scanned my body with their eyes.

"*She's a 7.8.*"

They knew they were good looking.

"*I'd tap that.*"

It didn't matter to me.

"*You should bang her, dude.*"

He should bang me. He should tap me. I'm a 7.8.

I've always been shy. I lacked the ability to speak up for my-self. I let boys at school talk about the things that they wanted to do to my body. And I wouldn't say anything.

I'm too much of a pacifist. Or too weak. Either works. But this time, my fists were clenched and I was ready to punch. Maybe if I give them black eyes, I thought, they won't ever talk about a woman like that again.

I kept my fists held to my sides and I turned. They looked at me with sheepish smirks. I glared even harder.

"Chill. We were paying you a compliment."

He should tap that. I should chill. I'm a 7.8.

"What you said was disgusting. I'm a human being, not an object to fulfill your sexual desires."

I laughed. They stopped smiling. But I wasn't done yet.

I launched into a spiel. *"Feminism"* happened more than once. Also, *"Misogyny"* and *"The oversexualization of women."* I took my time. I got it out. I was soon out of breath but I was satisfied. I crossed my arms and gave them the same arrogant smirk they had given me. Here was the moment. What would they say?

"Sorry."

Sorry!

"We didn't know."

Like hell you didn't.

It wasn't much, but it was enough. For me, at least. They may have already forgotten that I answered back. But I haven't. And I won't.

I've changed. I always knew that men can say or do almost anything they want to a woman without repercussions. So it makes sense that they have no problem with the president grabbing at any woman he desires, Congress deciding who gets to decide, rating me.

These thoughts cloud my mind. A year ago, I was on the brink of losing hope. I thought feminism was a lost cause and that the only choice I had was to tolerate the way boys at my school spoke about my body. About me.

What changed? I found Girls Write Now. Suddenly, I had a community of loving, supportive women. They were strong. They made me want to be strong.

A year ago, I probably would've pretended not to hear my

score on the bagel line. Not anymore. Women need to speak up. For one another and ourselves.

The cashier smiled at me warmly as she handed me my bagel. I thanked her as I walked past the two boys and to the door. They were silent. I felt strong.

Shirley Jackson Said It Best

KATHLEEN CULLITON

I wrote this piece after the recordings of Donald Trump bragging about his past conquests were leaked. I retreated into a favorite book and found a story that felt strangely familiar. Yes, we have risen, and yes, we have spoken. But what if nothing has changed?

Have you ever read Shirley Jackson? If you haven't, you should. That creeping, subtle panic you're feeling right now is in her books waiting for you. And when the next Trump scandal hits, and you ask yourself how much more you can take, remember this: *We Have Always Lived in the Castle.*

The worn paperback was waiting for me on my bookshelf. I took a big gulp of coffee from a red cup, curled up in a blue chair with a yellow cat, and finished it. I couldn't stop.

Constance and Merricat live in a beautiful house, in an idyllic New England village full of people that hate them. So Constance doesn't ever leave and Merricat buries a talisman in the yard.

The villagers' hatred boils over.

They storm the castle. The home. Every room is destroyed as the villagers grab and break anything they feel like grabbing and breaking. They do it because it feels good. They do it because they can. Then they leave.

Do they brag about it later?

Constance and Merricat board up the windows and build a wall of broken furniture around the house so that the villagers can never get near them again. The villagers picnic on their lawn.

"Listen to me, Constance," says Merricat, behind the barricade. "We are going to be very happy."

I put the book down on top of a magazine with a sketch of Donald Trump wearing a Miss Congeniality sash on its cover. I suddenly needed to brush my teeth.

There'll be an article about Shirley Jackson in the same magazine, one week later. The critics teased her by calling her Virginia Werewolf. She gave her earnings over to her husband who would then allot her an allowance. Her mother very much enjoyed reminding Jackson that she was much too fat.

Jackson wrote about women surrounded by people who hate them. Then hurt them. Donald Trump is your president.

Your president has appeared on soap operas and in beauty pageants and even pornography. Your president surrounds himself with women who cannot walk away when he grabs them wherever he likes. Later, they'll also appear in magazines. They wear elegant sweaters and stern faces, daintily photoshopped to show off their cheekbones. "He grabbed me. He broke me."

Their stories are repellent. But nothing you've not read before. Didn't you know?

We have always lived in the castle.

DIAMOND LEWIS

YEARS AS MENTEE: 1

GRADE: Junior

HIGH SCHOOL: Brooklyn College Academy

BORN: Brooklyn, NY

LIVES: Brooklyn, NY

PUBLICATIONS AND RECOGNITIONS: The Hank Aaron Chasing the Dream Scholarship for dance

MENTEE'S ANECDOTE: *My mentor had the idea to go to the Brooklyn Museum to see Marilyn Minter (one of the feminist exhibitions for "The Year of Yes"). I entered the museum thinking that it was going to be a quick look at the art, but I was wrong. I enjoyed looking at the many different sculptures, paintings and videos that examined the many stereotypes and roles of women over time. Most importantly I enjoyed the bonding time that my mentor and I had. We learned more about each other and I really liked hanging out with her.*

KATE MOONEY

YEARS AS MENTOR: 1

OCCUPATION: Editor, *Metro* newspaper

BORN: New Orleans, LA

LIVES: Brooklyn, NY

MENTOR'S ANECDOTE: *Diamond and I are hilariously similar. I had noticed this before but it really clicked the night we showed up for Girls Write Now pair check-ins. There were all these activity stations set up and the two of us were aimless, struggling to follow directions, cracking jokes, losing focus. We took ten minutes just trying to figure out how to pose in our picture together. Our brains are the same combination of spacey and amused, inspired and indecisive. We have a good time, and I have loved getting to know her.*

My Random Autobiography

DIAMOND LEWIS

I never write about myself, so with this piece I wanted to try that. It's an introduction to who I am and explores who I am becoming.

I was born at 11:20 a.m. on a rainy Wednesday, November 29,
    2000, and not in February.

Premature, I fought for my life in an incubator and received my
    name,
a little yellow with acid in my gut but I came out okay.

I was the securely attached child who cried when my parents left
    and held onto them until I couldn't anymore,
then cried until they returned.

I found comfort in the books I read and expressed my creativity
    in writing.
Even wrote a book at eight titled, "Don't Eat Me at
    Thanksgiving."

I was picked on in school.
I wonder if they knew . . .
they couldn't crack a diamond.
They took their best shots

and I never fought back
because my hard exterior was not going to crack.

In middle school I was a lame
but, I had great grades
and had already picked out my dream college
while everyone was dyeing their hair and losing all their
    knowledge.

I danced in the rain, always
wearing my big clunky rain boots
and carrying an umbrella twice my size.

I took pictures of everything
I'm one to hold on to memories
(I think that is why my phone never has storage).

I do my happy dance
and smile really big during math tests
because it stimulates my brain
while my peers watch me like I'm some kind of disgrace.

I am a very technical dancer,
I think ballet may be a gene.

I watch *Grey's* enough to yell "Scalpel!" before they do
and *Criminal Minds* enough to become the best serial killer of
    all time.

I sit on the floor in libraries and bookstores
to hide and escape the realities of the world—

like the little boy at the table making book towers and knocking
    them over
creating mini earthquakes within the stories.

I love fortune cookies as snacks
but the fortunes are wack.

I'm 5'1 & $^3\!/_4$s
116 lbs

I may be small,
but I will snatch the crown.

Now we are 30

KATE MOONEY

Here is an excerpt from a piece I wrote about dealing with the anxiety of turning thirty. It was a bonding moment when I shared it with Diamond, who told me she was writing poems about being sixteen.

When I turn thirty, I'll give so few fucks that by the law of supply and demand folks will be lining up outside my door just drooling for a piece (that will never come).

If you want one, it'll have to be a handwritten request sent in on the back of a circus dog with the scruffiest of hairs and then maybe I'll consider it (or just play with the dog and forget your vague desires).

See, when you turn thirty (I'm not sure how old you are as you're reading this), you ask yourself, where do all the fucks go? You are Holden Caulfield with the ducks, Langston Hughes with the dreams, Paula Cole with the cowboys. All the fucks you sent out into the hollow universe of unknown recipients, do they land anywhere? But there is no real way to get a tracking number on those fuck(er)s and follow them to a safe landing; they are like bullets or balloons, screams or dandelions.

When I turn thirty, I'm gonna be like, 'bye twenties. 'Bye all two-digit numbers with a 2 in the ones place and a 0, 1, 2, 3, 4, 5, 6, 7, 8, or 9 in the tens place. It might be a while before I can even look a twenty-dollar bill square in its Jackson; I might have to change them all out for fives and tens and ones. Get these feckless greenbacks out of my pocket, out of my sight!

But I will still be cool with *people* in their twenties. Age doesn't mean anything; everybody knows that.

Like when the twenty-three-year-old barista says to me, "I think you should do *all* the things you want to do."

When I turn thirty, I will stop asking. Tell me it's your birthday, I'll say, congratulations, you're alive.

You see, everybody to me will exist in a spectrum of all the ages at once. A prism of priors and posts. What's happened, what's on its way. ROYGIBIV but for a lifetime. You are the ages you've already lived, the ones you might never reach. Eyelashes a four-year-old flutter, voice a forty-five-year rasp. Ankles of fifteen, crow's feet not a crease over thirty-nine. And we haven't even gotten to interiors. You add up the ages of the parts and divide:

The mean is how old you are inside.

MARIAMA LOUCOUMBAR

YEARS AS MENTEE: 2
GRADE: Senior
HIGH SCHOOL: International Community High School
BORN: Dakar, Senegal
LIVES: Bronx, NY
PUBLICATIONS AND RECOGNITIONS: Sharing a poem in poetry club and overcoming shyness when publicly sharing my work

MENTEE'S ANECDOTE: *We had a lot of fun working together on poems using all five senses. Some were silly, like the one about pizza. My favorite line was, "If a man ever asked me to choose between him and pizza, I will remember him whenever I order a box of pizza."*

SUSAN SIMONDS

YEARS AS MENTOR: 2
OCCUPATION: Office Manager, Melvin Capital
BORN: Milford, CT
LIVES: New York, NY

MENTOR'S ANECDOTE: *I think one of my favorite moments this year was sharing Chimamanda Ngozi Adichie's essay on feminism with Mariama. This sparked a discussion and many poems about feminism! It was great to not only share our thoughts, but express them creatively together.*

The Forgotten Diary

MARIAMA LOUCOUMBAR

I wrote "The Forgotten Diary" thinking of how I had abandoned a diary because I now have friends with whom I could share my daily life. This kept me from daily writing, so I wanted to think about what my diary might have to say about this.

I am sitting on her desk, long forgotten
She hasn't touched me in that sensitive way that makes my pages
    glue together with
Her long, cold fingers
I am disgusted by how she ignores me like a painful memory
I wish she could see me like a naked canvas and draw memories
    on my pages
Her tears used to land on me and dry on my weary pages,
Now they dry on a napkin and land on a garbage can
I was her first,
She made love to me with scratches on my pages
Scratches so painfully full of emotions that her next lover would
    be jealous
I was her go-to whenever there were emotions
But she has a new go-to
One that could tell her she will be fine
One that could laugh with her and catch a movie night
But one could never stay silent and

Welcome her grief like I did
One could never hide her secrets like I did
I wish she could remember that I was her first
And during nights when he doesn't come home
She could open me up and tell me how tired she is of his shit
I wish she could remember that I was here, I am here and will
    always be here.

Forest Found

SUSAN SIMONDS

This poem imagines the transformation of self-empowerment. Girls Write Now helped to remind me how important it is to be a strong role model to young girls, and has also shown me I still need role models today. The transformation doesn't end in this poem, it begins.

On my way through the wind
I catch a spirit
begging to tell me a story

It rattles my ears
and bites my fingers
and sings of a young girl
who grew to be so fierce
her teeth turned sharp
her voice became a growl
and finally

with the muscles of a beast
became a tigress
and into the wild she ran

At first my eyes do not understand
and blur at the thought
of this girl astray
so far from home

But the wind swept up
and corrected me:
she was not lost
she was forest found

WINKIE MA

YEARS AS MENTEE: 3

GRADE: Senior

HIGH SCHOOL: Stuyvesant High School

BORN: Brooklyn, NY

LIVES: Brooklyn, NY

PUBLICATIONS AND RECOGNITIONS: Scholastic Writing Awards: Gold Key

MENTEE'S ANECDOTE: *It is with bittersweet feelings that I realize in a matter of months, I won't see Stephanie every week. In the past three years she has taught me to think a little deeper about the world. Whether we were bouncing ideas for a new piece or exploring the latest art exhibits, her wisdom, experience, and guidance have shaped me into the writer that I am today. I will forever treasure the Wednesday afternoons in the Target cafe where we have shared writing and laughing together, and I know she will still be my mentor for many years to come.*

STEPHANIE GOLDEN

YEARS AS MENTOR: 3

OCCUPATION: Freelance author and journalist

BORN: Brooklyn, NY

LIVES: Brooklyn, NY

PUBLICATIONS AND RECOGNITIONS: Published e-book, *Mermaid No More: Breaking Women's Culture of Sacrifice*

MENTOR'S ANECDOTE: *Winkie and I had great fun with found poetry. When a friend sent me a single long sentence from a speech by Donald Trump, we each wrote a poem from it. Our two poems, with their similarities and differences, reflect the closeness we've developed in our three years of working together. Both of us focused on the sound and rhythm of the language, more than on concept—me to distill an essence of the speaker's destructive voice, and Winkie to shift his abrasive tone to give a new feel. We are—and will remain, I know—on the same wavelength.*

Welcome to Madame Zhu's; In the Words of Mr. Trump

WINKIE MA

The first poem came from a New Yorker *restaurant review; the second, from one long Trump sentence. In the second, I wanted to use Trump's words but give them a different tone and meaning.*

Welcome to Madame Zhu's
The pan-Chinese unicorn,
the stuff of fantasy and forlorn foodie dreams.
Start with Sichuan peppercorns
and spicy mung bean jelly:
slippery, tremulous slabs of mung bean starch
steeped in a magma-like vinaigrette,
and chewy chili peppers transform
a tender main event.

Marry sweet with savory,
glaze the meat subtly,
taste every dish
and then eat endlessly:
this is no idle dream.

In the Words of Mr. Trump

Look—a great professor and scientist and engineer,
good, very good genes,
smart, very,
very smart—
you know,
they would say I'm one of the smartest people—
It's true!
—but oh, do they always start off:
good student, went there, went there,
did this, built a fortune—
it would have been so easy.
These lives are powerful;
explain
the power of what's going to happen
and who would have thought when
you look at what's going on with the four prisoners—
used to be three, now it's four—
even now, I would have said
fellas, fellas,
you know,
it's gonna take them about another 150 years
so they,
they just killed,
they just killed us.

Two "Found" Poems

STEPHANIE GOLDEN

In one workshop this year I discovered a knack for found poetry. The first poem below is based on a single endless sentence in a Trump speech. The second comes from a Vogue *article.*

Trumpery

Having nuclear . . .
My uncle, a great professor and scientist, very smart, very good,
    very smart,
Went to Wharton, was a good student, went there, went there,
    did this, built a fortune.
Look at the nuclear deal, nuclear is powerful; my uncle explained
    to me many, many years ago, the power,
The power of what's going to happen.
It's all in the messenger . . .
The Persians are great negotiators, the Iranians are great
    negotiators, so they, they
      just killed,
They just killed.

Dangerous Bargain

We are always the same age inside. But one day,
    you will be invisible.

If you start altering your face so you resemble a Cubist painting?
   (But I know what it's like to hate your reflection some
   mornings.)

Now there is no turning back.

Two weeks later, my face glowing, I am flooded with elation.
It's dangerous—delusional—yet I want
more, more, more.
I feel an almost sickening sense of hope . . .
I begin a cosmic bargaining.

NADA MAHMOUD

YEARS AS MENTEE: 1

GRADE: Senior

HIGH SCHOOL: Susan E. Wagner High School

BORN: Brooklyn, NY

LIVES: Staten Island, NY

MENTEE'S ANECDOTE: *I was not sure what to expect before meeting Mink because I have never had a mentor before. But she turned out to be someone who constantly pushes me to challenge myself. Mink also taught me to speak louder and clearer because it got pretty loud in the Starbucks we met in. She helped me have a deeper understanding of myself and was not only a writing mentor but a friend I could always rant to (which happened a lot during the past election). Mink turned out to be one of the most interesting, kind, and understanding people I have met.*

MINK CHOI

YEARS AS MENTOR: 1

OCCUPATION: Literary agent

BORN: Raleigh, NC

LIVES: Queens, NY

MENTOR'S ANECDOTE: *This is my first year in Girls Write Now and I was nervous about what I might have to offer. But when Nada and I had our first pair session, we immediately bonded over what it is like to come from an immigrant family, to be a woman of color in America, and we discovered that we are both passionate about social justice issues, like the Black Lives Matter movement. I continue to be inspired by Nada's openness and her confidence in being a Muslim Arab-American woman. I know that Nada will go on to do absolutely brilliant things in her life.*

Three Things Right-Wing America Should Know

NADA MAHMOUD

This senior year, I experienced a horrifying election. Its results have had a forceful impact on many minorities in the United States. This is a poem I wrote after feeling fed up with the rise of Islamophobia.

My government has indirectly waged a war on my
    religion
The Americans vs. the Muslims
But what if you are one of the 3.3 million Muslim
    Americans,
If your very own politicians and neighbors were the
    ones who had the power to define you.
Stop politicizing my identity.
Right-wing America, if you want to ban an entire
    faith from a land
A land built by slaves that you took by force
And immigrants that you have sold a lie to
Then maybe you should know three things

1- *Jihad* does not mean holy war, it means to strive
    and struggle.
2- *Shariah* means a path to be followed; it refers to

the law of God. It does not preach the cutting of heads or harm of any innocent person. Also, please stop saying *sharia law* because you're really just saying *"law law."*

3- The physical *hijab* is part of an Islamic principle of modesty that I and millions of other women in the world choose to wear proudly. It is not a form of control or oppression.

So please do not define a woman's freedom and worth by how much she decides to reveal to the public eye. Do not define who I and the other 1.7 billion who share my faith are to satisfy your political agenda.

Otherness

MINK CHOI

I was inspired to write this piece after conversations with my mentee about growing up in an immigrant household.

It's hard to explain the desire to be white, to have pale, translucent skin, prickly blond leg hair, sparkling blue eyes. When you're a small child growing up in a small Irish-Catholic town, you dream about blending in, about not being complimented on how well you speak English. When I was ten years old, my mother stuck small strips of Scotch tape to my eyelids. She was trying to create an artificial fold in my monolids—she wanted me to have big, Western, Barbie eyes. Because the thick-lidded eyes I inherited from my father were too ugly for her to look at.

At school, my white classmates told me to go back to my country, called me chink and gook and egg-roll while flattening their faces with their palms. My teachers tripped over my foreign-sounding name, and friends couldn't understand why I wasn't allowed to sleep over at their houses or paint my nails or shave my legs.

At home, my parents spoke to me in a mix of broken English and scattered Korean phrases. Father taught me ancient proverbs about living a full life and which well to drink the cleanest water from; he told me Korean folk tales of foxes and tigers, while mother sucked on a thin white cigarette and beat the backs of my legs with a wooden stick because I forgot to clean out the rice cooker.

I didn't learn about double-consciousness until I studied Edward Said in college. It was then that I realized I had been navigating these two sides to my identity my entire life, that I couldn't reconcile one with the other: my Americanness and my Korean heritage. My otherness had become a part of my identity but I struggled to embrace it—I resented it. I wanted to erase it.

My mother told me to stay quiet, to be polite to white people, that racism wasn't a part of my reality, of my existence. It was a complete denial of the stereotypes that society had imprinted onto my skin. But I know now that it is the anger and the quiet rage that fuels me, that pushes me to love myself and my skin color, my heritage, my culture, my Korean side and my American side; it is this anger and rage that has been with me since I can remember, that tells me I can't stay silent.

VERONIKA MARQUEZ

YEARS AS MENTEE: 1
GRADE: Sophomore
HIGH SCHOOL: The High School of Applied Communication
BORN: Queens, NY
LIVES: Queens, NY

MENTEE'S ANECDOTE: *My mentor and I have a very comfortable relationship and she helped me to* Rise Speak Change *by talking to me about the world around us and our positions as women in modern culture.*

ANNETTE ESTÉVEZ

YEARS AS MENTOR: 1
OCCUPATION: Poet, office manager
BORN: Brooklyn, NY
LIVES: Queens, NY
PUBLICATIONS AND RECOGNITIONS: Accepted into the Pink Door Writing Retreat and the Tin House Poetry Winter Workshop.

MENTOR'S ANECDOTE: *I was impressed by Veronika's creativity and talent from day one when she completed her first writing prompt, which was an erasure poem. She opened up to me pretty quickly and was always fearlessly up to the challenge of taking on new writing exercises and techniques. It was a great experience getting to know her interests and tailoring my choice of reading materials and writing prompts to suit them. We mesh very well and it has been a year filled with learning from and with one another, laughing together, dissecting the day-to-day issues in the world, and having heart-to-hearts.*

I Find Myself in Blue Envy

VERONIKA MARQUEZ

This poem is about how I, as a teenager, express myself through my hair.

I define me.
Hair in fist, snapped at ends
soon to have another life
razored into layers.
Side-swept.
Pixie cut.
Cowlick.

I shed each version of myself
I color them to match me—
I find myself in blue envy,
chocolate brown, blond, highlights

My girlfriends' hands
through my hair,
impossible softness
its shattered ends
against my pillowcase
Soft roots, rough edges

Ice-breaker. Mood-changer.
Autumn leaves falling into winter.
Each strand, an hour hand
twisting around my finger.
These locks, my endless canvas.

How to Make Use of Barbie

ANNETTE ESTÉVEZ

*This piece is based off of an observation I made on my daily commute.
It is about a girl creating a new world with the help of her imagination and the repurposing of her Barbie doll.*

After failed attempts at asking Mom for her smartphone,
a little girl squeezes Barbie's calves together
in her fist in protest
tilts her lilac-haired head
toward Mom's mouth
like a microphone and digs:
"In 1972, you dated
a werewolf. Tell me, how
was that?"

KIANA MARTE

YEARS AS MENTEE: 1
GRADE: Senior
HIGH SCHOOL: Cathedral High School
BORN: Brooklyn, NY
LIVES: Brooklyn, NY

MENTEE'S ANECDOTE: *I went into the Girls Write Now program with high expectations and the program ended up exceeding them. Girls Write Now matched me with the best mentor I could have asked for. She is one of the funniest people I have ever met. She has helped me construct my work with humor, and that has developed my writing in extraordinary ways. Additionally, we have worked together on the editing process, which is an area I struggled with in the past, and I feel a lot more confident with that now.*

MAEVE HIGGINS

YEARS AS MENTOR: 2
OCCUPATION: Writer, podcaster
BORN: Cork, Ireland
LIVES: Brooklyn, NY
PUBLICATIONS AND RECOGNITIONS: *The Irish Times, The New York Times,* "Maeve in America: Immigration IRL"

MENTOR'S ANECDOTE: *Kiana is a blast to work with. Her prose is thoughtful, honest, and right when you least expect it, really funny! Seeing how naturally poetry comes to her, as we worked on her CHAPTERS submission, was a true Girls Write Now highlight. Alongside college essays, workshops, and our busy school/work lives, I've been lucky enough to spend some downtime with Kiana. We discuss politics, culture, the future, and just swap stories about our lives. She is insightful, whip-smart, and irreverent. I can't wait to see what she does next.*

Easy-Bake Oven

KIANA MARTE

I set up a club in my school that brings awareness to mental health issues and how they affect families. Here, I've captured the first moment I felt that impact myself.

I woke up to the smell of bacon and eggs and a feeling in the air I could not quite understand. I didn't have the words back then. Today? I know exactly what it was: tension. I put on my SpongeBob slippers and investigated. Every day was something new, but it wasn't *exciting,* it was chaos. Random, sporadic, and never-ending. I walked through the narrow, gray hallway with my doodles on the wall. I knew my family could hear my steps because the air got lighter. I saw my grandparents and my cousins in the living room with their smiles high, but their eyes droopy and their hands clenched. I knew something was wrong, but they wouldn't tell me . . . like always. "I can't believe we're getting kicked out and Mom isn't even here to help us move," my sister said, rolling her eyes. My grandma—we called her Mama—gave my sister the evil eye, like she had blurted out a secret. I didn't know what eviction was, but I knew whose fault it was: my mother's. I was used to my mother going on extravagant trips and never taking us. I created my own life and detached myself from reality. My secret home was with my toys. There was one toy that gave me the biggest sense of warmth, no pun intended: the Easy-Bake Oven. A pink plastic rectangle, one little shelf, and the magical ability to bake cookies, cupcakes, and pretzels at any time! My dad gave it to me. He knew I was going to be the best chef in the United States. And I was. I was a tiny, all-powerful chef. I didn't see my dad a lot, but through the Easy-Bake Oven, we could connect from miles away. I was the one creating a masterpiece every day, the one who called the shots. No one could take that away from me.

That morning, the living room was stacked high with cardboard boxes that reminded me of the signs homeless people used to beg with. My eyebrows furrowed at the fact that my Easy-Bake Oven looked like a piece of garbage. I snatched it up, away from the boxes, and held it close. I watched my cousins help Mama tirelessly go up and down the stairs, emptying the bedrooms. She was looking after us all, but she looked like she needed looking after herself. I wish we could have shared the power of the Easy-Bake Oven, but she would probably just end up cleaning it.

I didn't care about the house; home is where the heart is, right? So that meant home was in Puerto Rico, with my mom. My sister was mad that she wasn't here in Brooklyn, taking care of us, stopping those guys from taping up our door. But my sister was wrong, as always. Even if our mom were there, she wouldn't help. She would just sit in the living room awake for hours, scared of the aliens. I was only six, but even I knew there were no aliens. And as for the "people in her head," they were useless; I bet they wouldn't even help us move!

Mama stood, surveying all of the boxes. "*Aye mis niñas, hay demasiados juguetes. Necesito vender esas cosas.*" She called it there and then—a yard sale. And it turned out a lot of people were happy to buy our junk. Mama was happy; she told me and my sister to go settle in at her place five blocks away and put some of my clothes away in our new room. I put my Easy-Bake Oven down and told my cousin to keep it safe. I walked through the neighborhood with my sister, into my grandparents' building with the elevator that reeked of pee. I looked at our room; Mama had put sheets on the bed, and that felt good. My sister and I unpacked our plastic bags and stacked the clothes in the drawers, then we took the stairs down, counting as we went. 218! The yard sale was winding down when we reached our old building. I skipped up to my cousin, but she was looking at the ground as if she'd broken her neck.

I knew immediately what had happened. They'd sold my Easy-Bake Oven, and there was nothing I could do about it. I knocked over the ugly lamp sitting on the table in the yard and Mama yelled at me to pick it up. The thing is, I wasn't even mad at her. Or my mom. It crystallized for me right there and then. None of this would have happened, us losing the house, my sister being sad, my dad living miles away, my grandparents selling my toys, if it weren't for my mom's illness. Whatever was up with her got to us all. Losing my Easy-Bake Oven meant losing more than a toy. I lost the child in me. I didn't yet know what I was becoming: a young woman ready to speak up about mental illness.

Not Annie Moore

MAEVE HIGGINS

This is an excerpt from my New York Times *piece about Annie Moore, the first immigrant through Ellis Island. I think and write a lot about immigration, and what "home" means.*

In January 2014, a girl from Cobh, Ireland (formerly known as Queenstown) journeyed across the Atlantic, skipped rosy-cheeked off an airplane at John F. Kennedy International Airport to start her new life. That was me, compensating for my indoor ghost face with too much blush in a shade aspirationally entitled "orgasm." In January 1892, a girl from Queenstown (now known as Cobh) skipped rosy-cheeked off a boat at Ellis Island to start her new life. That was Annie Moore, flushed with embarrassment at the unexpected fuss being made of her by the officials on the island. She was the first immigrant through the new processing center that opened its doors on January 1 of that year.

I know she was rosy-cheeked, because *The New York Times* said so, back in the day. I'm only guessing as to the reason. Maybe she wasn't mortified by the attention, and the redness was simply caused by the icy wind whipping through the harbor. Maybe she just lit up with the anticipation of seeing her parents for the first time in years and the relief of no longer being her little brothers' sole guardian, as she had been on their voyage. I have no idea. I grew up knowing all about the people that left my hometown, but nothing about what happened next.

Cobh is an island in the mouth of Cork Harbor, the departure point for more than two million Irish people between 1845 and 1945. It was the last place the *Titanic* stopped before it, well, I don't want to ruin the movie. While other children went to amusement parks, our school trips were to replicas of coffin ships, so named because of the death rate onboard as they transported people to America during the Irish famine. My classmates and I filed into the wooden bowels of a ship to listen to audio of people groaning, and look at wax figures leaning over buckets. So you see, this whole leaving thing, it's in me.

KARINA MARTINEZ

YEARS AS MENTEE: 4
GRADE: Senior
HIGH SCHOOL: The Bronx
High School of Science
BORN: New York, NY
LIVES: Bronx, NY

MENTEE'S ANECDOTE: *After a hectic four-year journey, I'm glad to say that this final year with Rachel has been the best for me at Girls Write Now. Through our random talks at Whole Foods, I was able to get back in touch with myself and my writing after feeling out of place for a number of months. Rachel encouraged me to rediscover my love for writing and to approach it in a way that I hadn't before. Without her, I might have lost one of the most important parts of myself, and for that I am forever grateful.*

RACHEL COHEN

YEARS AS MENTOR: 4
OCCUPATION: Student,
Grace Hopper Academy
BORN: Concord, MA
LIVES: New York, NY
**PUBLICATIONS AND
RECOGNITIONS:** Sports Reporter, *Associated Press,*
2007–16; *Dallas Morning
News,* 2000–07

MENTOR'S ANECDOTE: *I didn't hear the phone beep and came back to see two texts sent a few minutes apart. "Also, Emily just asked me to emcee the March CHAPTERS reading!!! Should I do it?" And then: "I just told her yes! I'm so excited." I'm glad I missed the first, because sometimes the best mentoring is not to. Of course I would have responded supportively—"What a cool opportunity! You would be amazing!"—and meant every word. Even better, though: Karina's "yes" came completely from her, the culmination of her four years in Girls Write Now and our two together. I'm so excited, too.*

people watching

KARINA MARTINEZ

Something I think everyone is guilty of is "people watching," and lately I have begun to wonder if, when people look at me, they can see the conflict in my eyes.

i've found that i'm afraid to smile at people.
whenever i make eye contact with someone i don't know
my first instinct is to look away
and i don't know why.
i want to be the girl that smiles back
and yet i'm the girl that spends her days watching,
listening in on stories far more interesting than her own.
everyone is so close,
their embers burning so bright,
and i guess i want to know how it came to this,
me craving more than i've been given,
me wanting more than the memories in my head.
i see *them* more than i see *myself.*
i've always been a faded photograph,
my skin washed out as if someone had left me out in the rain,
so why do i want them to see me
if i know that if i saw myself
i'd probably turn away?
is it because i want to know what they think?

do they see the world in the shades of red that i do?
or do they see it all in fantastic shades of yellow?
so bright and beautiful.
it's untouchable.
it's magical.
i'm sick of all the smoke.
sure fire looks nice from afar
but even the warmth of it isn't enough
to keep me from seeing that it's moving towards me,
it's gonna burn me if i don't move away.
but i like it when they're happy.
it makes me happy,
and yet i know it isn't good for me
'cause they don't see me,
and just this once,
i think i want to smile back.

Participation Trophies

RACHEL COHEN

In my years as a sports reporter, I always found it intriguing that how Americans talked about sports often reflected how they thought and felt about many broader issues.

The fourth game of the day was more than an hour behind schedule, and the parents sat in an empty corner of the bleachers, heads bowed down to the screens of their phones. In the game that needed to end before the Lone Stars could take the field, bat struck ball with the dull ping of aluminum on leather, and parents of that team's players shrieked as the home run cleared the fence. No one from the Lone Stars looked up.

"Hey, you've got to see this," Caden's dad told Beckett's mom in a near-shout to be heard over those other parents stomping on the stands in celebration. "My boss's son plays in some Dallas city league for the kids who didn't make travel teams. Always wants to talk to me about it—like that league and this are the same thing. So his kid's team lost in the first round of the playoffs. Well, check out this photo from their end-of-season banquet. Can you believe the size of those trophies?"

Beckett's mom leaned over to peruse the picture and shook her head gravely.

"Participation trophies," Dawkins's mom chimed in from one row above. "Everything that's wrong about this country."

"God forbid we hurt little Johnny's feelings by pointing out that the point is to win," Gage's dad added. "That's how they grow up into these oversensitive, politically correct crybabies."

"And get this," Caden's dad said. "My boss is convinced his kid is going to make Lone Stars next year. I keep trying to tell him that if you aren't good enough to make even the joke travel teams when you're six, you're never going to make Lone Stars. But somehow he thinks his kid is going to be different."

Snorts of laughter.

Just then, Austin F.'s mom came clambering up the bleachers.

"The tournament director," she paused to catch her breath, "just said they're canceling our last game," another pause to compose herself, "because they won't have enough umpires."

Every parent looked up.

"How are they going to determine the champion?"

"Winning percentage. So Houston Elite is going to get it."

"That's ridiculous!"

"Completely unfair. Our kids worked just as hard as their kids. Not their fault the organizers are so incompetent."

"They should just name co-champions."

"I'm going to email the regional chair right now to let him know what a fiasco this is."

KAMILAH MAXWELL-BOWDEN

YEARS AS MENTEE: 3
GRADE: Senior
HIGH SCHOOL: Vanguard
High School
BORN: Brooklyn, NY
LIVES: Brooklyn, NY

MENTEE'S ANECDOTE: *Ashley and I have passionate conversations that branch off in many different directions. We have a great ability to connect anything to everything in an inherently political and controversial way, which is befitting of the times we are in. We talk about religion a lot, since it is the foundation of our world and society and where world-building starts. This is the greatest thing for me because I believe Girls Write Now is the place for women to connect and make sense of our ever-changing world in a safe, friendly environment that does not judge by race or creed.*

ASHLEY SCHNEIDER

YEARS AS MENTOR: 1
OCCUPATION: Associate
Teacher, Saint Ann's School
BORN: Philadelphia, PA
LIVES: New York, NY

MENTOR'S ANECDOTE: *Recently, Kamilah sat across the table, coat still on, and said, "I have to tell you this story. Okay, so, it follows this character Lena . . ."* *For the next hour, she took me through "somewhere in Mesopotamia or beyond. It could also be Africa" as I asked questions and her characters blossomed with life. Each time Kamilah and I share writing, we dive into these culturally diverse, imaginative conversations, sailing too quickly through our time together. Girls Write Now provides a powerful community in which to nurture this relationship and discover the strength in writing.*

A Quote from Jessie Redmon Fauset

KAMILAH MAXWELL-BOWDEN

When studying Jessie Redmon Fauset in school, this quote made me realize I didn't learn about any African-American authors. I felt deeply bothered, so I wrote this poem, hoping to inspire change.

A QUOTE FROM JESSIE REDMON FAUSET

"When I was a child I used to puzzle my head ruefully over the fact that in school we studied the lives of only great white people. I took it there simply have been no great Negroes, and I was amazed when, as I grew older, I found that there were."

—Jessie Redmon Fauset

They don't teach you about my people
Our achievements have been conveniently obscured from history
As descendants of slavers and slave masters efface our legacy
From our native land
I recall my elementary school years
Where the only black poet we ever heard of
Was Langston Hughes
Mind you, I went to a predominantly black school

And a younger me found poetry to be the language of the
    oppressed
Schools ought to teach about black writers—*survivors*
From the time of mass African-American revolt
So black kids can know their ancestors through a cultural lens
I would have liked to learn much earlier
The music of my people
The language of love and loss and *longing*
Known to those members of Harlem
Should we ever forget where we came from,
Or the trials we faced—*they* faced
Along the way
We lose more than just a few songs and a dark past
We lose the love our ancestors knew for one another
Their hope for freedom and change
We lose the importance of fighting
The understanding of our resistance
So I ask you:
Rise,
While you still can
Speak,
Even if you are the only one
And Change
Because history proves it is possible.

Legacy

ASHLEY SCHNEIDER

Inspired by Kamilah, my mentee, and her submission, I tried my hand at poetry to examine my role in history, both personal and global. I hope with this piece to advocate for change and inclusivity rather than be complicit with the negative rhythms of the past.

a history we inherit,
mine wrapped up in roadside tomato stands,
ripe red emblems of my great grandfather's hard work,
sold for profit after working the land, like the human beings
my ancestors must have sold
(though I'm not told; my kin believe
it was always someone *else*)—like the land
my ancestors stole, ravaged, like the history
my ancestors stole, ravaged, warring.

Sam Houston (remember the Alamo?) falls within my
history, imposing the glory of his legacy,
he charged in honor of democracy, beating
back Mexico from Mexican land, for the sake of
our potatoes; tomatoes, ripe, red,
sown and harvested in good ol' Tennessee,
(y'all come back now), fifty cents.

Great Grandma Grace taught my mom to sew.
She prayed, sang hymns, collected honey from the
honeybees—my honeybee, that's you, Lucinda, it's you

who can do anything, it's you who can
change our legacy, the first woman in our history to
have full political agency, owned by
no husband, no father; able, at last, to disagree;
It's this my mom passed on to me.

So rise, I say collectively
give voice to those who our history
has left without a chance to Speak.
Legacy, a chance to Change
the way we are, the way we will be
with each other, on this land,
each with equal opportunity
to sell potatoes, tomatoes, fifty cents,
to sow, to sing, to pray, to love—

It's you, Earth's honeybee,
It's you who can do anything.

TATIANA MEZITIS

YEARS AS MENTEE: 1
GRADE: Freshman
HIGH SCHOOL: Hunter College High School
BORN: New York, NY
LIVES: New York, NY

MENTEE'S ANECDOTE: *Going into Girls Write Now, I never thought I would meet such an amazing person as my mentor, Christina. As well as being a talented writer with great style, she is a wonderful friend. We've had many good times, but one of my favorite memories was when we visited the Emily Dickinson exhibit at the Morgan Museum. I got a glimpse into the life of a female poet (and we also shared a delicious cheese platter). She taught me not to limit myself in my writing and to expand my horizons. I always look forward to seeing her!*

CHRISTINA DRILL

YEARS AS MENTOR: 1
OCCUPATION: Freelance writer
BORN: Teaneck, NJ
LIVES: Brooklyn, NY

MENTOR'S ANECDOTE: *Tatiana and I meet at Alice Tully Hall every Friday afternoon, and it's my favorite part of the week. Our weekly meetings are filled with drive and new frontiers—they inspire me to be a more curious writer. I can give Tatiana literally any prompt, even a boring-sounding prompt like the one I once gave her about a table, and she will weave together a brilliant poem from it that is filled with wonder and thought. And I second what she said about the cheese platter. That was the best day. :)*

Kingdom Out of Hope

TATIANA MEZITIS

This is my reflection on a world between two people. Although surrounded by destruction, being in each other's presence provides them with hope. We shouldn't be afraid to surround ourselves with people who bring out the best in us. Regardless of the world's chaos, there's always room for love.

i imagine kingdoms.

i imagine a world where i find solace in your presence, nothing but silence and softness and light, light like a morning where we can start over. the air is frigid on our skin, but your touch surges like wildfire through my veins.

one touch, one kiss, a soft dance where i turn away and you come closer. the distant roar in my ears is all the music i need. it is an approaching tidal wave, enveloping us in its shadow, but we dance under death, we waltz in a gilded courtyard built above tectonic plates and beneath a hurricane.

peace replaced the fear in our eyes, a soft glow dances above the pallor of our skin.

the world is turning slower and slower, until the universe itself seems to stop. beneath the stars, beneath the moon, beneath the receding sun and the incoming waves, time stills in our kingdom as we dance.

we built this kingdom out of hope. we are safe.

i imagine us above the clouds, i imagine kingdoms where hope reigns.

Wick

CHRISTINA DRILL

This is a love poem! There should be more love everywhere.

When I miss you I pretend we're happy alone together. In a field, or in rosewater. Or near a big wall with books. Where there is no city. And everyone is cycling, with fat yellow metal over their tires, in forest green vests. They're kind. And everyone cooks for every meal. Hot hearty things with spice. Everyone is there, on their yellow bikes and in their vests. And then afterward we light a candle.

If I could touch your forearm for forever, I would. We didn't even put the music on. It's okay. There are love songs, that's why there's music in the first place, on the first bikes. It's okay. None of them are ours.

NATALIE MOJICA

YEARS AS MENTEE: 1

GRADE: Sophomore

HIGH SCHOOL: Central Park East High School

BORN: New York, NY

LIVES: Bronx, NY

PUBLICATIONS AND RECOGNITIONS: Scholastic Art & Writing Awards: Gold Key (2); New York City Youth Poet Laureate finalist

MENTEE'S ANECDOTE: *I think the first time I met Gabriella outside of the Girls Write Now office was the most important. I was terrified that she would be someone I would never be able to talk to or want to share my writing with. However, from the first moment we started speaking I quickly realized the opposite would be true. She is someone who cultivates my creativity and inspires me to work on writing more. She doesn't dismiss my opinions or input and supports me in more ways than one. I owe many of the writing projects I am working on to her.*

GABRIELLA DOOB

YEARS AS MENTOR: 1

OCCUPATION: Associate Editor, Ecco/HarperCollins

BORN: New Haven, CT

LIVES: New York, NY

MENTOR'S ANECDOTE: *One of the first things I noticed about Natalie is that she liked to quietly read even when a lot was going on around her. While I could certainly relate, I worried I wouldn't find enough things to connect with her. Quite the opposite—I have been consistently inspired by her creativity, her robust opinions, and her many, varied interests. She has introduced me to writers, ideas, and—crucially—the show* Riverdale. *We've spent a lot of time talking and debating—over coffee, burritos, books at the Strand. It has given me a lot to think and write about.*

Skinny Girl Memoir

NATALIE MOJICA

Growing up surrounded by women of color, I always felt isolated by the fact that my body was different than those of the beautiful women around me. This poem was my moment of solidarity; my body is no one's but my own and I don't need anyone else's approval.

I know distance more than I know company,
and when my family pinches at the fat around my
waist I am taken back to the motherland for a
brief moment. my grandmother is sitting in the
backyard, drinking the cafe bustelo my mother
sent her and smiling, she beckons me towards her
and I sit on her lap blissful and naive to what the
next twelve years of my life will become. the moment
ends almost as quickly as it started and my aunt is
questioning if I eat enough at home, my cousin is
grimacing as her curves are compared to the angles
my body is made out of and both of our bodies
have become spilled coffee stains on the floor for
other people to step on; everyone in my aunt's
too small kitchen is laughing and I feel as if somebody
has set me on fire. my skin becomes paper
and my skeleton becomes full of the debris I tried
so desperately to sweep under the rug; my twelve-

year-old insecurities come flying out again like a genie
from a magic lamp simply by the sound of drunken
family laughter and I cannot breathe. I have never
smoked before but in that moment I swear there is not
oxygen in the world and my lungs are filled with
tobacco made from the scars on my body that never
healed and nicotine-like unspilled tears. my cousin is
blushing and I know that it bothers her that her father's
friend is staring at her in a way less than appropriate because
it bothers *me* that *my* father's friend is staring at me as
if I were a blow-up doll made simply for his pleasure.
the twelve-year-old inside of me, filled with insecurities, is
screaming with shame but the fourteen-year-old me is
sighing because she knows—
we've been through this process so many times we
know it by heart, it is wrong but it is to be expected and
the newly fifteen-year-old girl I have become stays silent.
I pretend that my aunt's sharp fingernails poking me
don't feel like knives, I smile and laugh with them,
when my aunt says that my hips are finally growing in
I do not say that this is not an accomplishment, that
my body growing is not a trophy for the public to stare
at. instead I nod and feel my throat constrict with
anger so immense it is like a monsoon inside of me. but
I do not speak. my obedience has become a habit too
hard to break. I know distance more than I know
company because even if my body is an abandoned home
that grows only weeds in the backyard it is *my*
abandoned home.

The Monsters in My Head

GABRIELLA DOOB

*I began writing this irreverent poem a while ago as a sort of homage
to my childhood books, the reason I'm a reader and editor. Re-reading
those books, I felt freed by the playfulness of the forms and reminded of
the many ways—serious or whimsical—to express oneself in writing.*

Aside from all the creepy-crawlies that live 'neath my bed,
There are all the creepy-crawlies that I keep inside my head.

First you have my tongue,
a serpent decked in slime,
it slithers 'round my back-of-throat,
in restless, pulsing time.

Then there is my nose,
a looming, lumpen den,
with sticky little putrid trolls,
that burst from their damp pen.

And don't forget my jiggling eyes,
rolling, swollen balls of gooze,
that could fall out at any time,
made flat by careless shoes.

I don't need to remind you
of those monsters called my ears,

with their twisting, windy pathways
they capture groans and sneers.

Back to the mouth we travel,
with its lips like quivering slugs,
that wrap themselves with gusto
'round cups and coffee mugs.

Those pudgy slugs are creepy,
but are nothing, don't you see,
to the glittering, clanging, scraping teeth,
I nightly gnash in sleep.

But by far the scariest monster
that I keep inside my head,
is the clumpy, dumpy mash of brains,
I'll have until I'm dead.

Those clumps are icky, sticky,
and worst of all they host
the fears and pains
in my mind and brains
that torture me the most.

But if my brains are rotten,
filled with demons, ogres, elves,
they are also what can free me
from my monstrous, mutant selves.

See, my brains are wondrous creatures,
sprightly, roaming trickster fairies,

that mark the time,
or tell a rhyme,
and ward away the scaries.

So, of all the precious monsters,
that live inside my dome,
I'll take my brains,
with all their pains,
and never be alone.

ANGLORY MOREL

YEARS AS MENTEE: 1

GRADE: Senior

HIGH SCHOOL: City College Academy of the Arts

BORN: Santo Domingo, Dominican Republic

LIVES: New York, NY

PUBLICATIONS AND RECOGNITIONS: 2016 Questbridge College Prep Scholar; Questbridge National College Match Finalist; Semi-finalist for the Coca-Cola Scholarship

MENTEE'S ANECDOTE: *I am thankful I met Laura. Girls Write Now is filled with amazing mentors and mentees and Laura was the perfect match for me. Girls Write Now and my mentor have given me confidence in my writing. I have met wonderful writers and experienced being part of a community of empowering women. This year I have flourished. My writing has become stronger and I am more comfortable sharing my work. I thank my mentor for our weekly meetings and for her brilliance. Being a part of Girls Write Now is an invaluable experience.*

LAURA GERINGER BASS

YEARS AS MENTOR: 1

OCCUPATION: Author of many books for children and young adults, including *A Three Hat Day* and *Sign of the Qin*.

BORN: New York, NY

LIVES: New York, NY

PUBLICATIONS AND RECOGNITIONS: *The Girl with More Than One Heart* (Abrams, 2018.)

MENTOR'S ANECDOTE: *It has been a joy to get to know Anglory and I'm grateful to Girls Write Now for the opportunity to work with my mentee on her writing. It has been a deeply satisfying and rewarding experience. For Anglory, high school has not been a "crystal stair" but she has navigated it with grace, diligence, and great humor. I hope to keep up with her during her college years and after as she rises, speaks, and discovers how her talent, intelligence, and loving nature can indeed change the world.*

Joyful

ANGLORY MOREL

In dark times, when poisonous politicians call immigrants snakes, revealing only their own reptilian nature, it is important to rise and speak, remembering the joyful times—the times when love triumphs, when families come together.

In the Morel house Christmas was no joke. The smell of pine filled the air. The aroma of roasted chicken escaped the kitchen where the counter overflowed with delicious treats for our house guests.

Our small NYC apartment located on the second floor of a thousand-year-old building felt tight. We all paced back and forth in the kitchen, in the living room, and in the bedroom making sure everything looked presentable. *"Anglory, guarda tus zapatos y ayúdame a recoger,"* my mother yelled as she gestured towards the shoes lying against the Christmas tree.

The Christmas tree—what a sight! Overstuffed with decorations. It was tall, too tall for our small apartment. It scraped the ceiling and covered half the wall. Adorned with huge glass balls of all colors, the huge pine tree was more decorated than the Macy's tree or even the Rockefeller skyscraping tree.

A buzz filled the room. They were here! Our guests made their way up the marble stairs and towards our door decorated with wrapping paper. Soon they would see all the green, red, gold, and silver hanging from every corner of our small space. A grin overtook my face. A little piece of home was coming to visit. Our beloved family, a reminder of the life we left back home on La Quisqueya, was at our doorstep.

Every year it was the same. We watched as people from all over the world, of different religions, races, and ethnicities, came together to be with their families in a land where differences were accepted and celebrated. Every year my cousins would call to tell me how happy they were to visit the United States, how lucky I am to live here, how many opportunities I have, how everyone from everywhere wants to be here. Christmastime was when we got to mix the love and culture from our little Caribbean island with the rush and buzz of New York City. We celebrated coming to this free country of hope and promise. Once a year we had the opportunity to see the ones who weren't as fortunate, to share this diverse land with them. At Christmas, joy filled every corner of the city and excitement raced in our hearts as we waited for them to make their way to us.

The door flew open and there they were, the family we all missed and loved. My eyes were set on one particular person, Ken Morel, my cousin, a caramel-colored boy whose facial hair was beginning to grow above his upper lip. His hat was way too big and sat awkwardly on his head. He was much taller than the last time I had seen him. I bet he could reach the star on the tree without even fully stretching his arms out. As soon as his eyes met mine, he let go of his luggage and rushed towards me. Memories of going to school with him and riding bikes flashed through my mind as we hugged. I stood back and admired my beautiful family. They only came once a year and now they were here. The thrill of seeing them melted like Christmas snow into pure joy, the joy that only they could bring me. *Feliz Navidad!*

Pig with Wings

LAURA GERINGER BASS

Anglory and I are both children of immigrants. Our parents came to America hoping for a better life. Let's keep that hope alive. Rise, speak, and remember the love and joy in our human hearts.

In the Geringer household, Hanukkah was no joke. Eight nights meant eight presents—eight surprises for my brother, my mother, and my father—building to the biggest and best of all on the last night.

Originality was prized in my family and it wasn't always easy to be original.

Sometimes I collaborated with my brother, who was five years my senior, on ideas for my parents. One year, when the heat in our apartment spluttered off and the bedrooms were icy cold, we sent away to L.L. Bean in exotic Maine for two matching pairs of scotch plaid sleeping pants. I asked my mother for my own mail key and strung it on my wrist with a ribbon so I wouldn't forget to check the mail every day. When the package finally arrived, I thought the pants looked kind of ugly, but my mother said she loved them and bestowed on the gift her highest compliment: *so original!*

One year, I complained to my brother. Why eight nights? Why didn't we just have a Christmas tree and presents all on one day like my best friend Eva? She had to think up only one present for each member of her family.

On the eighth night that year, my brother surprised me. He set up a little tree on the Hanukkah table with three decorations he had made himself: a witch, a snowman, and a pig with wings. (It had started as an angel but had turned into a pig in the process of construction.)

It became a Geringer tradition to celebrate Hanukkah with a menorah and a tree. The tree was set up on the first night of Hanukkah and each night after that we made decorations. The best we saved for the eighth night and we saved the best of the best for the following year. It was so much easier to be original when we made the presents ourselves.

When I grew up and had children of my own, I continued my family's tradition of menorah and tree. To my surprise, last year while going through boxes of homemade decorations, I found my brother's pig with wings—only now it looked to me like the angel he had originally meant it to be.

BRITTNEY NANTON

YEARS AS MENTEE: 3

GRADE: Senior

HIGH SCHOOL: Landmark High School

BORN: New York, NY

LIVES: New York, NY

PUBLICATIONS AND RECOGNITIONS: High Honor roll throughout all four years of high school; admission into the College Now program for English 101 and Psychology 101; accepted to the Brandeis University summer program.

MENTEE'S ANECDOTE: *My relationship with Amy is something that I am extremely thankful for, since we have developed a very close bond over the past two years. She is someone who helped me through some of the challenges that I have faced throughout my years of high school, and was always there to support me. With Amy's guidance, I learned how to use my voice and speak up for what I believe in.*

AMY FLYNTZ

YEARS AS MENTOR: 5

OCCUPATION: Founder, Amy Flyntz Copywriting LLC

BORN: Bridgeport, CT

LIVES: Brooklyn, NY

PUBLICATIONS AND RECOGNITIONS: Several essays published recently in *Thoughtfully Magazine.*

MENTOR'S ANECDOTE: *Conversations with Brittney have continued to open my eyes to issues of social justice. Our hour-long meetings often turn to heartfelt discussions of feminism, activism, and politics, and she has helped me understand what it means to navigate the world as a young black woman. Together, we have supported each other as we each try to make sense of the world around us, and what it means to be a woman in society today. I can't wait to watch Brittney make her own mark on the world. She is a constant source of inspiration to me.*

When Does a Black Boy Turn into a Monster

BRITTNEY NANTON

I've been thinking about the system our society has created specifically to bring black men down. This connects to Rise Speak Change *because I feel like people should start to question these ideals as well, raising awareness for an issue that has been going on for decades.*

At what age does a young black boy turn into a monster?
When his innocent smile is replaced with claws and fangs
A monster to the society that keeps him chained to the ground?
When the voice of his ancestors cries out for a change
Only to be silenced by the shine of a badge or a man with a gun?

At what age does a black boy lose his rights?
Is it when his mind sprouts and questions his surroundings
Or when he has no choice but to become another victim to
    a system
That has been set up to keep him locked away forever?

You see, in my eighteen years of life, I have seen many of my
    friends
Dragged to the back of a police van

And I have prayed that they made it to the station
With their hearts still beating
Fearful that they'll lose their life before they even get the chance
    to fight for it.

At what age does a black boy deserve to lose his life?
When does his mother have to bury her child?
When does his name become a hashtag filled with rage and
    anger?

At what age does a black boy become another forgotten figure?
When all that is left of him is a newspaper article
And the question,
Why?

Bystander

AMY FLYNTZ

I wrote this poem as an emotional response to Basquiat's Dustheads
*painting, and the grotesque epidemic of police brutality against
black men. We are all responsible for rising up and speaking out if we
have any hope of enacting change . . . especially now.*

I find him haunting, the one on the right
and I think he could make me lose sleep
with that gaping, toothless maw
that could be mistaken for a smile:

Tumbled-out teeth
now resting in a deliberate row
guarding his face like the bars
of a jail cell.

His concentric eyes avoid
my gaze or maybe
I am the one to look away
from that preternatural focus

And turn instead to his body
Bifurcated by his hands up
Don't Shoot!
feet already headed in the direction

Of freedom or at least
a few more breaths
of it.
I wonder why he's wearing red?

I can't tell if he's unlikable
The one on the left
or if he's just making me nervous with his
quiet authenticity

Turning toward the eyes
sizing him up, his own pools blackened
with depth, round like the barrels
he's been forced to stare down.

That left cheek dappled by
chit marks to remind him

and me of
the debt he owes society

His mouth struggles to form
a shape easily recognized
as a rectangle: even, sturdy
but he can't quite make it fit

And I wish he would raise
his fists instead of covering
his body with that one bony hand
like a skeleton.

MILENA NARANJO

YEARS AS MENTEE: 1
GRADE: Junior
HIGH SCHOOL: The Renaissance Charter School
BORN: Queens, NY
LIVES: Queens, NY

MENTEE'S ANECDOTE: *Thanks to Andrea, my mentor: she has made my experience at Girls Write Now unforgettable. When I first joined the program, I thought that I was only going to work on essays and developing skills for my college application personal statement. But I have gotten exposure to other forms of writing such as memoir writing, poetry, and short stories. I have gotten better at editing my own writing and identifying my own mistakes thanks to my mentor. Now we even finish our own sentences when revising! I feel more confident about my writing compared to before.*

ANDREA CUTTLER

YEARS AS MENTOR: 1
OCCUPATION: Talent Booker, *NBC Studios* Late Night with Seth Meyers
BORN: Los Angeles, CA
LIVES: New York, NY

MENTOR'S ANECDOTE: *I think my experience with Milena at the Girls Write Now program has been fun. I have gotten to know a little more about her every time we meet once a week. We have developed a good relationship, share our ideas, and talk to each other as friends when we need to. I have been able to support her when she is struggling with applying her thoughts to her writing and make her feel more confident with it. She has better developed certain skills in different genres of writing. It has been a great experience.*

Wickery Town's First Dream

MILENA NARANJO

This is a short story about a young female who is thirteen years old and has been living in a town for her entire life. But this will change. Her best friend takes her on an adventure where she meets a woman who gives her life purpose.

It was a hot summer day in Wickery Town. Bailey woke up at seven in the morning, and turned on the radio. Nothing. She smacked it. Again, nothing. It was broken. She opened her curtains and stared out the window. Like most mornings, she gazed up at the sky, not wanting to leave her bed.

"Bailey! Breakfast is ready," her mother screamed up to her room.

She put a pillow over her head and sighed into it, then jumped out of bed, rushing down to greet her family.

"Mom, there's really no point in waking up every day for school just to end up working at John's Pub."

"That's just the way it is," her mother responded.

"Hurry up, Bailey!" her father yelled. "I have to be at the mechanic shop in thirty minutes and have to drop you off at the restaurant first."

Bailey arrived at school and rushed to her locker where, to her surprise (not so much), her best friend, Allison, was right behind her. "Bailey, Bailey! Guess what? You're not gonna believe it. We're going out of town to a carnival where there will be boys . . . and boys!"

Allison had been so excited about going to the carnival that she had been talking about it for the past week. She observed the construction of it from her porch. But Bailey was not ready to get out of town, especially behind her parents' backs, and having to cut school. "I have to go home and start dinner, Alli. Then I have to get ready and go to the bar for work. You know this."

"It's just three miles out of town. All we do is walk straight down the road and we're there," Allison told Bailey. Shortly after, they found themselves on the road, walking.

They reached the forest, as it was part of their trip to make their way across town. The beauty of the forest comforted their hearts and the sudden peace of the morning was soothing their souls. There was life around nature.

"I wish I were able to see this back home," Allison told Bailey as she looked up at the clouds. They couldn't help but to feel amazed by the trees that were skyscraper tall. And finally they reached Dreamland Town. There were large mansions that set beyond the sidewalk towering over them.

They stepped onto the sidewalk and noticed beautiful fountains standing on both sides of the well-cut lawn as they walked along. All around, there were houses with statues of angels looking up towards the sky and water gently falling onto the crystal blue pool.

"Come on, we have to get going, we're almost there," Allison gently said to Bailey, who was easily amazed by the architecture in the town. They walked down the streets in shock without a word being exchanged.

There they stood right in front of the madness of the carnival filled with the bright and colorful lights of the booths that shined, even at a distance. It was loud. All you heard were screams and shots and dings of teens testing their luck at the can knock-down booths and soda toss, among other games, and the people trying to shout over the noise of the music.

"I'll catch ya at this very spot, twelve-sharp. See ya!" Allison yelled, already feet away from Bailey. Bailey walked around, astonished by every little thing that surrounded her. All the vibrant colors.

The atmosphere was different from home, a raggy old town with colorless ancient homes around, with shattered windows and rotting doors, where only a gust of dry wind passed through the rolling hills. But in Dreamland Town, everyone was full of life. Everything was full of life.

Out of everyone and everything that there was to be fascinated by, there was a tall woman that stood out. Although she did not face Bailey, she could tell how elegant this woman was. Fashion owned her; it expressed the way she lived. How could she possibly miss that long, thick, dappled coat that hung on her shoulders? Despite its obvious weight, it floated around her shoulders so delicately.

She turned around and, to Bailey's surprise, the woman noticed Bailey staring at her. The woman began to walk towards her and caused her to blink quickly as her eyes adjusted behind her glasses.

"Do I know you?" she asked Bailey.

Stuttering between her words, she responded, "No ma'am. But I'm Bailey and I've never been here before. You see, my friend brought me and I don't know anyone around. Pardon, I simply got lost in that coat of yours. I should get going."

The woman immediately stopped Bailey and said to her, "I'm Madonna, and I happened to make this coat myself, actually. You like it? It's yours now." *How could one possibly give away such an expensive-looking coat to a random girl she just met!* is the immediate thought that crossed Bailey's mind. And for the rest of the day, in the middle of the craziness going around, they spoke and exchanged their thoughts. Madonna uncovered parts of the world that Bailey had never before imagined. She told Bailey about her job as a fashion designer, creating, and traveling the world for a living. She told Bailey about places Bailey didn't even know existed—beaches covered with soft golden sands, islands that looked like fairy-tale gardens with exotic flowers and trees.

The woman fascinated her. Bailey's eyes glowed like a Christmas tree as she stared at the woman telling her story with such confidence. She watched her every move. From the way she tapped her nails against each other, to the way she moved her cherry red lips as she spoke so smoothly.

That night, Bailey didn't say a word to her best friend on their trip back home, whereas her best friend spoke all the way back. She was lost in her own thoughts and imagination. She pictured herself entangled in the beauty of traveling the world.

She felt inevitable excitement and got jittery butterflies that fluttered through her stomach as she imagined packing her bags. There was more to the world she lived in. There was color to everything she saw from then on.

Once at home, she observed every little detail of it. The old wooden couch, the rusty alarm clock next to her bed, and the colorless picture frames. She imagined what could replace them instead.

Bailey closed her eyes as hard as she could and thought to herself for the first time, "I want to travel the world and get out of town. I want to come back home and tell my grandchildren that I have visited every place they could think of. I want to be big." And that was the moment thirteen-year-old Bailey was the first young person to ever have a dream in her town and want more to life than what was offered.

Untitled

ANDREA CUTTLER

It is hard not to think about where your family came from amidst the political climate of today. The past few weeks in particular have had me thinking more in-depth about my mother's journey from South America to the United States, as well as what it means to be a woman. Herewith, a little slice of her story and why it inspires me every day.

My mother is an immigrant. She came to the United States from Bogotá, Colombia at the age of sixteen with five siblings, her mother, and not much else. My grandmother worked double shifts, including the graveyard, at the local Howard Johnson's in Miami scooping ice cream.

"Thank God we were able to go to high school for free," my mother once told me of her public school education. She took classes, went to school, and worked forty hours per week at the local drugstore, followed by a long-running stint at a shoe store, appropriately called The Wild Pair. [One of my all-time favorite stories, that I had her repeat to me ad nauseam as a child, had to do with a pair of shoes that she used to sell with water and a goldfish in the Plexiglas heel. Without fail, every time a new shipment of this particular shoe was delivered to the store, the fish were dead on arrival.] She dated American boys, learned to speak English fluently in less than six months after her arrival, and, as she tells me, "studied nothing." This is not an exaggeration. She graduated high school with a 1.4 grade point average.

Though neither of her parents ever went to college, her *not* going to college was oddly never an option. Luckily, Miami Dade Junior College South accepted anyone and everyone. And so she went.

At Miami Dade, she took art classes, architecture classes, and English classes. She began to understand the language more fluidly and thus came to care about her studies more passionately. I asked her recently what else changed between high school and junior college; what motivated her to study harder? "It's not a great story," she told me. "My older brother was at Vanderbilt University, studying there on a full scholarship. He told me he'd give me $1,000 if I got straight A's. So I did." But of course, there was a bit more to the story. "He pushed me to work harder," she said. "And finally, something clicked."

After two years and a 4.0 GPA, she graduated from the junior college with an associate of arts degree and a full ride to the University of Miami to finish the remaining three years that would earn her a full bachelor's degree in architecture.

During her first semester at the University of Miami, she was told by her professor that she should consider another career because she had zero talent. "Nothing was going to get in my way," she said.

During her time at the U of M, she met my father. (At the Dadeland Mall, no less; he worked at a clothing store called The Male Ego.) He was a divorced Jew, a single father, an aspiring musician, and twelve years her senior. Her very Catholic mother, who has come around since, was not terribly pleased, to say the least.

But she graduated, they moved to Los Angeles, and she was hired by a small architectural firm in Westwood, Rochlin, Baran, and Balbona, where she worked during the day. She received scholarships to both the University of Southern California and the University of California, Los Angeles (she ended up choosing USC) and spent nights and weekends taking classes to complete her master's degree in urban planning. She spent four years living and breathing architecture, sleeping under her desk many nights just to get all the work done.

After graduating from USC, she was brought on full-time by RBB Architects Inc., where she has remained for the past thirty-two years. She has had just about every possible job title and position that one is able to have, from drawing up posters to actually putting buildings together. She became a licensed architect while pregnant with me, passing a test that approximately 11 percent of people pass each year. She is LEED certified (meaning that she can build environmentally friendly structures), and she is a member of the American College of Healthcare Architects, of which there are fewer than 700 members, only seventy of whom are women. And today she is the only female partner in the firm's sixty-plus-year history; it is a position that she has held for more than fifteen years.

She builds hospitals almost exclusively. She is the president of the company, and she is in charge of human resources. She is the office caregiver. She is the first person employees go to when they are having problems, personal or professional.

On vacation for the week, I went to visit her at her office on Wilshire Boulevard, a place where I have visited her since birth. It happened to be International Women's Day. She did not take the day off. I say this respectfully, but that is just not her style.

She shows up. She gets business done. She knows that 100 percent of the employees in her office, herself included, are not in the position to take the day off to march or protest, even if the cause is an incredibly worthy one. Because there are hospitals to build, and patients to care for, and people who need her. People who she has never met and will never meet and who likely don't even know that the reason their hospital rooms are laid out the way that they are is because of her work.

I sat in her office that day, staring at her in awe as she finished a conference call with a client, wondering to myself how a woman who came from nothing ended up here, the odds stacked against her at every turn.

She loves to talk about the American Dream and her love for this country. How it was this country that made her a success story. And while I do very much believe that this country afforded her every possible opportunity, it was she who grabbed it with her all and refused to settle for less. It was she who simply continued to show up every day, determined to make a better life for herself than those who came before, never realizing the impact she would have on those who came after.

STEPHANIE NAUT

YEARS AS MENTEE: 1
GRADE: Senior
HIGH SCHOOL: Manhattan Bridges High School
BORN: Santo Domingo, Dominican Republic
LIVES: New York, NY

MENTEE'S ANECDOTE: *My mentor Arielle and I have shared so many experiences, like going to bookstores together, doing freewrites, and consoling each other, like when I met poet Rupi Kaur. She taught me different (and funny) ways to think about grammar while we were working on our writing pieces.*

ARIELLE BARAN

YEARS AS MENTOR: 1
OCCUPATION: Senior Account Executive, Derris
BORN: Los Angeles, CA
LIVES: Brooklyn, NY

MENTOR'S ANECDOTE: *My mentee Stephanie has taught me what it means to read with passion and write with whimsy. She is a bookworm with an affinity for young adult novels. Together, we traveled to bookstores around Manhattan where Stephanie helped me explore the stacked shelves of Russian literature, poetry books, and novels, among other genres. I'm so grateful and proud of her and all her writing this year.*

Your Voice

STEPHANIE NAUT

This piece is about how the language barrier I faced coming to the United Stated was not my challenge. Instead, my struggle was figuring out how to express my voice as a young woman and stand up for what I believe is right.

Over the last two years since moving from my home in the Dominican Republic to my new home in New York City, I escaped from my bookish world and fell into the real one. Growing up, I was never a reserved person, but I was always scared that I would say the wrong thing. Sometimes it felt that the world was telling me to "shut up." I became more shy and estranged from everyone around me. But when I came to the United States, I realized that my voice matters and that people welcome my opinions.

There are still certain circumstances when I revert back and just close myself to the world. I try to pretend that I am present but, in my mind, I am thinking about words that could work for a story I am writing or a character I want to create. I was always fascinated with reading. My interest in books later led to my ability to write. It happened when I had to write a story for a contest in my AP Spanish class. At first, I was a little insecure about it, but when I passed my first draft to my teacher, he said, "I really like your story and you have the potential to become a great writer." Those words inspired me to keep writing.

Writing and reading were a sort of escape from my fear of speaking and sharing my voice aloud that was built up after years of being told to shut up by the world. All those years of holding back, of not expressing my feelings and ideas, had alienated me from the real world.

The only people that I talked with freely were my family and my closest friends. My mom always told me, "You do not have to worry so much, you are fine just the way you are." My friends didn't seem to mind my quietness, but deep down I had this feeling that by not talking, I was missing something. There were times when I really wanted to speak up—to say what was on my mind. But I felt like something was stopping me.

I came to New York City because I wanted to get a better education, so I could be independent and confident. The real change in me came when I realized that I am not supposed to please everyone. I just have to do what I believe is right. That is why I want to study international studies when I get to college. I want to connect with people from other cultures, so I can have more empathy and see the world from a different perspective.

What Do We Ask of Him

ARIELLE BARAN

I wrote the first draft of this piece the day after I was assaulted. Writing it down was a source of catharsis—a way to process what happened. While hard to share, publishing this part of my story is my Rise Speak Change.

This is hard to share, but I was sexually assaulted for the first time this past year. *Powerless* is the best word to describe how it felt. I have always intellectually understood the position women have in this world. We can be smart, successful, driven, and independent, and yet, for a very scary moment, none of that can matter. I learned that feeling of disempowerment firsthand for the first time when he put his hands on me.

I was walking the few blocks from dinner to a jazz show with two girlfriends when a man came up behind me, grabbed me, and aggressively gyrated on me. My first brief thought was that this person touching me must be a friend, although no friend would ever grab me that way. But when someone touches me, I assume I have given that person permission because I control my body. After the quick realization that I had lost that control, I let out a scream and luckily scared the man away. Only catching sight of his back running around the block, I am left to assume this stranger is a sick and confused young person.

It all happened so fast that my friends initially thought he was trying to steal my purse. I wish he had been there to steal my purse because you can cancel credit cards, repurchase a cell phone, and track down phone numbers, but it is a lot harder to shake off the feeling of being violated.

I cried and shook for a while after it happened. It was the type of raw crying and shaking that I rarely experience in myself. I am very fortunate and blessed to feel safe and secure most of the time—not everyone gets to live with that sense of calm. But having that security taken away for a brief but assaulting moment is a truly terrible feeling.

Just because I am a woman, I should not have to be afraid to be alone. As women, we have to think about how and where we will walk at night. We are asked to feel responsible to pay for the extra cab home, to dress a certain way, to walk down the right, bustling street, and to hold keys between our knuckles, because that is what we were taught. The onus is placed on women to control for various factors and to be "smart." But what about this man who got to run away? What do we ask of him?

KIZZY NELSON

YEARS AS MENTEE: 2
GRADE: Senior
HIGH SCHOOL: Urban Assembly School for Green Careers
BORN: Port-au-Prince, Haiti
LIVES: New York, NY

MENTEE'S ANECDOTE: *I met Maryellen after my first mentor could not participate in Girls Write Now. At first I was sad and afraid to open up. After meeting Maryellen a few times, I discovered she is easy to talk with. She became a counselor to me. I talked to her about my problem at school, and the advice she has given me has worked. My mentor inspires me through her strength—she does not give up on herself or me, which inspires me to not give up. I think that her smile is contagious because whenever she laughs I want to laugh.*

MARYELLEN TIGHE

YEARS AS MENTOR: 2
OCCUPATION: Assistant Editor, Debtwire Municipals
BORN: Council Bluffs, IA
LIVES: New York, NY

MENTOR'S ANECDOTE: *One of my favorite parts of my Fridays is walking with Kizzy back from the coffee shop we meet at. After writing and editing we just talk and laugh about friends, parents, or school. I am amazed by how smart and level-headed she is. The stories she writes, even in our quick freewrites, are often profound and inspiring. I look forward to watching her continue to grow as a writer and a woman.*

She Realized She Deserved Better but She Still Followed the Trick of Her Heart

KIZZY NELSON

When a woman cannot identify true love it can affect her daily life.

Every day when she saw him, a smile crossed her face like he was the only person on earth. How could she leave the years they had shared as if they were nothing?

She looked at her reflection in the mirror and examined every scar he left on her. She cried because she did not understand how she would be able to make that decision.

Zzzz

His phone kept vibrating on the table and she knew better than to unlock it and check the messages. But she did anyway, and discovered that the messages were from another girl. She saw them—the promises, the "I love yous," and, finally, "You are the only one for me; there's no one else that has my heart like the way you do." Those words hurt her heart as if someone was squeezing it inside.

That is when she made her decision. She would leave; she would try to heal herself even if it meant dying before getting out.

He came out of the bathroom, his gaze upon her like a mad dog about to attack, especially after she said, "You don't love me anymore; you're keeping me just because you like the way I treat you. I am tired of all this—let me go. Don't you see you're slowly killing me?"

He slapped her after hearing those words. Gaetan never believed that Nefertiti would talk back to him. She had stayed quiet for years, even though he would beat her until she bled. The only thing you could hear was her screaming while the tears slid down her cheeks. Nefertiti had forgotten everything, her friends and her family, for the love she had for Gaetan.

Something hit her hard, behind her head. She felt metal as the pressure threw her to the floor, knocking her out.

I am sitting in a crowded room and everyone is looking at me. I wonder—is it my clothes? Is there something on my face? Or did someone call me?

I hear a thump thump in my mind, like someone is knocking on the door called my brain. I recognize this voice; it has been inside my head for ages.

It says:
"There's nothing wrong with you; maybe they are looking at a scene behind you."
And the other one:
"They are staring at you because of your self-doubt."

. . .

But wait, what kind of doubt? I ask myself.
*   Is it because I believe negative things?*
*   Is it because he makes me believe I am not worth much?*
*   No no, maybe all of this is just a dream.*

Then the world flips upside down; a color I have never seen sur-rounds us—me and the crowd.

"What is love?" a woman with reddish hair asks us.
*   "Love is food," a tall handsome man with blue eyes says.*
*   "No, love is when the happiness of others is yours," the woman with reddish hair says angrily.*

I have started to think about the reply of the woman.

Is love really the happiness of others?
*   I did not understand her reply. But did I really know the mean-ing of love?*

"OUCH!" I scream. I felt as if something was biting my feet. I looked down confused, but there was nothing.
*   "OUCH!" It bites me again. I close my eyes and reopen them carefully . . .*

. . .

It was just a dream. If my mind was a person, would it be the woman with reddish hair? And would the handsome man be my stomach?

I woke up with the sound of a woman crying near me. The only thing I could see was the light, which seemed like a room in a hospital.

Nefertiti's mom visited her for months in hopes that her dear daughter would one day recognize her, but she didn't. Nefertiti only wanted to see her lover, but he never came to the hospital. And she will never realize that the condition she is in is because she was afraid of moving away from this man who tortured her every day.

From those painful days she learned something—to never confuse the knowledge of a mind with the feelings of a heart. If your mind tells you something is wrong with the relationship you should never stay. The heart always tries to play with our emotions, or tries to ask advice. Do not be afraid of moving on from something that keeps hurting you every day. Because it could hurt not only you but also your surroundings, ruining the better future you could have had.

Shell

MARYELLEN TIGHE

This is a poem inspired by the PostScript mentee session Girls Write Now hosted this year. It is about learning to find your own voice when no one is listening, so you can be clear when you want to be heard.

I read my poem to the turbulent ocean
    The crashing waves my only applause
    The sharp wind snatching the words out of my
        mouth half-formed
I have never had an audience more hungry.

The wind and the waves were equally appreciative the second
    time
    When I moved off the break wall to walk along the
        sand
    When I added dance steps between the words my
        feelings contained.

In the third recitation my words came more strongly and
    powerfully
    The wind still grabbed them with a fierce intensity
    This time rather than crashing into the ocean, my
        words skipped like a pebble.
By the end the wind was cutting through my coat and my eyes
    were clear.
I was shivering and raw and it was time to go home.

The ocean had not asked me to hurry.
    It let me take my time.
    The cold winter spray and the early spring rain
        blended on my cheeks for hours before I said
        the first word.

And after letting the wind carry my thoughts out to sea, it
    returned them with the tide
        The edges softened.
        The feeling refined.
Ready for a smaller, more human audience.

LESLIE PANTALEON

YEARS AS MENTEE: 1
GRADE: Freshman
HIGH SCHOOL: Midwood High School
BORN: Brooklyn, NY
LIVES: Brooklyn, NY

MENTEE'S ANECDOTE: *I recently read a letter I wrote to myself six months ago. It reminded me how strange I had found the concept of suddenly adopting a stranger with whom I could share my writing, my most private self. Today, I am happy to say that Lauren is far from a stranger. She is a mentor I also gladly call a friend. It is only fitting that the first piece I worked on with her is the same one you now hold in your hands.*

LAUREN HESSE

YEARS AS MENTOR: 4
OCCUPATION: Digital Marketing Manager, Penguin Random House
BORN: Albany, NY
LIVES: Brooklyn, NY

MENTOR'S ANECDOTE: *When I was told I was working with a freshman mentee this year, I was nervous! What if she didn't like me? What if she wanted to switch mentors? What if she left the program after our year? Of course, the second I met Leslie those fears dissipated. Though she is just starting high school, Leslie writes prose beyond her years. Her language is poetic and tells rich stories, and every week I look forward to reading what she is working on. I cannot wait to see what she creates next!*

Two Broken Pieces Don't Make a Whole

LESLIE PANTALEON

Characters should be complicated, just like humans. Clifford embodies the theme of Rise Speak Change *because he could not summon the courage to do any of those things. He is somewhat of a cautionary tale.*

At first, I only came to see Her. I loitered dutifully like a man in prayer at the MTA booth where She worked. Being around Her became intoxicating and, even on the platform, the knowledge that She was near made me feel less lonely. It became a bad habit, and I hung around the train more than I really should have.

One night I happened to have off from work, She ran onto the platform. She was crying, a small ball of black fur in her hands. There was no one else, it was quiet, and, miraculously, She sat close to me.

"Hey," I said softly. "Please don't cry." She whimpered. "Hey," I said again. "Hey. Don't cry. Please?" She tilted her face tentatively and awkwardly. I tried to smile. She laughed. Another miracle. A soft meow from Her lap caused Her to introduce me to Moon, a cat She explained to have been left at the station this morning. Moon is a little black thing with wide eyes that reinforced the idea of the kitten he still was. He would let me scratch his tummy as he, faced toward me on my lap, pawed my wrist for more affection.

"My supervisor wants me to take him to the pound. I know they won't treat him right there. I wish I could take him home, but I don't get off for a few more hours tonight. And I can't leave him at home when I work because my husband stays home. He has a temper that I can't say Moon will be protected from."

She sniffled a little more and, afraid that She would cry again, I quickly offered to watch him while She finished Her shift. She seemed startled.

"Thank you," She said, quietly embracing me, almost discomforted with our conversation as if just realizing She had burdened a stranger with what should be Her problems. Still, She carefully dropped the little black ball into my lap, even bothering to ask my name.

It's Clifford if anyone is interested.

We met again in a few hours when Her shift was over and She took Moon home. Tired for the first time in weeks, I went home dreary but invigorated by the attentions of the woman I admired.

In the following months I did notice, though, a strange phenomenon. As Moon grew bigger and out of the kitten we could no longer call him, he began looking more tired, more worn, when he was brought back from Her care. Moon began getting mysterious scratches and began losing hair.

One weekend, though, when noticing a particularly deep gash on the side of his leg I offered to take Moon home for the week, taking off from work in order to nurse him properly. It was during that week when I noticed a big change in Moon's behavior. He slashed me on my right arm when I tried to replace his bandages and hissed when I offered him the foot of my bed. No longer the kitten that I knew to be cuddly and warm, Moon contained a trembling, a crazed look in the eye that conveyed a sense of fear that kept him panicked all week.

I returned to the train station the following week on a sunny day, when I discovered that the woman I adored so faithfully left Her job. I'd seen the bruises on Her face and Her scarred arms, but I had looked away and chosen to keep to myself what I hoped not to be true.

I sat on the train bench with Moon nested in my lap, too weak to look up when trains passed, too hopeless to pay mind to the small tokens of the private lives of others. My emotions seemed to imprint themselves upon Moon, who curled up underneath the bench in which I was sitting and laid his head down upon the floor.

Not long after, Moon and I decided to go back home. This train station was making me sick. *She left you*, I thought, once home. *She couldn't care less of a damn about you.* My mind wouldn't stop turning, and it was with this thought that I angrily kicked Moon, tears spilling down the sides of my face like the sides of a broken bottle.

I looked at Moon. *She left the both of us.* He lay at the threshold of the kitchen when, suddenly throwing myself down upon the floor, I cradled the twitching animal. *I'm sorry*, I whispered. *I will never, never hurt you again*, I promised on the way to the veterinarian.

We are two broken pieces, I tell Moon now, months later, *but maybe that means, together, we can be whole.*

Moon and I continue to visit the train station where She left us every day.

We sit on the waiting bench looking at the skyline, waiting. Because maybe if we continue waiting together, She will feel us somewhere, perhaps sitting on a similar train bench waiting for a day She can come back to us.

Witches of the Resistance

LAUREN HESSE

My first writing prompt with Leslie was to think of a person we had seen in passing for a flash fiction piece. I had just read about a group of women looking to use witchcraft to hex Trump and my story was born.

Online, it said that my garden would need "just a few basics." I did not even know what mugwort was. Rebecca at the greenhouse hadn't the slightest clue either. She knew exactly what plants would make my three-year-old tabby cat sick but had no idea how to obtain the roots needed for spellwork. Earlier in the week, I had crafted box planters on my fire escape from pallets that the previous tenant had left in the backyard. Now, I stood armed with a twenty-pound bag of potting soil on my hip and a handful of seed packets: basil, mint, hot peppers, lavender, and rosemary.

I hauled the bag onto the counter and dropped my seed packets as the bag split. My eyes welled.

"No use in crying over spilled dirt! We use this in the greenhouse and the rain caused a lot of runoff last week so, thank you, I guess?"

Relieved at the cashier's kindness, I grabbed a slightly smaller fifteen-pound bag off the front door display and brought it to the counter, faking a smile. I walked out with the supplies in my backpack and the dirt balanced on my hip like a fat toddler. Thankful that my mental health day afforded me a trip to the plant shop at 2:00 p.m. on a Tuesday, I got a seat on the train and opened the preloaded browser page on my phone. The message boards had conflicting opinions; High magik called for a ritual bath before planting. For this I would need to purify with an array of personal artifacts and oils. Others, so-called "kitchen witches," felt you should work with what you have, that your magic came simply from everyday objects.

After a sweaty walk home, I decided a ritual bath was worth it. Hovering over my sad selection of talismans, I selected an amethyst crystal and lavender oil. I added a few drops of anointed oil and some salt, plus a drop of honey to "sweeten" the bath and my intentions. I was literally dipping into my first shot at spellwork. I soaked in silence for what felt like an hour but it was closer to three minutes.

After I rinsed and changed into all black, looking more like I was heading to a 5K than like a witch, I laid out the seeds and set my intentions. I ripped two pieces of brown paper bag. On one I wrote "Rise" twenty or so times, and on the other I wrote "Trump" just once. The second paper was burned, leaving only ashes to mix in the soil. "Rise" was laid in a middle layer of the box, covered with dirt and eventually seeds. Now, all I had to do was water and wait.

SABRINA PERSAUD

YEARS AS MENTEE: 1

GRADE: Sophomore

HIGH SCHOOL: Richard R. Green High School of Teaching

BORN: Queens, NY

LIVES: Queens, NY

MENTEE'S ANECDOTE: *When Stacie and I first met, I knew that we would do great things together. We both wanted "unsweetened tea" or in other words, honest critiques, and we aimed to tackle our bad habit of procrastinating. Throughout these past few months, she has helped me overcome writer's block and express my voice. Stacie sees me as the writer I want to be. Girls Write Now has helped me find a great mentor, but it has also given me a great friend.*

STACIE EVANS

YEARS AS MENTOR: 4

OCCUPATION: Literacy Advisor, Mayor's Office of Workforce Development

BORN: New York, NY

LIVES: Brooklyn, NY

PUBLICATIONS AND RECOGNITIONS: Featured guest, cHURCH of Monika Pop-up Dinner: Freedom of Speech Is Paramount, 2017; "Brave New World Indeed," JustNoMore .com, 2016; "Please Allow Me to Introduce Myself," *After Ferguson*, Mourning Glory Press, 2015

MENTOR'S ANECDOTE: *Sabrina and I have similar writing habits. And that has been fun to discover. . . . but I have discovered that we also share some of the same writing procrastinations! That means we have spent a lot of time this year learning how to encourage one another and spur each other on, and I have spent a lot of time thinking about my process and how sharing that with Sabrina can help her. Working with Sabrina this year has made me a better mentor and a better writer . . . and has been wonderfully fun!*

Salt on Old Wounds

SABRINA PERSAUD

Sometimes we are hurt by the ones we love the most. It is important to rise above that pain; turn it into something powerful. This is for everyone who has grown up in a broken home.

For a long time, it was all about you. Everything I did in my life—from the way I tied my shoes to the way I wore my heart on my sleeve—revolved around you. I didn't realize this until you were gone.

I don't remember much about that house on the corner of 110th Street. The memories are foggy; some good, most bad. The household was always a battlefield for two lovers who forgot how to love. My sister and I used to wave white flags for them, hoping they would see each other and surrender. Hoping he would take her hand to dance the way they used to, but it never happened. Instead, my sister and I took cover in our bedroom, holding each other so close it almost blocked the sounds of our family breaking apart.

After that, everything sort of fell to pieces: my happiness, confidence, faith. I was young, I'm still young, but I didn't know the kind of effect losing you would have on me. I was your little girl for a long time, and then I wasn't. You probably don't know, but it was my choice not to speak to you for those three years. Not Mom's, not her family's, not her friend's; it was mine. You only called when you'd had at least three drinks and you liked to cry, *a lot*. I think that's where I get it from, you know? You taught me how to wear my heart on my sleeve, but Mom taught me how to shield my heart from the world. Together, you created a child who is both rough at the edges and soft to the touch.

I sort of had a mantra during those years when I blocked you out; I find myself whispering it sometimes. "If you don't believe, he can't hurt you." If I didn't believe that you would get your act together, be the man I always wished you would be, then there would be no room for disappointment. I didn't have faith in you at all. I didn't believe that you'd be a good father, and a part of me didn't want you to be. Old wounds never seem to heal.

It was that night where everything took a turning point. My sister was turning twenty and she deserved a good birthday party. I knew I didn't want to be around you when you were drunk. It would set off something in me, a fear that was at the back of my mind. It made me uncomfortable when you had a drink in your hand. You thought it was okay to cry to me, or stop me from leaving, or hug me when I didn't want you around. I never stopped you even though I wanted to.

The music was loud and the smell of alcohol danced across the room. I was the only one who didn't have a cup in my hand. I knew I could have a sip if I wanted to—maybe it could have calmed my nerves—but the thought made me more anxious. The kitchen was small, too small, and I couldn't seem to find refuge. You were drunk and I was at the edge of a cliff. You were dancing all across the room and I was trying to hide. I didn't want to be around you—not when you were like that. Memories from years ago came to mind. I saw you in the same state in a different setting; at my uncle's house, at the old apartment, in your mother's home, at the other end of the phone. You found your way close to me and I looked down. I avoided eye contact in hopes that I would become invisible. It did not work. You put your arms around me and swayed back and forth. I felt every fiber in my body tense up. I felt my eyebrows crinkle. I felt a shiver run down my spine. You pressed a kiss to my head and I needed to scream. It was all too much: the smell of alcohol, the music, your arms, your words, *you*. You couldn't understand how badly I needed to be away from you. I had to do something; it felt like the earth was closing in on me. So I pushed you. I stretched out my hand and placed a distance between you and me. It was soft enough to avoid a scene, but strong enough to make you stop. You stepped back and looked at me with your head tilted to the side. I looked you right in your eye and shook my head. *No.*

I don't want to be in a constant battle with that bottle. I shouldn't have to ask you to put the drink down, put our broken relationship first. I was a little girl once and I needed you to be my hero, but that's not the case today. I don't need to be saved, not by you.

Rapprochement

STACIE EVANS

Sabrina and I decided to write about our relationships with our fathers. We have both had to navigate creating new father-daughter relationships—Sabrina is still navigating that path—and through that work we have risen, spoken out, and changed.

My father and I did not have a good relationship. To be clear, it isn't fair to say we had a *bad* relationship, at least not at the start, when I was a child. It wasn't bad then, it just wasn't *any* kind of relationship. We shared space, charting similar orbits in our family universe. He knew I existed but could never really see me, understand who I was.

When I was in high school, he and my mother split, a break that translated into a divorce from her . . . and from my brother, my sister, and me. Whatever non-relationship we had dissolved to complete disconnection.

A few years after college, I wrote him, attempting to get us talking, get us to know each other. And just like that—snap of fingers—we were talking, not easily, but semi-consistently. An awkward, stiff, uncomfortable conversation.

Then his cancer was diagnosed. We had been taking slow half-steps toward each other, and his diagnosis was like a riding crop on our backs, forcing a quick-march.

That quick-march was awful, but it was good, too, creating the need for weekend drives upstate with my sister and brother to visit as our father declined. Those afternoons hanging out in his living room did what the letters could not. That time together, talking about nothing or remembering the past, was stilted, but our discomfort came more from our inability or refusal to talk about his cancer, our insistence on pretending he was going to get well. It's hard to relax when you're acting as though the dying man in front of you is merely suffering from indigestion. Once he started talking about death, about the plans he was drafting for his funeral—as unsettling as *those* conversations were—the awkwardness faded. I wanted a relationship with my father, and for those short months, I had one.

In the more than half my life since he died, I have come to see him with kinder eyes, see qualities I could not credit him with when he was alive, see the ways I take from him that make me pleased and proud to carry him with me. Yes, I wish I could have found my way here while he was still alive, but it's not as if he's not still with me, not as if he doesn't know.

JULEISY POLANCO

YEARS AS MENTEE: 1

GRADE: Senior

HIGH SCHOOL: Bronx Studio School for Writers and Artists

BORN: Bronx, NY

LIVES: Bronx, NY

PUBLICATIONS AND RECOGNITIONS: Scholastic Art & Writing Award: Honorable Mention

MENTEE'S ANECDOTE: *Girls Write Now is something that crept into my schedule and influenced me tremendously during this last year of high school. It got me into college by helping me solidify my personal statement, find out more about myself, and accomplish my goal of strengthening my writing skills (teaching me the power of short statements). The program did an amazing job pairing me with a mentor that helps me embrace my flaws and allows me to elaborate my thoughts, even when they are not fluent. I could not have asked for a better preparation for the journey I have ahead.*

DIANE BOTNICK

YEARS AS MENTOR: 2

OCCUPATION: Fiction writer

BORN: Akron, OH

LIVES: Cold Spring, NY

MENTOR'S ANECDOTE: *Juleisy approaches life with such excitement that she makes me excited for each week's session. Whether in the library or at her favorite Spanish restaurant, we talk about everything. We were brainstorming ideas for this anthology piece when she told me about the tattoo she plans to get. The mother in me was ready to shout NOOOOO, but the mentor in me won out. I held my tongue and encouraged her to write about it. Her piece not only changed my mind about her tattoo, it made me want to get one, too.*

Diamonds

JULEISY POLANCO

After a Girls Write Now workshop, I told Diane that I eventually want to get a diamond tattoo. She suggested that I write about it. In this piece, I give my perspective on diamonds, the good and the bad, and how their symbolism relates to the journey I am on.

Today my mother got me diamond earrings as a graduation gift. Today is February 22, not June 23. She was so excited she could not wait. She kept saying things like, "Don't lose them, they're expensive . . . diamonds are a girl's best friend," while I read the message she wrote on the box: "To Juleisy, from Mami, this is your graduation gift. You deserve it for all your hard work."

I wish I could say my excitement matched hers. I would never buy myself expensive *things* like that. I admit it: I love diamonds. But for me, they are symbols to be admired, not objects to be worn and shown off. I wonder if my mom would have been as excited if she had known that what I really want is a diamond tattoo right in the middle of my chest.

This gem has many dimensions, like the sides of an argument or chapters of a story. Their qualities make them rare and desirable prizes that everyone wants but few will ever have. Men have risked their lives to mine these stones. People have stolen, killed, cheated, and lied to get their hands on the wealth associated with them. I know that greed is the driving force that has made so many willing to put aside their own morality to fill the void that comes from wanting. I know that my ancestors have been beaten and enslaved in pursuit of diamonds, and that in many countries this abuse continues.

Because of this, *every* diamond, even the ones in the earrings my mother gave me, represents great sacrifice. Maybe it is because of the sacrifice that we put these stones on such a high pedestal. That is raw. I want to wear that on my chest. I want to show the world that I think of my own values as jewels, equivalent to the biggest or brightest diamond there is.

The process behind this beautiful product is what intrigues me. It can take more than three billion years of heat, pressure, and darkness for diamonds to form. That is almost as old as the earth. When they are first dug up, diamond roughs do not look very appealing. Only with molding and shaping and careful cutting do they become the gems people find so desirable, bright, transparent, reflective.

The word "diamond" comes from the Greek meaning untamed, unbreakable, unalterable. Not all diamonds have the same qualities, however, and only those with the fewest impurities—the finest color and greatest clarity—are suitable for jewelry. But beauty is not the only thing that gives a diamond value. Diamonds are so hard they are almost indestructible, so not only do they shine brighter than all other stones, they are hard enough to cut through any one of them. This makes them very useful in manufacturing and industry. Diamonds can sparkle in rings and necklaces AND do the unglamorous work of cutting, drilling and grinding. How amazing would it be to marry both these qualities within ourselves?

With my tattoo, I hope to be branding myself with a different perspective on diamonds. It won't cost as much as the real thing, and I will not have to take special care of it or be afraid of losing it, but it will be the image of a valuable object I carry with me at all times. I want it in the center of my chest because that is the place from which my diamond roughs will be mined. This image will project my strength, signify that my values are unalterable, and show how close to my heart I hold my worth. Like a diamond, I hope to endure the pressures and darkness ahead to become a strong and valuable woman in my family and community. I hope to share my own light and also to reflect the light around me.

When people see my tattoo, I expect they will have questions about my choice. If they ask, I will tell them that my diamond symbolizes all the qualities I want to have: strength, resistance, transparency, and brilliance. I hope it raises questions about their own choices as well.

Pearls

DIANE BOTNICK

I set out to write a companion piece to Juleisy's "Diamonds." Are things beautiful because they are valuable or valuable because they are beautiful? That is the question we put to each other and, I think, answered from our own perspectives.

People say it takes only a grain of sand to make a pearl, but in truth it is usually a bigger menace that gets the process going. Consider the oyster. Its shell is rough-hewn and sharp enough to slice digging fingers, meant to be a closed, safe environment, a kind of cradle for the vulnerable being within. But in the ocean there are all kinds of parasites looking to make their home in that warm, safe place. The oyster's best chance for survival is to contain the invader, blanketing it with layers upon layers of a special, hard "skin."

The resulting gem, prized for its beauty, has become a symbol of purity, femininity, chastity, infinity, and perfection. Yet it begins life as a threat.

There is an elegance to their simple, round form. They have no flash or sparkle; they have no facets to deceive or edges to be caught up on.

Loose, they roll in the palm like garden peas. Strung together, like next to like, they bring the weight of their importance around the wearer's neck.

The more perfect the pearl, the greater its price tag. Yet cultivated pearls, perfect in form and color, lack the allure of natural pearls found in the wild.

Which makes me think of the girls of Girls Write Now. To all those pearls in formation, I offer the following encouragement:

To be the irritant around which beauty grows; the threat to comfort and complacency that becomes louder and stronger with time

To draw people in by your core of light

To protect that light under layers of understanding, each radiating its own luster, its own truth, its own message

To be one with many, like next to like, and in this joining, becoming weightier

To be alone, unafraid to stand out or to be singled out

To reach for perfection

To find pride in your flaws and come to see them as your strengths

To be a traveler who treads carefully, honestly, and respectfully, always mindful of all the others to follow

To be patient—anything good takes time

But never passive—anything good requires action

ANA PRIETO

YEARS AS MENTEE: 1

GRADE: Sophomore

HIGH SCHOOL: Richard R. Green Academy of Teaching

BORN: Duitama, Colombia

LIVES: Queens, NY

MENTEE'S ANECDOTE: *Coffee brewing, hard-boiled egg shell breaking open. We sit in Fika, a Swedish coffee shop in the Financial District of Manhattan, and explore the world of writing together. We write poems from issues revolving around everything from anxiety to romance, swapping our iPhones back and forth, writing one line apiece. We work on our novels and discuss ideas for story and character. And best of all, we get to meet once a week and just sit and talk about life.*

JULIA LYNN RUBIN

YEARS AS MENTOR: 1

OCCUPATION: Creative Writing MFA candidate at The New School & author of young adult literature

BORN: Baltimore, MD

LIVES: Brooklyn, NY

PUBLICATIONS AND RECOGNITIONS: *North American Review* (2014), *The Lascaux Review* (2014), *Dewpoint*, vol. 5 (2015), *Sierra Nevada Review* (2016), *Riprap Literary Journal* (vol. 39) [2017], *Burro Hills* (Diversion Books, 2018)

MENTOR'S ANECDOTE: *Ana feels like more than a mentee to me; she is like my little sister. Her creativity, wit, and ambition continue to leave me in awe every time we meet. I still cannot get over what a perfect match we are. She is an incredibly talented writer and I know that one day she is going to be a brilliant author. We have written some funny things, some experimental things, but to me, the best things we have written have been the emotional and—I really cannot describe this any other way—real.*

Day One
ANA PRIETO

This is the beginning of a novel that I started writing with my mentor during our sessions. The main character is a seventeen-year-old Colombian girl who just arrived in America in the 1920s, having lost both of her parents in a shipwreck.

"Where are you taking me?" Katerina asked the officer who was guiding her through a hallway that never seemed to end.

She was full of fright. The previous night's events kept replaying in her head. Katerina was alone, but it hadn't always been like this. She had come on a long journey with her mom and dad, but it wasn't their fate to step onto the soil of America together. Katerina remembered the way her mom screamed as the ship pulled her and her father down into the ocean. Katerina was already on a safe boat when she witnessed both of her parents die before her eyes. And to think, she probably would have her mom with her right now if it were not for love that made her mom sacrifice her life for her husband.

"You will stay here until you get a trial with the immigration officer," the officer said. He opened a door to reveal a small room that only fit a metal toilet, a small window that let in very little light, and a bed that looked like it was made out of bricks. Not to mention the smell; it smelled like piss and seawater. Katerina could feel the tears threatening to come. Was this her life now?

. . .

"Quiet, quiet!" demanded the man who held the fate of Katerina in his hand. Her own hands were shaking underneath the table from where she sat in the courtroom.

"I looked over your case, Miss Jones," the judge said to her. He reminded her of one of the homeless men that she used to see on the streets in Colombia. He had a black expression, his beard covered his mouth, and she saw no emotion through his eyes. "And I've decided to send you back to Colombia. You are a seventeen-year-old child who has no one to support you. You should be grateful you actually made it this far." His voice was laced with judgment.

Katerina could feel her lips trembling from fear and desperation. She blinked repeatedly to stop the tears from falling, but no matter how strong she tried to be, she couldn't hold it together.

"Please sir!" The words came before Katerina had time to think of what she was saying. "I promise you that I can make something up myself. I can work in the textile mills; just please don't send me back! Things back in Colombia are bad."

"My decision has been made," he said. "Now you are wasting time from other cases. You are dismissed. Get your bag ready; you will be sailing out on the first ship."

An officer appeared next to Katerina and began to lead her out of the courtroom. Katerina gave the judge one last look before she reluctantly followed. Suddenly, a light switch of an idea came on in her head.

"Sir," she said quietly to the officer. "Sir, please help me. The judge was wrong. There is someone here who can support me." She needed someone to listen.

"I'm sorry, miss," he said. "I would love to help you, trust me, but if I don't get you on the boat I can lose my job. My family depends on me." Unlike the previous officer she'd dealt with, this one seemed as though he actually cared.

"Please," she repeated. "I have a telephone number. You can call this man, he is rich, he can help me! He is practically my uncle. Please sir, you have to help me. If you don't, you would basically be sending me to my death." She knew that the man standing in front of her was her last hope.

He had stopped for a moment outside of the courtroom. They were alone in the long, empty hallway. He looked her over carefully.

"You aren't lying?" he asked.

"No, of course not! Why would I lie about something that can easily be proven?"

He frowned. "What is the name of the man, the one you say can help you?"

"His name is Ernest," Katerina said. "Ernest Hunt."

The officer looked at Katerina like she had two heads! He glanced over her outfit, her raggedy clothes that were torn and dirty and still smelled of seawater, her long and tangled hair.

"Ernest Hunt is one of the richest men in New York," he said with a huff. "How do you know him?"

"He is my—he was my father's best friend." The pain in her chest came back as the wall she had carefully built around her heart began to crumble.

"You don't need to worry about that," the officer said. "One of his offices is near the pier I pass by on my way home. I'll do what I can, but you must obey the rules and do whatever they tell you to. I'm one of the good guys, but not all are like me. You seem like a strong girl. You remind me of my own daughter, which is why I'm helping you, but I really hope you aren't lying. For your sake and mine. My job is on the line."

Burro Hills

JULIA LYNN RUBIN

This is an excerpt from my debut young adult novel, Burro Hills, *coming 2018 from Diversion Books. The main character is a seventeen-year-old boy named Jack who lives in the fictional Southern California town of Burro Hills. My mentee was one of the first to see this passage.*

The living room was wrecked. The stench of beer was everywhere, infusing the room with its sickly sour odor. Dad sat in his La-Z-Boy amid a smashed lamp, broken bottles, torn papers and documents. The coffee table was overturned. The remains of the ceramic pig Mom had painted for me on my twelfth birthday lay in a corner. I spotted a pink snout and a hoof.

Mom was gone. I knew this before I walked in. Her car had vanished from its ancient spot next to the sycamore, a trail of oil leaking across the pavement. And he just sat there, bloated and bleary-eyed in his stained white t-shirt and acid-washed jeans, staring at the carpet. Expecting her to come home once she'd cooled off, maybe fucked the pool boy at the nearest motel, downed a half-empty bottle of Vicodin. Expecting me to stay here and clean up the mess he'd made, once again.

"I'm leaving, Dad," I said. Just like that, one-two-three words, and I held my duffel bag close to me, as if daring him to stop me.

It took him a moment to respond.

"Your mother's gone," he told the floor.

"I'm leaving. I'm not coming back," I said again, trying to sound firm, resolute.

He finally glanced up at me with bloodshot eyes. I waited for him to tell me not to go, to promise he'd change and fix everything and it would all be alright again. But all he said was, "Take care of yourself, you hear?"

My dog whined from his spot in the corner, all curled up with his head down. My throat tightened. "I'm coming back for Gunther," was all I could manage to say. "When I find somewhere else to stay."

I turned and left him there, slamming the door, running as fast as I could from that awful fucking house that I hated loving. I didn't stop until I was back at the alley behind my grandfather's old building, where he'd died and left me here with all of the broken pieces. I slammed my fist against the cheap siding again and again and again, then crumpled to the ground and cried like I'd never cried before.

JENNIFER PUAC

YEARS AS MENTEE: 1
GRADE: Senior
HIGH SCHOOL: The Boerum Hill School for International Studies
BORN: Brooklyn, NY
LIVES: Brooklyn, NY
PUBLICATIONS AND RECOGNITIONS: Scholastic Art & Writing Award: Honorable Mention

MENTEE'S ANECDOTE: *Meeting Heeseung for the first time was a little nerve-wracking. I was worried about getting to know her and allowing her to read my writing. But, man, one hour every week in a coffee shop has really drawn us closer together. She has pushed me out of my comfort zone and given me the best constructive feedback one can ask for. One day, I realized we had built a friendship of curiosity and laughter while sitting and sharing stories from our pasts. I will never regret meeting Heeseung. I will truly miss her.*

HEESEUNG KIM

YEARS AS MENTOR: 1
OCCUPATION: Copy editor, *Cosmopolitan.com*
BORN: Buffalo, NY
LIVES: Brooklyn, NY

MENTOR'S ANECDOTE: *When I first began mentoring, I vowed to be a good role model for my mentee, Jenn. Little did I realize at the time how inspiring she would be for me. I have seen Jenn challenge herself by sharing her writing and reading publicly at a workshop. She has tried new things, such as writing poetry, and has not shied away from serious discussions about what is going on in the world. Jenn has reminded me to push myself just as much as she does—so the mentor learns from the mentee!*

Dear Struggling Writers

JENNIFER PUAC

If you are someone who struggles to write and are in need of motivation, take a few minutes to read my letter dedicated to you. Yes, you!

Dear Struggling Writers,

Ever burned daylight trying to figure out what to write? Or spent long nights stuck on a piece you wished to conclude? Have you ever had trouble expressing what was on your mind? Well, my friends, you are not alone.

To those who struggle with writing: It is natural to feel that way. But don't be worried that others may find it easy to produce a finished piece of work. Everyone has their own way of writing. In his guide *On Writing Well,* William Zinsser states that "there are all kinds of writers and all kinds of methods, and any method that helps you to say what you want to say is the right method for you." Zinsser stresses the concept that there is no "right" way in how you personally write literature. There are writers who need peace and quiet, writers who cannot work without music, writers who prefer using a computer, and writers who must work at a specific time of day to produce their writing, such as I, who have been known to stay up writing into the early hours of the morning. There is not one specific way to start or end writing; it's all up to you. But how do you find the way that best suits you?

When writing, finding your way may be a matter of just seconds, or it might take days. The process can be long and hard. Trust me, I've been there. The struggle happens to me almost all the time. I tend to overthink what I write and fixate on word choice when creating a piece of writing, and often, I fail to express my thoughts. And failure isn't a great state to be in.

George Orwell stated, "If thought corrupts language, language can also corrupt thought." According to Orwell, mind and language can affect the way you express your thoughts. Sometimes, your ideas may become cluttered, causing you to have difficulty expressing them. You may end up writing about an entirely different topic altogether. The mind can make it harder for you to write. Isn't it funny how the mind can take over what you truly want to say?

Diction takes on a major role during the process of writing. You may spend hours trying to find the right words to explain your thoughts. And often, we think that certain words will make our writing seem fancier. However, that is not the case. And so we must be open to rewriting our work because sometimes, due to a misused word, it might end up making no sense at all. We might even come to think that we may never become perfect writers and decide to give up. But the truth is, we should not.

We can agree that English is a tough language to master, especially through the art of writing. Yet that doesn't mean we should hate or give up on writing. English literature can challenge us, leading us to find our own methods of writing. Notice that writers all have different styles of writing. We may be tempted to use other writers' distinct styles, but you shouldn't feel the need to exactly copy any one person's style. It is best to learn from their methods and see why their methods of writing work for them. Be open-minded of others' works, and if you wish to be influenced by their writing, then do so. It can help you develop your very own method.

There is always a way to overcome the difficulties of writing. I am like you, Struggling Writers, an individual who spends hours thinking about what to write and more time still figuring out how to write it. Writing is a practice, a skill to work for. But it is also a form of art to communicate to an audience. The goal is to create writing that expresses you and reaches your reader.

Don't give up on writing because it is hard. Beginnings are always hard, and so are endings. But don't let that stop you! I bet you every piece of literature you've come across that seemed like it was easy for the writer to create probably took them a long time (like us). Start and finish strong. Have the mindset that you are someone who can do it, because you are. Successful writers all have their methods, and soon you will find yours too.

I wish you all the very best.

Sincerely,
A Fellow Struggling Writer

Others, United

HEESEUNG KIM

It is easy to think one voice does not matter. But writing allows each person to amplify their voice—so they can speak up for what is right.

Picture 130 kids, a nearly uniform sea of white. In the sea, three yellow dots. Zoom in—one of them is me. As one of just a few Asian Americans in my high school class, I grew up painfully aware of my otherness. It was something I worked hard to ignore, studiously avoiding any allusion to the fact that I did not look like everyone else. No rice or kimchi at lunch for me—it was peanut butter and jelly sandwiches every day. I wanted so badly to blend in. But over time, I realized I would never be able to change the color of my skin, the shape of my eyes, the fact that no one could ever pronounce my name on the first try. These things mortified me, until they didn't.

Unless you're a very specific kind of person, the kind of person who was born with the right skin color and the right body parts, who loves the right people and believes in the right religion and was born in the right place, unless everything about you is "right," then you are an other. America was built by others. Despite this, we are constantly under attack by those who wish to preserve the status quo of what is "right." And so we, the people who are different in one way or another, must protect our rights and the rights of others to continue to be so.

Otherhood encompasses many. We have different needs, different goals. Monolithic agreement is practically impossible. What's more, it's all too easy to succumb to the desire to compare one hurt against another, to tally traumas, to get caught up in resentment. And yet, just as you are able to have compassion for others, they are able to have compassion for you. Remember this. Compassion for others does not erase the experiences we have lived. If our individual pain has the potential to isolate us, compassion has the power to bring us together. And so, under duress and attempted diversion, we must stay strong, united. When people try to silence some of us, we must amplify each other's messages. People flood the streets, chanting, "The people united will never be defeated."

SARAH RAMIREZ

YEARS AS MENTEE: 1
GRADE: Junior
HIGH SCHOOL: Scholars' Academy
BORN: Queens, NY
LIVES: Queens, NY

MENTEE'S ANECDOTE: *I have nothing but feelings of accomplishment and appreciation when reflecting on the past couple of months I have been working with my mentor, Erica. This was my first year at Girls Write Now, and I was initially very hesitant, holding back in what I said and wrote. But, as the weeks went by, discovering that we share many things in common, I became more comfortable asking for feedback, accepting critique, and speaking my mind. Erica has helped me grow as a writer and push my creative boundaries to create pieces I did not know I was capable of producing.*

ERICA SCHWIEGERSHAUSEN

YEARS AS MENTOR: 1
OCCUPATION: MFA candidate, Hunter College
BORN: Harvard, MA
LIVES: Brooklyn, NY

MENTOR'S ANECDOTE: *One of my favorite parts of meeting with Sarah each week is learning about each other through writing exercises. One week, Sarah started writing about her interest in the Civil Rights Movement. She told me she had been reading a lot of Martin Luther King Jr.'s writing, and we started sending speeches, essays, and interviews back and forth. It was exciting to share and talk through ideas, learning from each other. Sarah is a thoughtful and ambitious writer, unafraid to take on challenging topics in her writing. Her quiet confidence inspires me to push beyond self-doubt in my own writing.*

Transformative Love

SARAH RAMIREZ

Through the course of my life, I have always seen love as something more than just romantic. This piece uncovers how I interpret love and its ability to create change.

Love is powerful. If you want to change something, the most effective way to go about it is with love. Love is universal in its ability to push past superficiality. It is not formulaic or structured. It is not written on a piece of paper and decided on over a handshake. It is not something that only those in power are able to use. Love is free of form and intangible—beyond limits and beyond definition. A word that is used incessantly can often lose its power; however, when experienced, love has the power to be transformative.

Growing up in church has taught me that without love, all that I do is meaningless. However, not everyone grows up in church, and many do not see love as necessary. In fact, many have become hardened by life's disappointments and obstacles, so they don't recognize love as something that is as important as life, something that is important *to* life. But it is. I say this urgently, because today's news demonstrates the necessity of love without limits. Subway platforms in New York City are riddled with angry voices and loud disputes. I believe that love is gentle enough to heal aches and console cries, but also mighty enough to combat injustice and oppression.

Love, according to Congressman John Lewis, is "a way of being"—meaning that whatever you do, you do with love. Love is the ability to recognize someone else's humanity—and resistance to anything that would degrade or diminish that humanity.

Love does not mean staying silent when you see injustice around you. In fact, it is the exact opposite. Love is correcting and fighting injustice, because injustice is a clear violation of love. We cannot say we "love" when we witness wrongdoing and choose to stay silent. Many people equate love with avoiding conflict, so they stay away from speaking out against it. However, you *can* show love by boldly condemning injustice; you *can* be outraged and still love at the same time. This is called "righteous anger." The anger is what motivates you to want to put an end to the injustice, but the love sustains you and keeps you going. If hate is your sole motive, it makes the quest for justice poisonous and burdensome. In the words of Martin Luther King Jr., "Hate is too great a burden to bear."

"Love your neighbor as yourself" is a well-known Christian commandment. There is no fine print to go along with that verse; there are no conditions. It does not say, "Love your neighbor as yourself, but *only* if they look like you, *only* if they are the same religion as you, *only* if they do good to you, and *only* when it's convenient for you." Our neighbors are not just people who we *want* to help, or who are *easy* to help. Our neighbors are refugees, people of different faith, skin color, and social status. We cannot sit still as we see groups of people being marginalized. Doing so makes us complicit in their mistreatment.

Yet Christians are called to love not only the victims of injustice, but also the perpetrators. We are to love our enemies, which is easier said than done. *How do you show love to people who don't know what it is? Who seem to be working so vehemently against it?* You love them because they are human. You see them as individuals, and you seek out the goodness in them, that "spark of divine," as John Lewis says, trusting that it's there. You try to understand what happened over the course of their lives that made them this way—angry, vengeful, cold. In a way, loving your enemies is revolutionary; it's righteous, it's radical. "That you beat me, you arrest me, you take me to jail, you almost kill me, but in spite of that, I'm gonna still love you," as Lewis says. Your enemies do not have to have a foot-hold on your consciousness. You can deny them the power and satisfaction of controlling how you feel, and how you act to-wards them. In the end, when all is said and done, love will win.

Love is something every human, no matter how hard and cold a heart, responds to. It digs down deep to the core and has the power to shift one's foundation. Love inspires people to rise out of the depths of neutrality. It urges people to speak out against injustice. It is universally understood and craved. It transcends language barriers and time zones. It is a common thread running through people of every nation, so it only makes sense to use love as a catalyst for change.

Small Kindnesses

ERICA SCHWIEGERSHAUSEN

This year, Sarah and I have been thinking about the potential for love to affect change. This piece was inspired by an unexpected moment of kindness that has stayed with me.

I was standing in line at an airport newsstand waiting to buy a bag of Chex Mix when the woman in front of me turned around. "Let me get that for you," she said to me.

"What?" I asked, not sure if I had heard correctly.

"Let me get that for you," she repeated, gesturing to the Chex Mix. "Oh," I said, blushing and confused. "You don't have to do that."

"I want to bless you," she explained. "The sermon in church this morning was about random acts of kindness."

"Oh," I said again, understanding now. "That's so nice. Thank you." I had the urge to reciprocate, to offer to pay for whatever she was buying, but instead I said, "I'll pay it forward." She smiled and nodded. "Exactly." It was just a small thing. But as we wished each other a safe flight, I felt lighter, and moved by our exchange.

I'm a shy and sometimes anxious person, so striking up a conversation with a stranger does not always come as easily to me as I would like. But in the past few months, I've found myself thinking back again to the woman at the airport. I'm grateful for her reminder that even a small kindness can inspire love and hope in someone else. On days when I feel overwhelmed and cynical, when I don't seem to be able to do anything besides compulsively read the news, I've been trying to find reassurance in small moments of generosity: sending a note to a new friend who's in the hospital; telling a student I recognize their hard work; even just giving up my seat on the subway, or sharing a smile. In my experience, love on a small scale can be powerful, too.

MEHAK RAO

YEARS AS MENTEE: 2

GRADE: Senior

HIGH SCHOOL: International High School at Lafayette

BORN: Malka Hans, Pakistan

LIVES: Brooklyn, NY

MENTEE'S ANECDOTE: *Protest, subway, pie, Girls Write Now gala, Koreatown, Brooklyn Public Library, tripping but did not fall. Esther and I are more like sisters than just mentee and mentor. We have grown super close to the point that I share almost everything with Esther. Like the time when I started to watch Korean dramas. When new Kpop songs came out. When I told her to wear heels because she is shorter than me. We laugh over little things. Time when I was being sassy. Time when we went to the bookstore. What else can I ask for from Girls Write Now other than a great mentor who is more like a sister?*

ESTHER KIM

YEARS AS MENTOR: 2

OCCUPATION: Publicist, Other Press

BORN: Yonkers, NY

LIVES: Brooklyn, NY

PUBLICATIONS AND RECOGNITIONS: I published a personal essay in *Brooklyn Magazine.* My first byline!

MENTOR'S ANECDOTE: *The year itself was a wild one due to political and personal reasons, which were crystallized in the Muslim Ban that kicked off the new year and new administration/regime. But through Mehak, I gained so much perspective on Brooklyn, Pakistan, and internet memes. From protests to workshops, we have explored New York City together. She possesses this dauntless spirit that is inspiring and infectious, so while it's sad that she's off to college this fall, I am sure we will keep in touch.*

Love Poems?

MEHAK RAO

This eraser poem is about a girl who visits Times Square for the first time, seeing many things that change her imagination. She takes the subway alone by herself once a week. She grows up from a girl scared of traveling to a woman who just wants to travel alone.

Love poem,
Raised her hand, or loss poem?
Her first trip to Manhattan
Times Square like it is no big deal.
All people representing
Sticking out as a rainbow.
The rainbows in life can judge
The show
Over the Manhattan Bridge in his brain.

Confessions

ESTHER KIM

This was inspired by a Wellesley alum asking the girlgang: "What are some of the awful/embarrassing/horrific things you've done to an ex after a breakup?" Our year's motto goes: Rise Speak Change. *I cannot claim to have risen above, but I can claim here to speak and change.*

The truth is after our breakup I kept going to your holds shelf at the Brooklyn Public Library and moving your books to other parts of the library. For months.

The truth is this is how you introduced me to Yukio Mishima's *Confessions of a Mask.* Inadvertently. By requesting it at least four times.

The truth is I stopped moving your books once I found a pocket-sized guide to my favorite country that you had requested. I shoved it back onto the shelf as if I had found dead bed bugs pressed into its pages.

The truth is sparrows still remind me of you. One summer you pointed one out, sitting in someone's garden, saying, "I love when they take dirt baths," and we watched as it shimmied its little breast into the sun-dappled earth, forming a cloud of dust.

The truth is when planning the venue for my birthday festivities, I considered Doris, the lovely Bed-Stuy bar where we broke up and you consequently ruined. I wanted to reclaim it with a happy, drunken party, but R wisely said, "No! You should burn it down, and go to the bar *across* the street to watch it burn."

The truth is this memory-soaked map of Brooklyn and Man-hattan does not burn.

EMILY RINALDI

YEARS AS MENTEE: 1
GRADE: Sophomore
HIGH SCHOOL: Susan E. Wagner High School
BORN: Staten Island, NY
LIVES: Staten Island, NY

MENTEE'S ANECDOTE: *Although my whole life I have had a love for writing, I have never had a stable environment to get my work out there and to get real, genuine criticism until I joined Girls Write Now. Now not only do I get both stability and feedback with the help of Molly, but I have dived deeper into some more unconventional topics, like the world of conspiracy theories, the artwork of Chelsea, and embarrassing anecdotes from our lives.*

MOLLY McARDLE

YEARS AS MENTOR: 1
OCCUPATION: Books editor, *Brooklyn Magazine*; regular contributor, *Travel + Leisure*
BORN: Washington, DC
LIVES: Brooklyn, NY

MENTOR'S ANECDOTE: *Though it may sound strange to some New Yorkers, my favorite part of the week is driving to Staten Island Wednesday afternoons. Emily and I meet at a little café called Fab Cub and talk about our lives—work, her school, and an internet meme or two—and work on our writing together. We have eavesdropped on a few patrons for dialogue exercises and navigated a couple of others who have wanted to get in on our conversations. It has been amazing watching (and reading) Emily's writing: every new project we tackle, her voice gets stronger.*

Cliché Teen Crisis

EMILY RINALDI

This is an excerpt from Cliché Teen Crisis, *which I would love to expand into a novel. This represents* Rise Speak Change *because in the extended version, both main characters Jane and Everett defy stereotypes and lead a life they feel is worth living.*

"Everett! Your alarm has been going off for the past twenty minutes, get up!"

The voice is thick and resolute and comes directly outside the thin, hallowed walls of my bedroom. Typically, if I oversleep, one of the maids usually roars up the staircase to awaken me. This is definitely not a maid. That is when I really wake up and hear the boisterous and ear-splitting "marimba" ringtone blasting from my phone across the room. I must have accidentally kept it connected to the speaker all night. I get up to turn the alarm off, still confused as to who the voice was possibly resonating from, and precariously pull the sheets of my tall and lanky body. I call to the outside voice, "I'm up, I'm up!"

I glance quickly in the mirror to see my evidently narcoleptic eyes along with my dark, brown, curly locks—frizzy and filled with tangles and knots. It is frankly a reflection I have not seen in months, more specifically since school ended. I run a dollop of curl-shaping product through my hair and splash cold water on my face to wake me up a bit. After, I slip into my maroon St.

Jude's Prep school uniform, I rush downstairs to see a face I have not seen in weeks . . . my father's.

"Good morning, son! Before you go I would love for you to have dinner with me tonight . . ." he says abruptly.

A growing silence lingers between us. I am waiting, I think, and I know that the next words that roll off his tongue will be about his current love interest. "Just us?" I say with a slight rise in pitch.

"Yes, just us! Some father-son bonding! What do you say?" he says with a questionable amount of enthusiasm, especially considering the time.

"Yeah, sure, I will see you after school then," I say as I leave the house and he smiles at me with the corners of his mouth ear to ear. I make a left turn after skipping down the steps of my Upper East Side penthouse as I replay that conversation in my head. But I brush off his strange behavior, as I usually do, and walk to the nearest train. Bikes weave through traffic and people run across the street. I soon find myself walking down the flight of stairs leading to what many consider the underground armpit of the world: the subway. I make like the bikes I have just seen and weave in and out of the human traffic.

I see wads of gum stuck to the floor, maybe once chewed to ease someone's test anxiety, and multiple shoes, like the running sneakers maybe worn when another person finished a marathon or the black stilettos a third person wore to her dream job interview. That's when I remember my vocabulary word this summer's homework. *Sonder.* That is the emotion you feel when you take notice that every person you pass has a life as complex as your own. Maybe the man performing reggae music on the pans has had a dream to be a professional musician his whole life. Perhaps the man dressed in fancy attire angrily yelling at someone on the other side of the phone is stressed because he needs that promotion.

I hear a loud scraping noise and snap out of my daze. The train is approaching the station. I hop on the least crowded car where I sit across from a man, dressed in pajamas and with obvious bed head, angrily grunting and texting. I reach for the copy of *To Kill a Mockingbird* in my bag, to read some last-minute pages in case of a quiz. The train makes a very abrupt stop and my attention is no longer on my book but the girl situated on my lap. She has big green-hazel eyes, and long, wavy, brown hair that runs down her back along with a black blazer with the letters "SJP" written below the shoulder. That stands for St. Jude's Prep, my school. I don't recognize her—I know everyone.

She quickly gets up and says, "I'm so sorry, are you okay?" as her face turns incredibly red. I reassure her that it is no big deal and say, "I'm fine—don't worry about it." In a blink of an eye, she is scurrying to the opposite side of the train when I realize she has dropped her book, *To Kill a Mockingbird*. I open the book to see the inside flap: "Jane Rosenthal, Class 1121" appears in feminine, detailed handwriting. 1121—that is my class. I walk over to her, holding the bars so I don't pull a Jane Rosenthal, and say, "Excuse me?" She looks up from her phone, a deer in headlights. "I think you dropped this . . ."

She bends her head down and says quietly, with a slight laugh, "Thank you, I need this."

I sarcastically say the words, "No problem, Jane."

Maps

MOLLY McARDLE

Emily's work on her novel this past year has helped push me with my own fiction. This is an excerpt from my novel-in-progress, Geography.

He opened the atlas to "Washington—District of Columbia" and tore out a perforated sheet of lined paper from a school notebook. He laid it over the city and began to trace it. A broken diamond. A clenched fist. A beating heart.

These were the maps he made: first crude outlines of the city, then street maps of DC—though none of the paper he used was large enough to accommodate the level of detail he desired. The east-west streets: letters. The north-south streets: numbers, then two-syllable names (alphabetical), then three, then the names for flowers. Favorite names: Quankebos, Jonquil, Aberfoyle, Quesada (it reminded him of quesadilla), Ingomar, Fessenden, Brandywine, Klingle, Call, Prout, Brothers, Golden Raintree, Xenia. The rules were numerous: the city split into four quadrants and each had its own set of streets, the same ones but mirrored. He pressed down so hard on the paper it tore.

His notebook began to fill with them. Soon he stopped having to take pages out for tracing; he could draw the scraggly line of the Potomac, DC's western edge, by heart. And he narrowed his scope: to draw the streets of Tenleytown, or Columbia Heights, or Mount Pleasant, or Cleveland Park. Then he began to make maps of stores he liked, and then buses he took, then field trips he had gone on, then places all over the city where he had thrown up. He preferred maximalist maps: thick with detail, everything layered. But he also began to draw more sparing images: all the water in DC sketched out without reference to the land, or the routes of his walks without reference to streets. He started to dig up books on topography.

So much of it was copying: let us be clear here. To look at a map and then reproduce it, its spidery lines or the blush of elevation. Many looked a mess, with streets gone crooked and blocks blurred into nonexistence. Sometimes the whole city seemed, in his hand, to have collapsed on itself, like a deflating balloon. He drew the maps again. In time, they grew more delicate. He learned, with shading, to be gentle. The lines all intersected at the Capitol, which was off-center, but Bobby conceded that there must have been other, more pressing motivations for its placement. It was the axle on which the city turned.

After filling his school notebook, he began another.

CATHIOSKA RODRIGUEZ

YEARS AS MENTEE: 3
GRADE: Senior
HIGH SCHOOL: The Bronx School for Law, Government and Justice
BORN: Bronx, NY
LIVES: Bronx, NY

MENTEE'S ANECDOTE: *My mentor, Kate, had a mentee a few years back but they were not able to complete the program due to personal reasons. I used that to encourage a great relationship with her. She is extremely understanding, open-minded, well-rounded, and funny. She is very supportive of my future. She is excited about what might be the best four years of my life. I enjoy going to our check-ins, despite how I feel physically or mentally. I'm very thankful to have a great mentor like her. I am excited to graduate from Girls Write Now and high school with her.*

KATE MULLEY

YEARS AS MENTOR: 2
OCCUPATION: Playwright
BORN: Boston, MA
LIVES: New York, NY

MENTOR'S ANECDOTE: *Cathioska and I had a meeting on Election Day at the Girls Write Now office. We were both nervous, but just wanted to get through the night, get to the next day. Late that night on the train, knowing that I would wake up in a different America, I wrote a poem and shared it with her at our next meeting. She also shared a piece about her experience on the night of the election and the day after and it became a jumping-off point for us to talk and write about this new state of the world.*

The President-Elect

CATHIOSKA RODRIGUEZ

"This piece needs to be out there. People need to hear your political voice because it's not being said. It needs to be heard!"
—Mr. Connolly, my U.S History teacher

The 2016 presidential election was an eye-opener, and I am going to tell you why.

June 16, 2015 was the day he announced he was running for president. Americans across the country laughed at what we thought was a humorous action, but quickly found out that it was not. After his primary election win, it dawned upon me that he was one step closer to becoming president. His name *might* be the one written above the "Forty-fifth President of the United States." His name *might* be the one written under the "Winner of the 2016 Presidential Election." The idea of seeing those letters . . . scared me, along with 2.9 million American citizens.

February 1, 2016 was when the joke turned to the horrific reality. The primary election declared him as the Republican nominee for the Presidential Election of 2016. Not only was it Barack Obama's last few months as the *official* president of the United States, but in a few months the United States might have another history-making president, or just a business boy in a suit. The clock was ticking as all of our nightmares were slowly being turned into what might be a reality. But there was still hope. Just a little of it was being held. The country was holding onto this little piece of thread. And we all prayed it wouldn't snap.

The votes have been counted. The people stared anxiously at the stage. Waiting for the man with a red tie to walk up, waving—oblivious to the power he's going to have at the tip of his fingers. His minions standing right beside him, with the exact same mindset. The room was dim and crowded. When he came to the stage, red, blue, and white confetti blasted. The people cheered and cried tears of joy. These people were a part of the 46.1 percent that voted for that man waving, and walking across the stage. The stage he shouldn't have been walking across.

No one wanted this.

We the people spoke louder than this. We acted louder than this. Yet, we weren't being heard. Better yet, we were ignored. And we won't let that fly by. Not like his hair or wrinkly skin. We the people refuse to give up (like his fashion sense).

We refuse to speak without thinking, like him. Yet no matter how hard we kick, scream, hit, curse, and punch, he still signs executive orders against the orders we fought so hard for, against Planned Parenthood, abortion, and health care.

All the money that was being used to save lives, keep people safe, and keep families together is being used to put us in danger, destroy lives, and divide us. Literally. His stance on every issue screams, "THIS IS INHUMANE!" But he only hears the ignorance and the rustling of money. Not the outcries of worry and demands for change.

Why is that? How did we let this happen? How did we let money take us this far? How?

Money is the root of all evil.

Look at us now. Worried sick. So sick that we're going to have to pay for doctor visits because this monster wants to take health care away from us.

He is more concerned with "Making America Great Again." *Do not* fucking jack that.

That slogan of yours just shows every single person in America what kind of little boy you are.

You claim to fix everything for a better future.

I can see the future, too. I know in the future, I will say "thank you" . . . thank you for showing me how strong and determined I have to be to fight a beast like you.

And there will be a happy ending . . . for **ME**.

You cannot sit on that desk, pick up your fancy black pen, and sign your nauseating name at the bottom, expecting for changes to be made in two hours. That is not how this works.

Your cowardly manner to not focus on the obvious shows that you are completely capable of running this country STRAIGHT DOWN THE DRAIN.

her voice

KATE MULLEY

After Cathioska brought a first draft of her anthology piece to me, she suggested that I write about Hillary for mine. I am glad she did; I never would have written this otherwise.

i miss her voice most of all
i miss what it said
and how it sounds

i didn't realize i would
in that way that you don't
when you break up with someone
or lose them for good
but they creep into your brain
from time to time
and you have to keep yourself from crying

there's a crack in my heart
that feels like the crack in our country
that feels unstitchable
irreparable

that aches when I see her
in the woods
in a suit
at a show
smiling

waving
laughing

and I want to shout,
"we didn't deserve you!"
and I guess we didn't
and so we didn't get her

SMEILY RODRIGUEZ

YEARS AS MENTEE: 1
GRADE: Senior
HIGH SCHOOL: City College Academy of the Arts
BORN: Santiago, Dominican Republic
LIVES: Bronx, NY
PUBLICATIONS AND RECOGNITIONS: Scholastic Art & Writing Award: Silver Key

MENTEE'S ANECDOTE: *Lisa and I meet every Thursday at Hamilton's Café on Broadway and 146th Street. The place is very cozy, with dimmed lights and black walls covered with quotes. Every week we do The Squares: pieces of paper with prompts such as, "I will never do this again," or "The weirdest person I ever saw on the subway." We turn the papers over, spread them on the table, and pick at random. They can be crazy, weird, or funny. And as we sit, we come together. We get to know each other better, and we are inspired to write new pieces.*

LISA SCHWARZBAUM

YEARS AS MENTOR: 1
OCCUPATION: Freelance culture journalist; former movie critic, *Entertainment Weekly*
BORN: Queens, NY
LIVES: New York, NY
PUBLICATIONS AND RECOGNITIONS: Reviews in *The New York Times Book Review*

MENTOR'S ANECDOTE: *The Squares came about out of a desire to tell one another truths that are revealed in descriptions of small stuff: how we wake up, what scares us, what we love about a favorite sweater, what we think about our teeth, what our kitchens look like. Much of the fun comes from feeling free to be silly. But that same freedom and closeness between us, fortified by coffee and pastries in a cozy setting, has allowed for moments of lovely revelation and descriptions of simple beauty—the real privilege of working together as writers.*

Ten Things You Should Know About Me

SMEILY RODRIGUEZ

Everyone has a story to be told. Everyone has the power to rise and change—intellectually, emotionally, and in her writing. So I am going to speak out. But to get comfortable, I need to tell you some things about me first.

1. The first thing you need to know about me is that I over-think everything. With friends I think, "What if I offend someone?" In English class I think, "What if the professor doesn't agree?" I overthink at night, wondering whether something I just texted someone was the right thing to say. Crazy, right? But that's me.

2. I came to the United States from the Dominican Republic when I was eleven years old, almost seven years ago. I love and miss the people, the food, and the weather. I go back every summer, and I appreciate everything even more than when I was there. The beach sand is dry and yellow-ish; the cheese is soft and creamy. There's no place like home.

3. I do not know why I am not yet comfortable enough speaking English. When I do, I find myself planning what I want to say, especially in formal settings—classes, college interviews, meeting with teachers. Sometimes when I

meet new people, I stutter and struggle to find the correct words. That is why I do not like to speak in public: Inside I am all for rising, speaking, and bringing about change, but letting it out is a challenge. In front of a class, my hands sweat, I start touching my hair or the silver ring on my right hand, and I feel the need to constantly look down at my notes no matter how many times I have practiced.

4. Can you tell? I am a perfectionist. I have very high standards and I am very hard on myself whenever something goes wrong. I am very particular about my handwriting, I like my notes to be organized and neat, and I am also very particular about how and what I write in my Bullet Journal. That is why I draw pictures in pencil first and then go over them with markers and colored pens. This is time-consuming—but it looks good.

5. Lately, it takes me a long time to fall asleep. I lie in bed, staring at the ceiling. I never sleep with my cell phone next to me. My uncle always said that it emitted radiation, and that it was bad to keep it near you while you sleep. True? False? I don't know, but I put it face down on top of my dresser and next to my printer on the other side of the room. My favorite bed sheet has a pattern of orange and brown flowers. One side has the pattern and the other does not. The pattern *must* be facing up. Over the bed sheet, I put a white cotton bedspread. I like the "just washed" scent, and I hold it to my cheeks where I can feel the soft texture.

6. Now, this part is serious. My faith is really important to me. I started going to church when I was very young. I

loved the songs, the dances, and the Bible studies. Ever since I got to New York, I have not attended a church regularly, and I miss it. I wish people would understand that I believe in God not because my family told me to, and not because the church told me to, but because I have seen His greatness in creation, in miracles, and in the joy of song. And because I have chosen to. I find comfort in praying and in believing in something greater than myself.

7. I am passionate about volunteering. I have done so at the Presbyterian Hospital in New York and with a ministry in the Dominican Republic. I love using my skills to help others and to learn new ones. It is something I wish to continue doing in college and even after that.

8. I am a great listener. Although I am quiet, I am very attentive and make a big effort to understand the needs of others.

9. Okay, this is not so serious, but you must know: I *love* cheese. I like fried Dominican cheese with plantains, yellow cheese melted on white rice, mozzarella on my tacos, and white cheese with chicken and avocado. And this is my party story: When I was three years old, a boy in my class stabbed me with a pencil in my left cheek. The nurse held a giant syringe that she used to numb the area and take out the lead. I can show you the exact spot if you are interested.

10. So there you have it. I have been through a lot of changes, moving to a new country, learning a new language, and leaving behind all that I knew. But I have also been able to see and do more things than I ever

imagined—including joining Girls Write Now. I am thriving. And although there are things that I miss from the past, I am looking forward to what is ahead of me. I feel confidence rising in me. And that is a big change.

No Stones, Please, This Is Just My Opinion

LISA SCHWARZBAUM

This is a story that I have told many times in my long career as a movie critic, one that allows for some vivid writing. It explains a lot about what has built my confidence to speak out. Smeily has not heard it yet, so here it goes.

When I was a movie critic at *Entertainment Weekly*, I sometimes made readers mad. Mostly they were mad when I didn't like a particular movie or actor and they did, so they thought I was an idiot and told me so. Sometimes they were mad when I liked a particular movie or actor and they didn't, so they thought I was an idiot and told me so. Occasionally they told me I was an idiot because I was a chick writing about "guy movies." Those who agreed with my opinions thought I was a genius.

Do you want good practice at standing by your beliefs in the face of challenge? Be a serious observer of popular culture, and write clearly to explain yourself. Hold your ground with the grace to know that yours isn't the only right opinion, but it is yours and it is valid. Of course, you need intelligent arguments to back your position up. Otherwise, you are just a Tweet in the universe.

Well, sometimes my readers were the people who made the movies I was writing about. Which brings me to the day a messenger delivered a bulky package to my office. It was a giant cardboard tub—the kind you get when you buy the jumbo size of movie popcorn—and it was filled with round, polished, heavy, black stones. The note attached was from the wife of a Hollywood mogul famous for making noisy, mindless, blow-'em-up box-office hits. She wrote (I am paraphrasing), "Who are you to throw stones at my husband's movies? His movies have made a zillion dollars. What have *you* done? Have you won a Pulitzer Prize? No."

I was so dazzled by the grandeur and folly of this gesture that I proudly showed my bucket of stones to everyone in the office. They were *fancy* stones. I decided, by the way, that Mrs. Hollywood had a standing account at a garden store. And when she read a bad review of one of her husband's projects, she would bark at her assistant, "Order up another bucket of stones for the next idiot!"

With this story, I rise up to say once again say, thank you from the bottom of the bucket.

LUNA ROJAS

YEARS AS MENTEE: 3
GRADE: Senior
HIGH SCHOOL: Cobble Hill
High School
BORN: New York, NY
LIVES: Brooklyn, NY
**PUBLICATIONS AND
RECOGNITIONS:** Scholastic
Art & Writing Awards: Hon-
orable Mention

MENTEE'S ANECDOTE: *I thought I could never change my stance on things like being influenced by my mentor, the one and only, irreplaceable Sarah Todd, and on, for example, brussels sprouts. Sarah likes them and oddly, now I do, too. The topics aren't always so light-hearted. They range from politics, current events, and activism to reality television and food. She has taught me by example that my voice and those of others is what will bring change. Unlike myself, Sarah isn't a cynic. She's taught me that in dark times, it isn't just okay to laugh, it's necessary.*

SARAH TODD

YEARS AS MENTOR: 2
OCCUPATION: Deputy Ideas
Editor, *Quartz*
BORN: Cleveland, OH
LIVES: Brooklyn, NY

MENTOR'S ANECDOTE: *One of the things I love about working with Luna is that we always manage to make each other laugh—even when we're knee-deep in college application mode. At the height of application season, we saw each other almost every day, and every day, I was inspired anew as Luna wrote essays drawing on her incredibly varied experience as a daughter, sister, activist, artist, friend, french-fry slinger, and student leader. One common theme emerged from her writing: Nothing stops Luna Rojas from doing what she wants. And what she wants, always, is to make things better than they were before.*

Eu Su Espejo

LUNA ROJAS

Looking back on my childhood as I get ready to travel abroad and begin college has led to many profound discoveries, some to do with myself and some to do with others. This piece is about seeing my mother in a new light.

The first time I visited a college campus, I was six years old. I was there for my mother, not for me—or so I thought.

My mother, a first-generation Latina and single parent, walked into her economics class at a New York City college full of ambition and eagerness, with me in tow. She told me to read and say nothing until class was over. I took quick peeks at my mother, noticing how different she looked in the classroom. Eyes forward, hair up, she scribbled notes on everything the professor said. For the first time, she was devoting all her attention and focus to something that wasn't me. I felt jealous. I didn't understand my mother's drive to finish college back then, because I hadn't yet learned to see past myself.

Growing up, my mother fell prey to a common trap for children of immigrants—particularly women. Driven to provide for herself and help support her parents, she began working as soon as she graduated from high school, planning to attend college at the same time. But as a girl in a Latino household with traditional ideas about gender, she wasn't encouraged to continue her education. Meanwhile, her parents constantly urged her brother to think big, telling him that he could become a teacher, doctor, or lawyer. And so my mom was disadvantaged early on, because she was never taught to prioritize her own education. Soon she stopped going to school to focus on work.

After I was born, my mother realized she had to go back to school to support us both. It was a long process, with multiple stops and starts. She spent a year in school when I was six, then left again to be more present in my life. Then, as I began high school, she went back to academia again, determined to finish her degree by taking one class a semester. And although I still missed my mom, I was finally old enough to understand what she was teaching my brother and me.

Over time, watching my mother balance school and her job made me adopt a similarly serious work ethic. My final year in high school often made me fantasize about extending the 24-hour day by a few hours or so. An average day consisted of high school and a sociology course at City Technology College, after which I would do a 360, transforming into a sparkling sales associate at Banana Republic for the remainder of my evening. As a food-service worker, I also experienced what it was like to wash dishes for pay, then come home to wash even more. I babysat and cleaned other people's homes, and took orders from hangry customers—sometimes feeling more like a menu than a person.

During the last few weeks of my final semester in high school, I was so busy that I worried exclusively about myself, feeling that I'd taken on too much. Then I caught sight of my mother up late, making flash cards, and realized she had been doing everything I had—and much more—throughout my teenage years. In no way could I compare my hard work to hers. She didn't have the luxury to worry exclusively about herself. In that moment, I remembered the lunches she had packed for me every day, the snacks and inspirational texts she'd sent when I felt overwhelmed, and how the question "How was your day, honey?" never failed to come out of her mouth, no matter how tired or busy she might be.

Adulthood begins when you are able to look beyond the person you see in the mirror. Now, as I get ready to go to college, I know how much I owe to my mom. Watching her strive to complete her degree while raising kids and holding down a full-time job helped me understand the true value of a good education, and showed me that balancing work and study—while difficult—could be done.

My mother's drive came from her own confrontation with the realities of adulthood and motherhood. When she took me to that economics class years ago, she was learning to look away from the person in the mirror and toward the child who stood beside her. Now, as I look forward to beginning college this fall, I know that I do it for myself as well as my mother—who has done nothing short of everything to get me here.

Down These Mean Streets

SARAH TODD

Every time I've made a big change, I've had to get mad first. This is a poem about the fury that can become the fuel toward a better life.

"Down these mean streets a man must go who
is not himself mean, who is neither tarnished
nor afraid."

—Raymond Chandler

We're just three percent enemies
but I have a feeling it's the right percent.

Come here and sip my gloss,
it's so intuitive
like an oil slick
after the plane's gone down

I'm living in the wrong New York
(timed lights and tiny cups)
I've been unfaithful
to the dancers
with their heads bowed
just before the music flares

When I wake from a deep sleep
I know exactly how far away

I am from home
My only hobby is other people
what's yours

no, nothing's burning

I put on a blue dress
and leave to let the bad dogs in
I put on a blue dress
and do my best impression of a coin
that gives when bit
I put on a blue dress
and whirl toward your extended hand
I put on a blue dress
a bad dress
and I go out to listen
I think the cicadas may change my mind

DIANA ROMERO

YEARS AS MENTEE: 2
GRADE: Senior
HIGH SCHOOL: The Beacon School
BORN: Santiago, Dominican Republic
LIVES: Bronx, NY
PUBLICATIONS AND RECOGNITIONS: Scholastic Art & Writing Awards: Honorable Mention and Silver Key; Finalist for Urban Word Youth Poet Laureate

MENTEE'S ANECDOTE: *Working with Jan has been such an incredible experience. She is so supportive and super nice! I know that I can always count on her if I need any support. This year we've explored poetry more in-depth and discovered new and interesting styles in my writing. These past two years have been a blessing. I am so proud of the work that we've done together, the stories that we have shared, and the powerful writing that we have created together. I hope that this is not the end of our journey together and that we stay in contact forever.*

JAN ALEXANDER

YEARS AS MENTOR: 3
OCCUPATION: Senior Editor, *Strategy+Business* magazine
BORN: Chicago, IL
LIVES: New York, NY
PUBLICATIONS AND RECOGNITIONS: *Ms. Ming's Guide to Civilization*, semifinalist in Leapfrog Fiction Contest. Published in *34th Parallel* magazine and by Silver Birch Press. Fiction editor of *The Neworld Review*.

MENTOR'S ANECDOTE: *Diana is a brilliant poet. "I get started by writing down the feelings," she told me. I was awestruck. I knew only how to start with the story. But that was where our minds met. I've learned so much from my mentee. Diana pours sorrow, laughter, sounds, and colors onto the page. Then I ask, "What's the story?" Someday I want to write a first draft of a story and show it to her, so that she can help me turn it into poetry.*

The King of Atlantis

DIANA ROMERO

For most New Yorkers, this city is a whirlpool of craziness. But if we look closely and examine what's under the cracks, we can always find light and the powerful dreams of those around us.

It was around 9:00 p.m. and I was headed home from my school's choir gala: Our Americana. The night had gone well, and my mentor was in the audience cheering me on. I sang a solo, "Everything I Know," and somehow I didn't feel nervous. I was singing for my grandmother, and I could almost feel her presence, somewhere in heaven. But after the show my phone went dead. That rattled me; I wanted to unwind and listen to my playlist on the subway. But then, as I bolted into the express train uptown, I heard a rush of words inside the car. Little did I know that I was in for one of the most powerful rides of my life.

I planted a seed on this earth I'm forced to call home.
The sea grew nothing but out of wood it stood near the end of the
*   river calling to be sacrificed.*
I see them waving the white handkerchief across the evening song
*   and I prayed and I knew that the minute I walked across the*
*   ocean*
From the roots of my ancestors
They cried.

I was lucky enough to find a seat on the crowded train. I still had my earphones on, though there wasn't any music playing. A young woman and man got on at the next stop and began to dance for us. I smiled. They stopped, and an older African American man came around singing "(Sittin' on) the Dock of the Bay." It was beautiful, and I wished I had money to give the three performers.

I couldn't help but notice another man, an elderly African American, sitting across from me and talking to himself. A lady sitting next to me was looking out the window. She had a big bag of groceries. Across from her was a woman in her thirties; she looked exhausted, probably from working so much. Leaning on her shoulder was her daughter, who I guessed was around twelve. The daughter was asking in Spanish if the man was crazy. The mother didn't reply. A couple were arguing about Donald Trump and the state of the economy. The wife suddenly stopped, pointed to the elderly man, and told her husband, "Listen, hun, to the man. He might be homeless but he is speaking truth."

I pulled my earphones out and looked at the old man. To my surprise he stared right back. Then he said:

"I've known you my entire life.
I've sat on this train for three thousand years trying to save my
    people
But they put me in a box because they were trying to wear my skin.
His people had taken me and chopped me up into little pieces.
But, was it God or was it me? That is the question
It's not up to you to let me go.
They enslaved me. I don't understand how they are still l free.
Before the world was built,

I was holding a God
He had told me that eternity was the gateway to Heaven.
They made me dyslexic so that I would never speak their language
But honey, a Black man can't hide
And they are scared.
They found out that God was Black—and that he's my father.
But I ask myself again,
Why do I bury my own life source if they can't ever hear me?"

I looked around the car and it seemed as if everyone else had stopped talking. A voice in my own head sang its own words:

"I fight to not let anyone silence my voice
But sometimes, it seems that the more I speak the more my tongue
bleeds."

I think we all dream today to create tomorrow. The lady with the groceries, she dreamt of cooking a nice dinner for her children, and grandchildren, one they'd all remember long after. The mother dreamt of her daughter graduating from high school, going to college, and becoming a doctor.

At the Kingsbridge stop the homeless man got up and approached the door.

"What's your name?" I asked nervously.

"My name?" He laughed. "Do you really want to know?"

I nodded.

"My name is the King of Atlantis." And he walked out, laughing.

. . .

When I got outside, the sky was unusually clear, and the stars were bright. Walking up four flights of stairs, I couldn't help but stop thinking about the King. "Unfortunately, this is his sense of reality. It's different from ours," the woman with the groceries had said. But to me he was more than just "a crazy old man." He was real, and he was American.

In my living room, my family was gathered together watching a movie: *Atlantis: The Lost Empire*.

And in that moment I felt at home. Love, that's my American Dream.

Everyone's Moon

JAN ALEXANDER

My piece is fiction—sort of. My mother was never a Rockette. But when Diana and I began talking about how the rhythms of New York's streets have made us the writers that we are, I recalled a magical moon and how, for just a moment, all passersby seemed equal.

I came as a certain kind of immigrant to the big-city lights. I came with a message from my mother.

"The lights are alive, and the moon is bigger over New York," she promised me before I left home in Arkansas. My mother had run off to Manhattan herself once, and danced with the Rockettes. Even now, in the copy edit corner where I sentenced commas to oblivion and stalked renegade hyphens in celebrated writers' stories, I wore dresses with sprinkles of sequins.

"Why did you leave?" I'd asked my mother often. She had no answer except "I didn't have a lease."

On a certain balmy evening in October, I purged the last comma and decided it was a fine night to walk to my illegal sublet. That was when I saw it: the moon air-kissing Manhattan. A golden topaz moon, full and worldly-wise, grazing the skyscrapers like a penthouse no one can afford, bigger than anyone's dream.

Someone tugged my sleeve. I looked down, at a woman only as high as my chin, stooped and grizzled. She wore a coat held together with pins, and carried a tote bag with a hole in the bottom.

"Check out that moon, missy," she screeched.

The moon had paused, as if waiting for me.

"Wow. Awesome," I said. I was conscious that when I said "wow" it came out "way-ow."

"Thank you." She smiled, open-mouth, and stank of tooth decay. "This is my home. I painted my ceiling. I mixed the palette, oils not acrylics. A little harvest gold, and ochre and pink."

I pulled out a dollar.

She waved her hand at me. "No no no . . ." she insisted, as if warding off a hex. The light changed and I crossed the street. But I stopped just to look at the moon and the streetlights igniting my path. I turned around, and across the street I saw the woman tugging at a man in a suit and tie. I heard her screech, "Look at that moon," and I saw him look up.

"Beautiful," the man said.

SHANIA RUSSELL

YEARS AS MENTEE: 2

GRADE: Senior

HIGH SCHOOL: Bronx Academy of Letters

BORN: Bronx, NY

LIVES: Bronx, NY

PUBLICATIONS AND RECOGNITIONS: Scholastic Art & Writing Awards: Gold Key and Silver Key; NYC Tours and Photo Safaris blog contributor

MENTEE'S ANECDOTE: *Carol will argue that we only sat in the "audience participation" row of the theater because I was particularly stubborn that day, but there's so much more to the story. There's two years of her being at my side, encouraging me to write, to submit, to think, to explore, and, yes, to sit in the front row. Whether she knows it or not, she played as big a role in that moment as I did. That's why I look forward to being pulled out of my seat to partake in new things because I know she'll be there too.*

CAROL PAIK

YEARS AS MENTOR: 2

OCCUPATION: Freelance writer, editor, artist

BORN: Lowell, MA

LIVES: New York, NY

MENTOR'S ANECDOTE: *Shania and I decided that, right now, we most want to focus on writing that stretches our imaginations, refreshes our spirits, and makes us laugh. With that in mind, we came up with a project: we exchange writing prompts every other day, and must respond to the prompt we receive with a short play. We've been trying very hard to stump each other with increasingly outlandish prompts, finding inspiration in random photos, quotes, news stories, etc., but Shania, of course, is unstumpable. Our project has challenged, frustrated, energized, surprised, and delighted us and has also produced our contributions to this anthology.*

When Life Gives You Half a Lemon

SHANIA RUSSELL

Thanks to a basket of lemons, I wrote about the two things that we need for Rise Speak Change*: 1) the understanding that we can't change everything and 2) enough passion to challenge that belief.*

JACK *sits at his kitchen table, sipping coffee. He flips through a newspaper he is clearly not interested in and, after a moment, looks up at the audience. Nervous, he looks back at the newspaper, but he isn't reading it.*

JACK: I had this job once, working in a copy room. It was some magazine downtown—nothing too big, nothing you would know. But they had an audience. God knows it was probably made up of grandparents and bored housewives though—all they printed were fluff pieces about rescued rabbits and ridiculous scientific discoveries about what fruit could cure your depression. But then there was this one piece: it was about . . . d'you know that old saying, "when life hands you lemons" yada yada yada . . . Well, it was about that, but it had this whole science element to it. It was digging into the fact that lemons have a whole unknown origin and all we know is that they're bred from two different kinds of citrus. And that was the point. That they aren't naturally occurring—that life can't actually hand us lemons. Not on its own, anyway.

(CHRISTIAN *enters, ruffled with bedhead and sleep.* JACK *turns and looks at him as if he's hung the moon.*)

CHRISTIAN: Did you eat?

JACK: Just coffee.

CHRISTIAN: *(amused)* We finally get gas and electric in here, and your first instinct is coffee.

(CHRISTIAN *stops in front of him.* JACK *stands.*)

JACK: Hi.

CHRISTIAN: Good morning.

(They kiss.)

JACK: Do you want me to make you something?

CHRISTIAN: I've got it. Get back to your coffee and news. Let me know if anything interesting comes up.

(CHRISTIAN *goes to the kitchen, offstage.* JACK *sits and stares off in his direction. There is the sound of pots clattering and the stove turning on.* JACK's *smile fades; his brows furrow. He returns to his story.*)

JACK: It's weird. It's just never really left my mind, ya know? And it's really dumb to think that some article even *BuzzFeed* wouldn't publish got to me so much but . . . it just makes sense: the idea that whatever life gives us, we play a part in having gotten it. It's like . . . fuck the idea of fate controlling everything, but also, let's not pretend that we've been the deciding factor of our entire lives. Instead, it's both. Two things working at once. And honestly . . . that terrifies me.

(CHRISTIAN *walks back onstage.*)

CHRISTIAN: Asshole. (CHRISTIAN *steals* JACK's *mug, takes a large gulp.*) You drank the entire pot already—didn't you?

JACK: (*guiltily*) Maybe.

CHRISTIAN: (*amused*) You're the worst.

(CHRISTIAN *takes another gulp, then exits to return to his cooking.* JACK *doesn't watch him this time—he stares at the mug.*)

JACK: The thing is . . . even with all the fates in the world looking down on me, trying to orchestrate a happy ending, it doesn't make sense that I got him. No amount of luck or predestination could make up for all the shit I've put him through. So it's gotta be the lemons. It's gotta be that a little bit of my actions and a little bit of fate's help just worked in my favor. And that's what terrifies me. Who's to say that they won't change their minds, huh? Who's to say it doesn't all turn against me and take him away?

CHRISTIAN: (*offstage*) Vegetable omelet?

JACK: Sounds great! (*There's some shuffling. The fridge opens.*) I'm not gonna say that it would crush me if I didn't have him anymore. That would be too big an understatement.

CHRISTIAN: *(offstage)* Okay, scratch that—all we've got is eggs, and spinach, and tomatoes. *(Walks onstage, a tomato in hand.)* Is a tomato even a vegetable?

JACK: Scientifically speaking?

CHRISTIAN: Sure.

JACK: It's a fruit.

CHRISTIAN: You're so sexy when you know things.

JACK: You're so cute when you don't.

CHRISTIAN: *(pretends to throw the tomato)* Shut up.

(CHRISTIAN returns to the kitchen, offstage.)

JACK: So, for a while, I was scared. I was scared of the idea that things were half in my control: it meant either I fuck it all up myself, or it falls to shit and I can't do anything to fix it. *(Beat. Deep breath.)* But none of that's important, now. I don't want it to be. What matters is that we've made it this far. What matter is that we can make it further. But if I spend all my time trying to control it, or worrying that I can't . . . we won't make it anywhere. I'll let it all pass right by me.

CHRISTIAN: *(sheepishly pops back onstage)* Will you still love me if I abandon the omelet for some Pop-Tarts?

JACK: Always.

CHRISTIAN: What a relief. *(Returns to the kitchen.)*

JACK: *(looks at the audience, determined)* So I'll let the lemons do their part . . . and I'll do mine. A little bit of fate, and a little bit of me . . . and we'll be okay.

CHRISTIAN: *(offstage)* Oh! I found some lemons! Want a glass of lemonade?

JACK: Sounds amazing.

END OF PLAY

Of Course It Is, Mom

CAROL PAIK

Shania, outdoing herself in her efforts to make my life difficult, sent me a prompt that she took from a very odd Tumblr post about extra-terrestrial life. I tried to rise to the challenge.

ACT I

MOTHER *and* DAUGHTER *stand by a small spaceship.* DAUGHTER *wears a spacesuit and holds a helmet.*

MOTHER: We, our species, have spent hundreds of years looking up at the stars and wondering "is there anybody out there?" and hoping, and imagining. So much literature, so much science, all devoted—or wasted—on this pursuit. Why is extraterrestrial life so compelling?

DAUGHTER: Because we're lonely and we want friends.

MOTHER: We could look to our own kind. Why do you think our best hope for friendship lies—(*gestures to the heavens*) out there?

DAUGHTER: We're scared of our own kind. We're scared we're going to wreck our planet, blow ourselves up, ruin everything, if left to our own devices. We need help!

MOTHER: You don't know what you'll find out there. You imagine extraterrestrials will be like playmates, just our own size, who will teach us, learn from us, care about us, and whom we will care about.

DAUGHTER: I don't have any preconceptions or particular hopes. I just want to see what's out there. I've seen what this world has to offer. It's not enough.

MOTHER: So you must do this. All right. I will wait for your return. I'll wait—right here.

(*They embrace.* DAUGHTER *dons helmet and enters ship, which departs the earth. Lights fade.*)

   ACT II

MOTHER *is white-haired, stooped, standing in same spot. The ship comes into view and lands.* DAUGHTER *steps out.*

DAUGHTER: Mom! I'm home!

MOTHER: Darling! I was starting to lose hope.

DAUGHTER: Mom, I can't wait to tell you. I've seen so much! I've LEARNED so much! But most importantly, I want you to meet Josh. *(She reaches back into ship and* JOSH *takes her hand, a purple man with seven arms and fifteen eyes.)* Josh, this is my mom.

JOSH: *(emerges from ship, one hand in DAUGHTER'S, another three extended)* So pleased to meet you!

MOTHER: *(takes one hand gingerly)* Your name is Josh?

DAUGHTER: Mom! That's rude!

JOSH: Nah, it's cool! Josh is actually a common name where I'm from.

DAUGHTER: Josh is the love of my life! And the father of our eleven children.

MOTHER: But—!

DAUGHTER: Mom, what? I'm an adult, you know!

MOTHER: But this isn't why you left. To meet some—some *guy*! This isn't what you risked everything for.

DAUGHTER: Of course it is, Mom. Of course it is.

END OF PLAY

MAEVE SLON

YEARS AS MENTEE: 2
GRADE: Sophomore
HIGH SCHOOL: Harvest Collegiate High School
BORN: New York, NY
LIVES: New York, NY
PUBLICATIONS AND RECOGNITIONS: *Skipping Stones*, Moth All City High School StorySLAM

MENTEE'S ANECDOTE: *Like a sore throat that comes overnight, I sometimes wake up with my hands unable to write. It is worse than losing my voice. It is like losing my identity. When these days come around, I am not sure what to do. Meeting with Vivian helps. She helps me gain back my writer's voice. We might pass a computer back and forth writing a story that makes no sense or talk about the weather to spark ideas. I soon find myself with first drafts and able to write again.*

VIVIAN CONAN

YEARS AS MENTOR: 5
OCCUPATION: Librarian
BORN: New York, NY
LIVES: New York, NY
PUBLICATIONS AND RECOGNITIONS: New York Foundation for the Arts Fellowship, *New York Magazine*, *The New York Times*

MENTOR'S ANECDOTE: *I learn a lot from Maeve, both in writing style (she says a lot with few words; I tend to write too big) and her outlook on life (her quiet side is filled with trees and flowers, her passionate side with political and social issues, her playful side with finding the irony in things). I especially like the times we write a story together, each putting down a sentence, alternating until we come to the end, which we could not have predicted from the beginning.*

Past, Present, Future

MAEVE SLON

We can love things and hate them at the same time. These poems were written in winter and are about winter, the end of everything, but also a fresh start.

PAST

Winter is like a memory to me,
Always on the tip of my tongue
Or burning at my fingertips.

Winter is only a memory.
Snow no longer falls in December,
The air does not blow like I hope.

Winter always seemed warmer than summer.
The fire in our fireplace and family cheer
Would keep us dripping with sweat all winter.

But now, holidays are empty.
My fingers turn blue.
Winter is how it should be,
Long, cold, and dark.

Winter is like a memory to me.
Rosy cheeks and milky hair,
Snow that grows from the ground,
Warmer than summer,
But not any more.

PRESENT

We love winter but we miss the sun.
It will snow but our feet will get cold,
Our toes will turn blue to match the air,
And our skin will turn fair.

We love winter but we miss the sun.
The sun will shine but not warm our bones,
And the only way to reach you is over phone.

We love winter but we miss the sun.
School might get canceled,
We all will cheer,
But extra days in summer is to fear.

We love winter but we miss the sun.
The trees twist and shine at night,
But the trees are wired from Christmas lights.
We love winter but we miss the sun.

FUTURE

Are we alone?

The thick darkness
Devours us whole,
And we look around
With our eyes closed.
We hold our breath.

How can we be?

We are too small
In such a big place.
Were we born too late
To define our faith?
No one knows.
No one knows.
No. One. Knows.

We gasp for air
And search once more.
We are alone, aren't we,
In this place so big
And we so small.

Ceremony of the Records

VIVIAN CONAN

Maeve, my mentee, told me that last New Year's Eve her older brother went to a party with his friends. It was the first time her family had not celebrated the holiday together.

"I'll trade you *Tchaikovsky's Piano Concerto* for *Judy Garland at Carnegie Hall*," Marvin said, pulling an album from his stack.

"No way."

"How about the *Tchaikovsky* and *Schubert's Unfinished*?"

"Deal!"

It was past midnight in late August 1965, and my brother and I were sitting on the floor of his room, dividing our only communal property. We had started hours earlier, each selecting one album from more than 100, until we had two stacks equal in number. Now we were bartering. Even as we joked, I felt the solemnity of the occasion. It was the last time either of us would call Seventy-fourth Street home. Marvin was twenty. Tomorrow, he would stow his records in the trunk of my mother's 1958 Ford Fairlane, now his, and drive to Michigan State to begin work on his PhD in psychology. I was twenty-three, working toward a graduate degree in library science at Pratt. In two weeks, I would bring my records to the apartment I was moving into with my friend, a few miles away.

I was looking forward to escaping from my father's many rules. About the temperature and windows and cross ventilation. About never varying the arrangement of food in the refrigerator, so the nonexistent blind person who lived with us would be able to find everything. About noise we could not control, because it came from neighbors. When I had my own apartment, I would no longer have to tiptoe. I could even make a hamburger in the middle of the night.

Marvin and I made the last swap at 12:30, too late to talk. Carrying my records to my room in batches, I was happy, but also sad. In just a few hours, life as I had known it for twenty-three years would cease. The end of an era, I thought, placing the last album on my desk.

I whispered good night to Marvin and closed my door.

ROCHELLE SMITH

YEARS AS MENTEE: 1

GRADE: Sophomore

HIGH SCHOOL: Vanguard High School

BORN: New York, NY

LIVES: Queens, NY

PUBLICATIONS AND RECOGNITIONS: Vanguard Academic Award, Fall Term 2016–2017 in Recognition of Excellence in Art

MENTEE'S ANECDOTE: *This is my first year at Girls Write Now. The experience I have had so far is indescribable. Marie has been beyond amazing and I am so glad to have her as my mentor. Seeing outstanding authors at the workshops has been inspiring to me as a writer. This program has been one of the best experiences of high school.*

The pair session I enjoyed most was when Marie and I went to Strand bookstore, bought a stack of one-dollar books, and made found poems at Caffè Bene. It was my first time making found poems and I had a blast.

MARIE SCARLES

YEARS AS MENTOR: 1

OCCUPATION: Associate Editor, *Tricycle: The Buddhist Review*

BORN: Albany, NY

LIVES: Brooklyn, NY

PUBLICATIONS AND RECOGNITIONS: I had a poem featured on *Yes, Poetry*. My first chapbook, *Joy Machine*, will be published in April 2018.

MENTOR'S ANECDOTE: *Rochelle's enthusiasm and energy are infectious. It makes writing and editing together a joy. We have spent many evenings at coffee shops, combing through pieces Rochelle has written, snacking on grilled cheese, and writing side-by-side. One time when I was editing one of her stories, I noticed the person next to me peering over at my screen. When I told him what the story was about—it was a sci-fi thriller with a twist at the end—he was floored by the plot. As Rochelle's mentor, I am lucky enough to get that feeling every time I read her creative work.*

A Woman with Power

ROCHELLE SMITH

This piece was not planned in advance. One night, my mother came home after work and we had this exchange. I felt our relationship— one I had struggled to build—come together.

I heard the keys jingle as they turned the lock on the door. Quickly, I said goodbye to my friend and continued to do my homework. I sat there practically shaking in the wooden chair at the thought of my mother coming in and yelling at me. I kept my ears open to listen for her every action.

I heard her footsteps get closer to the door, and soon the door opened. She looked at me; I looked back at her. She showed me a small smile and asked, "Lots of homework?" I stared at her, confused, as she proceeded to give me a hug and a kiss on the top of my head. "Yeah, it's been quite the load this week," I answered.

My mother sat down on the mattress on the floor where she sleeps and looked up at me. Her makeup was smudged around her eyes. Her eyes were red with exhaustion. She started to take off her shoes, trying to get comfortable from all the walking she did with heels on.

She sat there and asked me about my day, asked about my homework. She started talking to me as if it was a normal afternoon, not one in the morning on a school night.

She talked to me like she had all the time in the world. Her lips moving. Endless chatter entering one ear and filtering out the other. She would smile her biggest grin, then her eyes would water, but nothing would fall. The red tint of her eyes made from the combination of exhaustion and sorrow.

"Rochelle, there's just so much to be done. So many things I have to do. I have to support you guys, your aunt, and your father and I'm only one woman. There is only so much I can do alone." I simply nodded. She continued to talk.

As she sat there, she looked so amazing—brave and strong—despite her unflattering appearance, her eyeliner smudged around her eyes, the roots of her graying black hair showing. I looked down at her thinking, *she deserves so much more than what she has now.* Seeing her on that mattress on the floor brought tears to my eyes. Tears she should have been crying. Every word she spoke was one of sadness, but still she chose to look at me and smile. She told me everything was okay.

"I'll do whatever I can to help you guys, but please try and help me out a little too, okay?" She phrased it like a question, but her eyes were pleading. With those eyes she was asking me to share some of her burden. Again, I simply nodded and gave her a small, reassuring smile as if to say, *everything's okay.*

She told me, *everything we're going through is temporary*; she told me, *it is all going to change.* After telling me this, she rubbed her forehead, the stress of the whole situation getting to her. The words she spoke were empty, waiting for the truth to be added to them. She said, *soon we will have everything we ever asked for* and *it is on me to change the life we live.*

The invisible pressure of stress was weighing her down; now I could see it. It was so clear to me. At 7:30 every night after work she would run around the house, vacuuming and cleaning up, struggling to keep everything together. Struggling without telling anyone.

She dropped her hands from her forehead. She leaned back on her palms and smiled at the ceiling. There she sat, holding a heavy weight with her bright smile. Even if she looks in the mirror and says, "Man, I look bad today," I would never be able to agree. Every time I see this woman, I see nothing but the unconditional love she shares.

She sat there, doing what mothers do best. She smiled and laughed when times were at their roughest.

True Beauty

MARIE SCARLES

This poem was inspired by a brave essay Rochelle wrote about beauty, body image, and friendship. She wrote about finding true beauty in her loved ones, not in what society tells women they should look like.

You know it when you see it, though men and women try to
    wear it
Like tailored coats, striding into lives where everything
Is worn in just the right way.

The city overflows with its approximated image—
In storefronts and on the sides of skyscrapers its glamorous masks
Catcall our weakest parts.

This image clutters us from within.

Sometimes, staring into the dark lake of the train's windowpane I
    feel I am the one
Smudging up the glass, smattering it with imperfection like flecks
    flung onto a mirror while flossing.
Other times, underground, I catch the eye of another girl staring
    too.
Her gaze floats up. Her head tilts back. The pout she had tacked
    to her mouth as if trying to lure herself back in closes, and
    we stand with the stillness of a reservoir.

We mirror its manmade depths until it yields.

Imagine now a mountain lake—no, imagine its source:
The seasonal shift from snowmelt to wildflowers, six months of
    powder-bundled rock
Giving way to warmth.

Picture the rivers streaming down its sides.

Feeding the springs
Filling the lakes
Calling green out from the stones.

EDEN DIAMOND STATEN

YEARS AS MENTEE: 1
GRADE: Senior
HIGH SCHOOL: High School of Art and Design
BORN: New York, NY
LIVES: Bronx, NY
PUBLICATIONS AND RECOGNITIONS: Scholastic Art & Writing Awards: Silver Key and Honorable Mention

MENTEE'S ANECDOTE: *More often that not, my meetings with Mara have given me something to look forward to. Thanks to her, I have learned how to set deadlines, accept criticism gracefully, and find even more confidence in my capabilities as a writer. Mara has also shown me that fear of rejection should never stop me from expressing myself—not only in writing, but in my everyday life. Whether it be helping me with supplemental essays for colleges or helping me celebrate my birthday, Mara has always been a consistent source of support not only as a writer, but as a friend.*

MARA NELSON-GREENBERG

YEARS AS MENTOR: 1
OCCUPATION: Tutor, Brownstone Tutors
BORN: Boston, MA
LIVES: New York, NY

MENTOR'S ANECDOTE: *Meeting with Diamond is always one of my favorite parts of the week. Over time we have developed a shorthand with one another. I first saw it when we were editing one of her poems. I gave her a note, but I was worried I wasn't articulating myself clearly, so I began trying to re-clarify my point. Before I could even finish, she said, "Like this?" and wrote a sharp new line that directly addressed the edit. This would not be the last time that Diamond used her writing to precisely respond to something that I was (imprecisely!) trying to say.*

In Search of Darker Planets

EDEN DIAMOND STATEN

For a long time I have struggled to verbalize how white supremacy has impacted my relationship to blackness. After many drafts, edits, and feedback, I have created a piece that not only illustrates this, but also the importance of rising up and speaking out against oppressive institutions.

In a piece for *The New York Times*, Claudia Rankine, a black poet and essayist, wrote that "the condition of black life is one of mourning." If you grew up as a black person in America, you know just how true and sad this statement is. You mourn for lost opportunities, lost futures, and lost histories. You mourn for all that has been denied to you and other people like you. Every black person I have ever met, liberal or conservative, knows to some extent that our history has been one tinged with suffering. Some may try to ignore it, but that shared knowledge still remains. We are reminded of it every day.

Growing up, the concept of racism was not foreign to me in the slightest. Internalized racism had planted its seed from an early age. In kindergarten, I used to squeeze the ends of my fingers until the skin there turned pale and bloodless, and wished for that to be my natural skin color. And I remember when a part of my morning routine involved waking up to updates on the Trayvon Martin case while getting ready for school.

However, it was not until the murder of Michael Brown that I started to truly interrogate the reality of systemic anti-blackness in America. I first learned about Brown's death through Tumblr, which was inundated with live streams of protests, articles about the shooting, and criticisms of America's so-called "justice" system. My Facebook was about the same. It was hard not to look away.

One muggy day in the summer of 2014, while at a bus stop, I broached the topic of Brown's death with my grandmother. She was not so much shocked at the circumstances of his death, but rather resigned. I expressed hope for a better, more racially tolerant future, but it felt meager, insufficient. She is a woman who grew up in the Jim Crow-era South; she was beyond surprise at the ways this country can mangle a black body. At that point, the shock was starting to wear off for me as well.

That fall, the grand jury ruled that Darren Wilson would not be indicted for the murder of Brown. In the nights that followed, I thought about how I, as well as my family and friends, could easily become another hashtag, another statistic, another memorial. There I was, at fifteen years old, contemplating how I would react if one of my older brothers had the misfortune of "fitting a description." But what struck me about this case in particular was not just the anger and despair it caused me, or the sheer brutality of it, even. It was that I finally had the words to articulate my fury; I had the power of knowing that there was a common thread between my desire for white skin and Brown's death at the hands of a white police officer. From there, the loosening of that thread could begin.

Since that summer, I have involved myself more in activism.

I have also learned the significance of shared, recognized pain. One of the most profound experiences I have had as an activist was attending a public wake for black women who were victims of state violence. To see such an outpouring of grief for those who are most likely to be pushed aside and forgotten was transformative. I learned how poignant it can be to put a name and face to our grief.

One day, I would like to become a professor and writer. I would like to reach other people like me who live with this anger and malaise they cannot name. I want to work to create a world where young black children never have to wish their skin bloodless in order to feel beautiful. This is a problem with no clear solution, a question with no simple answer. However, there is still meaning in this struggle. It has not been easy, but I must carry on.

Clio's Observation

MARA NELSON-GREENBERG

Recently, Diamond and I have been talking a lot about how to bring your unique point of view into your writing, a question that feels inextricably linked to the theme of Rise Speak Change. *This one-minute play addresses some of the things that came up during our conversations together.*

A living room. ERMA *tries to write, but she is stuck. She puts the pen down.* CLIO *steps out of a closet.* ERMA *looks up.*

ERMA: Clio! Where have you been?

CLIO: I was inside that closet for the past three years. I went in because I thought I would be able to observe interesting things about it from the *inside*.

ERMA: Sure. That makes sense.

CLIO: But then time passed. And the longer I was in there, the more the pressure mounted for my observation to be *really* interesting. So I kept not leaving. At one point I thought I'd never come out! But now I've finally got it. Closets are dork.

ERMA: Closets are . . . dork? Are you sure you don't mean . . . dark?

CLIO: Oh! That must be it. It's hard for me to write legibly when I'm in there, because it's so dork inside. Anyways, yes. Closets are *dark*. Trust me—I've been in one for three years.

ERMA: But I already knew that. I go into that other closet, over there, to get my coat every morning. It's always dark in there too.

CLIO: Hm. All right, then—so. Back into the closet for me! I'll try to come up with something more interesting next time. Wish me lork!

CLIO *exits into the closet and* ERMA *watches her go.* ERMA *looks around the room, sits down at the desk again, and begins to write.*

TASNIM TARANNUM

YEARS AS MENTEE: 1

GRADE: Junior

HIGH SCHOOL: Baccalaureate School for Global Education

BORN: Bogra, Bangladesh

LIVES: Queens, NY

MENTEE'S ANECDOTE: *From going with my mom on the subways to finally mastering them—well maybe not mastering them yet. At Girls Write Now, I met new friends who motivated me to write stronger pieces that I am proud of. I also have a mentor with whom I can share a saucer of molten hot chocolate as we discuss literature and politics. She says I should be proud of how much I have progressed and I concur. I have come a long way from that girl who stayed at home to someone who willingly ventures outside of the comfort of her home.*

NAN BAUER-MAGLIN

YEARS AS MENTOR: 3

OCCUPATION: Professor (retired) and writer

BORN: New York, NY

LIVES: New York, NY

PUBLICATIONS AND RECOGNITIONS: Coeditor, *Staging Women's Lives in Academia* (SUNY Press) and five other books

MENTOR'S ANECDOTE: *Tasnim has been fearless with her writing. She jumped right into trying out new genres: poetry and fantasy flash fiction. She is a hard worker. Simultaneously she takes IB classes in school and is applying to all sorts of scholarships, writing about personal change in a poem, a prose piece about a gift received, and recollection of a strange dream. Tasnim inspires me to risk more in my writing.*

Mother to Daughter: Don't Forget . . .*

TASNIM TARANNUM

This is not inspired by my mother, but by words I hear around me from the stranger-filled streets of Manhattan to my own community. It is a satirical piece that might speak for many women.

Don't forget to study hard.
Don't forget to tuck in the loose strands of hair
poking out from your hijab.
Don't forget to read the Holy Book,
it's your saving grace.
Don't touch that sliver of meat,
you don't know where it's been.
Don't take that first sip,
you don't know where it might lead.
Don't forget to cover up your rear with a long dress.
Don't forget to wear loose pants; others should not
    see your figure clearly.
Do not wear close-fitting shirts,
you don't want someone gaping at you.
Don't forget to wear your glasses,

---

*Inspired by "Girl" by Jamaica Kincaid, and "Rules for Being a Modern Woman in New York City" by Lauren Hesse from *(R)evolution: The Girls Write Now 2016 Anthology.*

you know
you can't see without them.
Don't forget to study hard.
But don't
forget to help others,
especially your sister.
Remember family is of utmost importance.
Don't forget to be in bed by eleven,
but by ten is ideal.
Don't forget to bring all your school supplies with you,
your notebooks and binders—
no matter how heavy.
We did not buy all of those
for you to leave
collecting dust
while you idly waste time
without a care in the world.
Honestly do you think the world
is so forgiving?
Don't forget your Metro Card.
Don't forget to be courteous
to all those around you,
yes even the annoying kid who
stole your class notes.
Well all I can say is I am glad
you took
your binder with you.
Don't fret over little things.
We want to make sure you
abide by the rules at all times.
Don't forget to wear a hijab

that actually goes with your clothing
and skin tone.
You know you can't pull
that white hijab off;
you're not pale enough.
Don't forget to comb your hair,
you don't want someone thinking
you came from the
streets.
But I don't look that bad!
We did not raise you like that.
Don't tell little white lies,
they may come back to bite you
when you least expect it.
Remember to look your best
so at least the illusion
that nothing is wrong with you
is always
there.

I Stand Here Weeding[*]

NAN BAUER-MAGLIN

At a Girls Write Now Persona Poetry workshop, we practiced writing from the voice of someone we did not know. I channeled my daughter's Colombian birth mother, a woman my daughter has not been able to locate.

Feet on the ochre earth
root vegetables sprouting
hoe in hand
I stand here weeding

days, months, years go by
I plant, I weed, I dig, I pull
and I miss her who
I never knew.

"Sometime I feel like a motherless child"[†]
sometimes I feel like a childless mother
as a girl I sang "Soy Colombiano"
and listened to Billie Holliday on the radio
not knowing her pain would be mine

wrapping my threadbare shawl around me
my feet on the ochre earth

---

[*]With reference to Tillie Olson's "I Stand Here Ironing."
[†]"Sometimes I Feel Like a Motherless Child," score by William E. Barton, D.D., 1899.

I wonder where her feet touch
somewhere far from here
some big city some fancy family.

I pull roots as she was pulled
red crying
from my fifteen-year-old body.
"Sometimes I feel like a motherless child
a long ways from home."

JANIAH TAYLOR

YEARS AS MENTEE: 1
GRADE: Sophomore
HIGH SCHOOL: Academy for Young Writers
BORN: Brooklyn, NY
LIVES: Brooklyn, NY

MENTEE'S ANECDOTE: *When I first started my pair sessions with Mel, we went to a library before going to our local cafe. One of the warm-ups that we did was to pick a random book, close our eyes, pick out a sentence, and write a new story using that sentence. I enjoyed doing this a lot because it helped expand my writing more creatively, and it was always fun to do.*

MELISSA STANGER

YEARS AS MENTOR: 2
OCCUPATION: Site Editor, *Revelist.com*
BORN: Rockville Centre, NY
LIVES: Brooklyn, NY

MENTOR'S ANECDOTE: *Since our first pair session together, Niah and I have been keeping a personal dictionary of new words we learn together. These are words we use to describe each other's work, words we read in writing examples from workshops, and other stories we share. It's been such an enriching experience to see that dictionary of ours grow as our mentor-mentee relationship has grown, too.*

The One I Need

JANIAH TAYLOR

I have noticed a change in my brother. It took six years, but he has changed. But when I look at him, I feel our connection, coming back slowly piece by piece. Only time will tell.

Kareem is quiet. Rarely ever speaking, and when you ask him a question, he will give you a low grunt, meaning either yes, no, or leave me alone. Though caring, he won't show it much. Try and touch him, he'll slap you. Give him a hug? Oh no, you get a rough push to the ground. That is his way of being nice.

He never seemed to care about life before; he was living just because he seemed obligated to do so. He never seemed happy . . .

When I was younger and I cried, which was a lot, he would always tell me to shut up. I would never go to him for support because he had what only seemed to be hate for me and he would always just push me away.

Yet this day was different.

I was about nine years old. My brother, only a year and a half older, was in charge. A few days before this, we went to see a Broadway Christmas show. Our mom got the last of a very delicate ornament as a souvenir. It was pretty large, about the size of a lightbulb. It was blue and had characters from the show on it.

That day we were putting up the tree, and Kareem and I were hanging the last of the ornaments.

"Let's put this one up," my brother said, pointing to the Broadway ornament.

"We shouldn't; Mom said not to touch it."

"We'll surprise her; it's okay."

I caved in and helped him unwrap it and bring it to the tree. We started to fight over who got to put it up and then CRACK. There it was, broken in half on the floor. At first, we tried to fix it with glue. Then my mother's footsteps came towards us.

Kareem threw the ornament in the box and I hid the materials. We bolted up the stairs and before I could lock myself in the bathroom, my mom's voice shook the house.

There was nothing my brother and I could do. In the old, dark, eerie hallway only the light from the bathroom aimed brightly at my mother's face.

"I ask you one simple thing, a simple task, and you can't seem to do that," she started. I stood there straddling the bathroom and the hallway barely looking at her, my eyes peered to the ground. My brother stood by his bedroom door, which was basically like a closet, giving the same blank stare as usual. I tried to open my mouth but her eyes stopped me. The look in her eyes gave me a feeling that you should never feel. It seemed so cold and heartless when it was unintended. I believed my brother felt this, too, for when she looked at him, he seemed scared for the first time.

"You should both be ashamed. When I ask something it should never be questioned. Do you know how much that Christmas ornament cost? Where will I find one like that again?" she went off.

She looked at my brother, who stood silent in his doorway.

"Nothing to say, Kareem?" she said sarcastically. He shook

his head without even looking up. "What about you, Janiah?" she said, glaring at my weak body.

"I'm sorry, Mommi," I sputtered out, holding back my tears.

"Sorry won't fix what you did," she said, walking away.

The stairs creaked as she went down to the basement. It was only silence, and I remember Kareem's heartbroken eyes towards me. The wind rustled against the window and the house seemed abandoned. Neither of us knew what to say. Kareem came towards me, trying to grab my hand, and I went into the bathroom and closed the door, only remembering the sorrow in his face before I was alone.

I sat down on the dull-colored toilet seat and cried my eyes out. The bathroom seemed sad like me, with the off-white tiles and the broken window that let in the draft and gave an ominous light. This was my safe space. The light brown granite sink was my armrest. I got up to look at myself in the three-paneled mirror. My eyes were bloodshot and my face looked drained. I could not bear to see myself.

When I opened the door it was just my weary shadow there to greet me. I turned, slowly, to find my brother standing there. The tension in his eyes made me nervous, so I looked down.

"I'm sorry," was all I could seem to spill out. I felt the tears creep up again, and thinking he would yell or just walk away, I felt his arms wrap around me so gentle like a blanket. He cried with me; I felt his tears fall on my shoulder. He held me tighter and he did not want to let go. And neither did I.

The Heron

MELISSA STANGER

This is an excerpt from a longer piece and was inspired by the life of Carrie Fisher, whose portrayal of General Leia Organa in Star Wars *inspired my own strength as a woman and as a writer.*

When Alder got back to Earth, he was different—which is to say, he was exactly the same.

The boy of seventeen I had known at military school, with the shock of red hair and smattering of freckles under the bridge of his horn-rimmed glasses, the stooped posture of an adolescent who couldn't keep up with the growth of his thin frame, he was the same. But the man of thirty inside, with the universe now in his pocket and the hull of a decade of loneliness surrounded by stars, he was a stranger to me.

I guess traveling at the speed of light will do that to a soldier.

I was hunched and squinting over my computer, working a bug out of a bit of code, when the call came in to Intelligence. *The Heron* had been found, they said, and my heart stopped. Staff Sergeant Alder Rosser, they said, was the only one left on board, and my heart started beating again.

When they guided *The Heron* down to base, I watched them escort Alder, gaunt and patchy with a five o'clock shadow, a Mylar blanket draped across his lean shoulders, out of the craft. It was him, but it wasn't; he looked like Alder, but he wasn't the same Alder standing there, a tremor about his entire body. I felt a rise of adrenaline, my breath catching in my throat, as I realized, this man . . . I didn't know him anymore. I stood, crowded with the other members of our class, as a couple of lieutenants held us back at a safe distance.

"Give the man some space," one barked, but he was looking over his shoulder at the bustling on the tarmac behind him.

I shouldered my way to the front of the crowd and Alder saw me—or, he looked like he saw me, my hand raised in a meek wave, searching his face, but Alder just stared back with hollow eyes as two medics guided him away by his bony elbows.

I felt the eyes of my fellow soldiers hot on my face as they tried hard not to stare.

"What happened to the others?" whispered one soldier, whose name, I think, was Cartwright, into the ear of another.

"Gone," she whispered back. I could hear the bounce of her curls against her shoulders as they turned and walked away.

MEEK THOMAS

YEARS AS MENTEE: 3

GRADE: Senior

HIGH SCHOOL: Uncommon Charter High School

BORN: Brooklyn, NY

LIVES: Brooklyn, NY

PUBLICATIONS AND RECOGNITIONS: University of the Arts Creative Writing Scholarship

MENTEE'S ANECDOTE: *My mentor, Carlene, has pushed me to take risks in my writing as well as in my personal life. This past summer, I was offered the opportunity to go to Philadelphia for a creative writing program thanks to Girls Write Now. At first, I didn't want to apply to the scholarship, for fear of being rejected, but since one of our pair goals last year was to take risks, I went for it. As soon as I got in, I told Carlene. She was beyond proud, as well as surprised at my leap of faith.*

CARLENE OLSEN

YEARS AS MENTOR: 3

OCCUPATION: Freelance writer

BORN: New Haven, CT

LIVES: Brooklyn, NY

MENTOR'S ANECDOTE: *My mentee, Meek, challenges me to be more creative, always. During one of our pair sessions, she shared some writing from her summer program at the University of the Arts, including an amazing screenplay. I loved the quirky, unique characters and the narrative tension. A doctor who lives in his car and eats greasy fast food? Yes, please. Thanks to Meek, I'm now working on a screenplay of my own and exploring a new writing genre. I'm so excited Meek will be heading to her first-choice college in the fall, though I'll miss our coffee chats in Brooklyn.*

Graduation

MEEK THOMAS

For the last four years, I feel like I have learned the least in the class-room and the most actually engaging with other students. In this piece, I touch on what is wrong with student/teacher relationships and why school is no longer fun, using my pen to rise, speak, change.

On June 8, 2017, I will prance across the stage and receive my diploma having absorbed bits and pieces of U.S. history, geometry, and health sciences, but what is that worth? Will it stick? Will it even matter to me in the next four, or forty, years? The only thing I'm certain of—completely sure of—is the way my fingers feel curled around a pen.

High school is meant to prepare students for the real world, but it has yet to teach me anything that matters. Like how to file taxes. Or snap my fingers with my non-dominant hand. Or how to feel safe walking down the street at night and still be a woman—still be strong. How to make an impact. How to sit in a classroom, stare at the board, and actually comprehend what they are saying. How to apply those lessons to real life.

Instead, I have learned to stay quiet and speak only when I am spoken to. I have learned the difference between love and ownership, and how to block out newborn wails at two in the morning. I have learned to scream in the silence, to be recognized. I have learned how to fall off a bike, never to ride one. I have learned to demand permission to go to the bathroom. I have learned to ask questions until I semi-understand. I have learned that "Did you do my homework?" has replaced "Good morning," and not to question why. I have learned babies speak half human and half God. I have learned they expect us to understand.

We are kept in lines. Like soldiers, we are told to stand head-behind-head and look forward. We are taught that being the line-leader is a treasure, a true prize. It is how they keep us moving forward. But I do not feel like I am moving forward.

On graduation day, I will walk across the stage. I will smile. I will laugh. I will tell my teachers I will miss them. I will lie and say it was the best four years of my life, I will lie and say I will visit, I will lie and say I feel prepared, ready to take on the world, ready to sit in more cold classrooms and learn from professors who do not look like me. But the one thing that remains true, above all else, is the power of a sentence and the way my hands fit around a pen.

High School Listicle

CARLENE OLSEN

Meek inspired me to think back on my high school experience, and I wrote this piece as a stream of consciousness, reflecting on the people and experiences that led me to rise, speak, change. These are the memories that stayed with me, much more so than my grades.

When I close my eyes. When I close my eyes and think about high school. When I close my eyes and think about high school, here is what I see.

Green dragons. Rows of pale yellow lockers in every hallway, around every corner. Rubber gym floors. The kind that make sneakers screech. The smell of chlorine. The way some girls got out of swimming during "that time of the month" with a nurse's note, and a signed note from home. Imagine asking permission to not do something—to not swim.

Italian class. True, our teacher played favorites. "Oh, Giustino!" she would say with a laugh, every time Justin spoke. But it was okay. We were the favored ones. Nutella. The smell of the cafeteria. Lunch tables. Fry day on Friday when we pooled our change and bought fries to share. But mainly, we brought lunch. Yogurts. Peanut butter sandwiches. Cookies—the home-made kind.

Textbooks. The weight of them, like lugging bricks. Notebooks with metal spirals. One page never left the rest without a mess. The bus. Saving a seat every afternoon, so the two of us could ride home together. He knew he could take his time, chat with friends, stroll in just as the wheels began to turn. But I didn't know he knew. I didn't know how to play hard-to-get when I so madly wanted to be gotten. So I would get there early and wait. Wait to hear him say, "Hey." And wait for an invitation to homecoming. And wait for an invitation to prom. An invitation that would not come.

Other invitations would, though. Invitations to birthday parties. The beach. Camping trips. And once, a Yale frat party. Our student teacher invited us. And we went. And felt grown up, for a moment, as we stood and watched games of beer pong. "Sippin' on Coke and." Coke. Graduation. Graduation parties. Jumping in the town fountain. In a dress. A rebirth of sorts. Or just a fun afternoon. Before the next step. Before college, and new addresses, and first jobs, and the rest.

SOPHIA TORRES

YEARS AS MENTEE: 1
GRADE: Junior
HIGH SCHOOL: Harvest Collegiate High School
BORN: New York, NY
LIVES: Queens, NY

MENTEE'S ANECDOTE: *Heather's awesomeness pushed me to develop my own writing style. Through that I was able to experience different types of writing styles in my own work while also learning from the girls in the program.*

HEATHER KRISTIN

YEARS AS MENTOR: 10
OCCUPATION: Writer at *Huffington Post*, public speaker, storyteller, advocate for the homeless, and violin teacher
BORN: New York, NY
LIVES: Brooklyn, NY
PUBLICATIONS AND RECOGNITIONS: *Woman's Day;* keynote speaker for the Get In Touch Foundation and Sterling House Community Center; Highlight of the year was being a craft talk speaker for Girls Write Now.

MENTOR'S ANECDOTE: *When Sophia and I began writing together, we had a lot of commonalities and had much to learn from each other. We had both been self-harmers and were ready to share our stories to help others feel less shame. We used Hillary Clinton's message and became stronger together.*

Superheroes

SOPHIA TORRES

When writing this piece I tried to cast a light on people around the world who continuously fight for their rights and to protect the people around them. I hope you enjoy my piece.

In the age of superheroes crusaders smash their comic book cages,
now dominating culture
These powerful superheroes devise a system
that impacts modern powers.

We define most in favor of their deepest cultural footprints,
have them individually averaged to create an overall for each.
The result will be from our own rankings,
your groundbreaking choice.

Just because each hero is ranked
we choose who will occupy that name.
They do not obtain imaginative abilities
but they carry something better.

Powerful superheroes appear to the world
as average people running through the streets.
One glance and the title "*superhero*" would not
have crossed your mind.

Sirens and gut instincts guide these people
through dangerous situations or threats.
They fight for what is right,
and they fight to make things right.

Powerful superheroes are not green,
they are not created with steel,
and their face remains bare.
Nothing stumps or conceals these crusaders.

Hate sweeps the nation
but heroes speak against it.
Bans are placed but they will not stand.
Walls are built but they will not obstruct.

Together they take each other's hands
and crush their jail bars.
They force themselves out of those cages
with their plans and determination.
With inspiration up their sleeves
they rise to the occasion to set it loose.
With confidence they chant their beliefs
using their skill to make their opinions known.

Crusaders fight villains across the country.
Those who exist within the government or out in the street.
They attract the attention needed to etch those footprints
deep into the ground.

Powerful superheroes make an effort
to understand a villain's point of view.
They do not shoot them down
unless it is apparent they need to take them down.

Crusaders protect the people around them.
Once purposely targeted because of gender, race, religion,
or sexual orientation, those crusaders use their capabilities
to protect and persuade.

To bring attention to human rights
they devise that system,
they use that system,
and they combat those who want to destroy it.

They can slap a couple of villains
with their words or with their palm.
They can inspire and can bring forth
more heroes willing to do the same.

As leaders we choose who is going to impact
our life positively or negatively.
As leaders we also decide who is going to impact
the world.

In the age of superheroes crusaders smash their comic book
    cages,
now dominating culture.
These powerful superheroes devise a system
that impacts modern powers.

We define most in favor of the deepest cultural footprints,
had them individually averaged to create an overall for each.
The result is *your* own rankings,
our groundbreaking choice.

I Am Wonder Woman

HEATHER KRISTIN

"If you are silent about your pain, they'll kill you and say you enjoyed it," wrote Zora Neale Hurston. That's why I wrote this personal essay about women's rights to rise, speak, change.

On the day of the historic Women's March in New York City, where blocks away, some 400,000 women chanted for President Trump to respect women, a lady screamed, "Help! This man is following me."

The woman, about my height at five-foot-five, dashed into the traffic. The man, six-foot-one, ran after her into Union Square Park.

I can either go home or I can help, I thought.

As a kid in New York, I had been followed, cornered, leered at, called names, attacked, and mugged by men much larger than me. I couldn't let this happen to another woman.

I thought about my two young daughters back at home. What if he pulled out a gun? I felt torn, but my gut said, *I'm not going to take it anymore. I'm standing up to this scum.* I followed them into the park.

I wouldn't be able to physically protect her if he attacked her. So, I filmed them on my phone. Even if it was blurry, I'd have a record.

Then they exited the park. She flagged a taxi and got in. The man stood in front of the car, blocking it. The driver honked.

The man yelled, "You bumped into me first!"

The taxi drove off and the man walked toward me. My heart

raced. I fumbled with my phone, still recording. He acted as if he had done nothing wrong. Like it was totally normal to chase after a woman.

I was beyond angry. I followed him down the block, determined to get a photo of his face to show the world what a screw-head he was. Finally, he stopped and turned. I walked up to him and snapped a photo. He glared at me. I ran into the subway and texted his photo to my husband, just in case something happened.

Later, over dinner, I told my young daughter about following and filming the not-so-nice man and how we must protect each other.

She said, "Brave, Mommy. Like Wonder Woman!"

I hope she knows, men don't have the right to control us, even if the woman bumped into the man first or said something nasty. Women should not be silenced like Senator Elizabeth Warren was on the senate floor when she read Coretta Scott King's words.

We, Wonder Women of the world, will put an end to the bullying, intimidating, harassing, and silencing.

You've been warned, Mr. President.

JAELA VAUGHN

YEARS AS MENTEE: 3
GRADE: Senior
HIGH SCHOOL: Richard R. Green High School of Teaching
BORN: Bronx, NY
LIVES: Bronx, NY

MENTEE'S ANECDOTE: *"It was the best of times, it was the worst of times . . ."* It is mostly the best of times when I am with my lovely mentor, Laura. We have spent the past three years learning to better ourselves and our writing. She encourages me to love editing, and I try to show her the joy of writing sad stories. I've learned to edit without becoming impatient and open myself up to different genres. Girls Write Now gives me inspiration to write and share my thoughts with the world. Without them I would not have met Laura; I do not know where I would be without her.

LAURA BUCHWALD

YEARS AS MENTOR: 3
OCCUPATION: Freelance writer/editor
BORN: New York, NY
LIVES: New York, NY

MENTOR'S ANECDOTE: *By the time you read this, Jaela will know where she's going to college, I will, hopefully, be done with my novel, and who knows where else we will be? It's been a pleasure working with Jaela over the past three years, watching her grow from a shy sophomore who wrote Sherlock fanfiction into a confident senior who has explored many different genres of writing, and who writes and experiments with confidence. And, dare I say, she has learned to value the editing process and to accept it as a necessary part of the writing life. Thank you, Girls Write Now!*

The "L" Train

JAELA VAUGHN

This is an idea for a longer work I intend to write. It revolves around two women who love each other, and learn how to rise, speak, change, and love themselves as well. My inspiration is the messiness that is the New York Metropolitan Transportation Authority.

> *Falling in love is a lot like taking the train. First, you must wait.*

Olivia nodded her head to the *Phantom of the Opera* theme song. She hummed it softly as she stared down the dark tunnel from which her train would emerge. The "5" train was coming in four minutes, adding to the ten minutes she'd already waited. She was going to be subject to another lecture from her boss: "You are an intern, you cannot afford to be thirty minutes late to work . . ." Maybe if she bought him a latte and a croissant the lecture would be brief.

"*That voice that calls to me . . . and speaks my name . . .*" Olivia mouthed as she tapped her foot in rhythm. She would have lost her mind by now if it were not for her show tunes. She had lots of Broadway musicals in her library.

The 5 was two minutes away. She moved to be the first to board and felt something bump into her. She took an earphone out and turned to see who'd almost pushed her onto the tracks.

It was a young woman.

"I'm sorry!" the woman said. "I didn't mean to bump into you—I was just so into my book."

Olivia shook her head. "Don't worry about it. Here, let me help you."

Olivia bent down to help the young woman gather her things and saw that it was schoolwork. *She looks a year or so younger than me*, she thought. *She must be a college student.* Her conclusion proved correct when the woman stood up and flashed her Hunter sweatshirt.

Olivia realized that she was holding all the schoolwork, while the student held just her book. She got to her feet and the young woman took her work and shoved it in her backpack.

"Good book?" Olivia joked.

"Oh, it is!" the woman exclaimed. "*The Picture of Dorian Gray* by Oscar Wilde. Have you read it?"

Olivia smiled, her interest piqued. "I love that book, and Wilde, too." Her smile grew as she saw the excitement rise in the other woman.

"You do? Everyone else I talk to only seems to have heard of the book, or know the gist of it."

Olivia paused her music, "My Friends" from *Sweeney Todd*. Her attention went back to this person who continued talking and gushing about Oscar Wilde, despite losing Olivia's attention briefly. She wore an afro, curly and brown. She was lighter than Olivia's chocolate skin, like caramel. Her eyes were big and round and brown. Her glasses were rectangular. Her face was bare, unlike Olivia's. Her lips were pink and soft and smiling. Her cheeks were plump and dimpled. She dressed casually. Olivia put her headphones away.

"Tell me, what do you think about it?" the woman asked.

"I wrote the majority of my college essays on *Dorian Gray*.

On the fragility of the human ego and the desire to retain youth . . ." Olivia blushed. The student laughed.

"What happened?"

"Nothing. I just realized that I sound like a professor. I didn't mean to." Olivia kicked herself.

"I asked, right? I would love to hear more about your thoughts on Wilde!"

The sound of the train halted their conversation and they moved to the side of the door to let the passengers off. They boarded and were about to resume when the loudspeaker went off.

Trains don't always run perfectly. Sometimes we need to figure out another route.

"Attention, ladies and gentlemen, due to a sick passenger, this train will be out of service. You must depart; this train is not in service."

Groans and curses filled the car as people filed out. Olivia was going to lose her mind. She watched anxiously as the doors closed and the train left the station.

"Hey!" the woman said. "The '6' is coming in three minutes; you can take it with me. I was only taking the '5' to save some time."

"Aren't you going to be late to classes?"

"Yeah, but chances are everyone else is going to be late, too."

"My boss is going to have my neck if I don't get to work soon. Of course, I'll be the only person late."

"I could try and be optimistic for you if you want."

Olivia laughed and shook her head. "No thank you. I'm more of a glass-half-empty girl."

Their conversation died down, and they looked down the tunnel waiting for the "6" to arrive. Olivia turned to face her new friend and said, "You know, I don't think we've introduced ourselves. I'm Olivia."

The student blushed. "I'm Grace."

Before either of them could say anything more, the 6 train came rushing into the station. It wasn't crowded; the rest of the express train crowd was waiting for the 4. When the doors opened, Grace took Olivia's hand and led her to a three-seater in the corner of the car. Grace opened her book and looked at Olivia.

"Now, let's pick up where we left off."

Olivia laughed and nodded. "Okay."

No matter the route, you'll get to your stop.

Aftermath

LAURA BUCHWALD

These are excerpts from my last two blog posts of 2016. The events of last November forced many of us to rise, speak, and change. It is said that creativity, too, is a radical act, and so I continue to work on my fiction and encourage Jaela to do the same.

November 11

No, walking the streets of New York today is not like the aftermath of 9/11. Back then we were a different kind of scared, and in New York at least, we were all on the same side.

Now, I've heard about aggressive, racist bullying of people in my community. I've heard about a young gay man who was attacked moments after the results were in.

Can you blame these bullies for acting out? When the future leader of the free world spends over a year mocking and insulting everyone in his path, when he does not condemn the violence at his rallies—the bullies, the racists, the homophobes are empowered.

This is not about politics. This is about human rights, empathy, and all that I and the vast majority of the people in my life hold dear.

December 25

I have been complacent for too long, and it is time to change that. In a strange way I feel as though I am finally finding my purpose in life. I know my strengths and talents, but purpose is an entirely different thing. My other purpose, at present, is to finish my novel.

This long road will begin in earnest after January 20. And while it has been argued that these forms of silent and vocal protests won't change things, in fact they will. They will prove to the world that not all Americans accept what this administration intends for this country. This will get many of us involved at the most local levels, so that we can change the course of things from the bottom up. We will do everything we can to maintain the things that make this country beautiful, and those include its ethnic, religious, and cultural diversity.

Today is Christmas and I am with loved ones in Paris. Despite all that this city and country have been through in recent years, Paris still offers the timeless beauty and romance that claimed me the first time I visited.

The Seine still flows, the Eiffel Tower still sparkles at night, the gryphons and gargoyles still guard Notre Dame. The sights and sounds and smells and tastes that I associate with this city remain, and this is comforting.

My goal for 2017 is to become stronger and wiser.

Whether you celebrate Christmas, Chanukah, Ramadan, Diwali, Kwanzaa, none of the above, all of the above, I wish you peace and joy.

SAMANTHA VERDUGO

YEARS AS MENTEE: 1
GRADE: Senior
HIGH SCHOOL: City College Academy of the Arts
BORN: New York, NY
LIVES: New York, NY
PUBLICATIONS AND RECOGNITIONS: Scholastic Art & Writing Award: Silver Key. Published brochure on adverse effects of microbeads and climate change on coral reefs on NOAA-CREST-HIRES website.

MENTEE'S ANECDOTE: *Lucy has not only been a great writing mentor, but also a great friend. I've never had a writing mentor, so this was definitely a novel experience. From visiting coral reef exhibits, eating Korean barbecue, to sharing funny stories about our life, she makes every moment personable and interesting. Having someone who has a critical eye (she knows what I mean before I even write it), is insightful, has great life advice, and strengthens my voice has been an invaluable experience.*

LUCY FRANK

YEARS AS MENTOR: 1
OCCUPATION: Writer
BORN: New York, NY
LIVES: New York, NY
PUBLICATIONS AND RECOGNITIONS: Author of eight novels including *Two Girls Staring at the Ceiling* (Random House/Schwartz and Wade); received the 2011 PEN/Phyllis Naylor Working Writer Fellowship.

MENTOR'S ANECDOTE: *I'd published two novels before I knew what it could mean to have a mentor—an interested, critical yet nurturing presence who believed in my voice, and more crucially, in me. "Surprise me," this editor said when I'd written something pedestrian, "I am utterly confident," when I sank into despair. I worked with him till he retired. It changed me forever. Now, as Sam's mentor, kicking around ideas, trading stories, helping her strengthen her already strong voice, I get to live that creative partnership from the other side. What a gift to be able to give back. What fun!*

An Extroverted Introvert

SAMANTHA VERDUGO

My first time at Buffalo Wild Wings was definitely wild. I wrote this on a total whim after I told my mentor, Lucy, about my experience and realized I had to share this heartfelt, unfiltered teen moment with the world.

We all slump into the cold metal chairs. Finals week always took a toll on us. My friends and I are in the Buffalo Wild Wings in Riverdale, ready to gorge on everything we lay our eyes on. In between bantering, we discuss the latest gossip in our high school—a tale of who cheated on who, and sip on iced tea while we wait for our waitress to arrive.

"Two orders of sweet BBQ, two teriyaki, and one blazin', please." My friend Ana never fails to speak with zest.

The waitress gives her a dubious look. "They're the spiciest wings in our menu and ya'll seem a little too young to handle it," she claims with a chuckle.

It only takes an assertive look and a "Let's fuck it up" from my friend Kat to convince the waitress.

"Ya'll remembered to eat right. You can't eat spicy stuff on an empty stomach," the meticulous planner, Ana, remarks.

My eyes widen. "I only ate a banana for breakfast. My burger will fill me up, plus I'm only going to have one blazin' wing. I'll be fine."

The waitress, a curvy woman with flexed arms and straight posture, holds up our food. Our eyes light up with joy as she sets the wings before us. We all take a bite of the blazin', partially wanting to test our limits and partially wanting to get it over with.

"It isn't that bad," my red-faced friend Brian, whose fair skin lights up like a stop sign, says with a wavering smile.

"This is a test of your will. This isn't meant to be enjoyed," another friend exclaims.

Half of the group finishes only half of a single blazin' wing, and I am one of them. I twist the cap of my milk bottle open, trying to decide if I need it to finish.

Most people have power songs, but I have power flashbacks. The milky way before me brings back vivid memories. I always woke up to the scent of boiling milk in Ecuador. My grandma and I got to know each other over warm milk and her honey-sweet words. With wrinkly hands, my grandma would turn the dial on the stove, and the crescendo of the open flame echoed throughout the halls. She wore her technicolored apron and wobbled over to the silver pot to sift the fresh milk from the residual pieces of creamy blob. As I walked in, she greeted me with a kiss on the cheek. School was always the motif in my "small talk" conversations with family members. But she had an admirable way with words. She was the kind of woman that turned small talk into big talk. *Sabes que eres mi orgullo. Pero, tienes que seguir así, no solo para superarte, sino también para mi Anita Lucia.* She would always tell me to continue working hard, that my efforts would pay off one day, and money would no longer be an issue for my mother and me.

I chug my mini bottle of milk and shove cold celery and carrot sticks into my mouth to ease the spiciness. I am determined to finish this four-centimeter piece of chicken, which contained six fresh habanero peppers (with seeds), five lemon drop peppers, and eight jalapeños (also with seeds).

Memories rush to my brain once again: the stress of college applications, disagreements between my father and me, all those times Calculus made me feel stupid, and the countless college interviews. The ones that made me suck up my shyness and get over the uncomfortable feeling of detailing my life story to a stranger who determined my future. "Own that shit. You need to go up there and tell them why you deserve to go there," Ana had said when I refused to meet my Cornell interviewer at the Cornell Club because I thought it would break my spirits, because I thought I wasn't good enough.

Taking a deep breath, I chug a second bottle of milk and finish my last bite of the blazin' wing. It's the pivotal moment. The burning sensation in my eyes from the spiciness coupled with my memories makes me burst into tears. "I can accomplish anything, dammit," I say in between sniffles.

"If you managed to finish that, then I can do half of what you can in life," Ana jokingly proclaims.

A compliment from the biggest go-getter I've ever met brings a smile to my face—the reassuring feeling left me wanting more. I didn't even touch my burger, to say the least, but I'm sure as hell ready to see what else I can accomplish.

Rise

LUCY FRANK

I'd planned to write something political, there being so much to rise and speak, if not scream about now, so much demanding change. Instead I found myself writing a quieter, more personal poem, about hope.

Overnight,
planter boxes reappear
outside the income tax store.
In last year's dirt
half a fortune cookie blooms.
Between bare oaks
still wound with Christmas lights
forsythia shows signs of yellow.
On a Broadway bench
a blear-eyed man lifts his face
to flimsy morning sun.
Out in LA, in March
jungle-bright begonias
strut their stuff beside primroses.
Lipstick-hued hibiscus nuzzle up
to pansies, dahlias to daffodils.
And everywhere, roses.
Here in New York
I lie on my yoga mat,
plant a cat atop my chest
and try to remember

how to breathe.
Tomorrow is my birthday,
the day the sun crosses the equator
for the start of spring.
I washed the windows yesterday.
Today I'll buy a brand new pack
of yellow writing pads,
paint my toes hibiscus red.

MAGGIE WANG

YEARS AS MENTEE: 1

GRADE: Senior

HIGH SCHOOL: Hunter College High School

BORN: Queens, NY

LIVES: Queens, NY

PUBLICATIONS AND RECOGNITIONS: Scholastic Art & Writing Awards: Gold Key, Honorable Mentions (3)

MENTEE'S ANECDOTE: *When we're not working on writing pieces for Girls Write Now, we're jamming out to old pop songs at cafes, struggling to connect to the WiFi, bringing mannequins to life, or staring at strangers. As we share our feelings on politics, irrational fears, and M. Night Shyamalan, I've realized how lucky I am to have Denise as my mentor, because she always listens to me without judgment and shares her advice and experiences with me. Her optimism and approach to life has made me more excited about trying new things, and she continues to inspire me.*

DENISE ST. PIERRE

YEARS AS MENTOR: 1

OCCUPATION: Agency Assistant, Jill Grinberg Literary Management

BORN: Halifax, Canada

LIVES: Queens, NY

PUBLICATIONS AND RECOGNITIONS: "The Beginner's Guide to Gardening," Indie Theater Now, 2015

MENTOR'S ANECDOTE: *Maggie is one of the most naturally gifted writers I've ever had the pleasure of working with. It has been a privilege to watch her grow, and in turn, be challenged by her. We've had so many amazing moments: trading favorite writers and artists, writing wacky monologues, and fashioning elaborate lives for strangers in Starbucks, all of which culminated in seeing her recognized with a Scholastic Gold Key for her work. The time we've spent together has been extraordinary, and while I'm gutted that we only got one brief year together, I can't wait to see what she conquers next.*

Model Minority Girl

MAGGIE WANG

As my senior year comes to a close, I wanted to focus on the way my environments and experiences have changed how I think of myself, to translate the feeling of not belonging into words.

Being a first-generation immigrant is often aligned with the struggle of balancing two different cultures—the impossible battle of trying to fit in and conform to both cultures while molding a separate identity. While culture is inherited, it is cultivated through one's environment. My inheritance of Asian and American identities has been shaped and molded to fit the environment I am in—a conflicting resolution to my sense of self.

As a Flushing native, I grew up surrounded by Asians and Asian Americans. My parents fit in perfectly with the boisterous crowds rushing past the test prep centers and bubble tea shops—a homogenous mesh of Chinese dialects and yellow skin. However, even in such a non-diverse community, there were still small differences that my parents draw pride from. As an East Asian, I was always told that I was simply superior. My parents claim another level of superiority, often looking down on other Asian immigrants who are not as well acclimated to American ways, have "country" dialects, or are less educated. For them, becoming Americanized was not the goal, but rather adapting and becoming successful in a foreign country. For them, having an Asian American daughter meant that I had an advantage over regular Asian immigrants and that I could be the perfect, obedient child.

My parents' ideals were reflected in elementary and middle school, where "Asian American" was synonymous with the best kind of conformity. My fellow classmates in the "Alpha" class and I saw ourselves through an elitist lens, as "the model minority"—superior because of our intersectionality, as if being Asian American was a superpower that separated us from everyone else. We looked down at the "FOBs"—the immigrants with the broken English and homemade lunches who we constantly sought to distinguish ourselves from. While it was bad to be an immigrant, it was also bad to be Americanized and called a "Twinkie": yellow on the outside, white on the inside. We began to try to top one another with the most ethnic experience we could regale. We shared the pains of Tiger Moms and forced lessons, be it violin, ballet, or Chinese folk dance, and the pressures of upholding the standard of the perfect Asian child.

We wanted to be exotic because we, with our perfect English scores and Lunchables, were still trying to figure out how to balance this duality of cultures. We did not know what it meant to be an Asian American, afraid we had conformed too much to the American lifestyle, and had lost sight of our Asian culture and traditions. I clung to what my parents expected of me because I thought their expectations reflected what a true Asian should be. So I committed to violin, even when my fingers became callused; committed to Chinese folk dance, even when my teacher grabbed my stiff, inflexible legs and forced me down; and committed myself to being the perfect Asian daughter with an English tongue, even when the only words I was allowed to say were: "Yes, I will do better."

When I entered Hunter College High School, I learned that not only did I not know what it meant to be Asian, but I also did not understand what it meant to be American. It used to be easy to be an Asian American. But at Hunter, there are no immigrants with broken English, and the desire to prove that we belong in this elitist, Upper East Side school was suffocating. For the first time, I wanted someone to call me a Twinkie. Among the Asian Americans, there were clear distinctions of popularity based on the ability to conform with American culture—TV shows, neighborhoods, stores, and music—nothing I had experienced before. I was afraid of being grouped with the girls who watched Korean dramas, who tried to emulate Japanese culture, or who tried to be the best in class. I did not want to be categorized in the subgroups for Asian girls, as if they were the only identities we could ever possess—never equal to the popular kids and their boundless identities. I felt like I had to prove myself every time I went to school, as if what I wore, where I went for lunch, and what kind of music I listened to meant that I was more than my skin. I grew ashamed of my Asian identity. Ashamed that every time I looked in the mirror, I could see why that white girl in my class confused me with my friend, even after being in the same class for a year.

This suffocating desire to conform over the years has made me realize that there is no guide to being an Asian American. No matter how many ways I try to distinguish myself, to perform for other people's perception of me, no one can tell me who I am. Being Asian American is my blood and birthright. I am not your Twinkie, your lesser, your copycat. I am not your Model Minority girl.

Better to Break

DENISE ST. PIERRE

I wanted to tackle the small shifts within ourselves in this poem, taking on moments both personal in their interiority and universal in their prevalence for so many women. We can rise above our fear, speak our truths, and change, but only for ourselves.

I was quiet once, unmoving
Let roving eyes, hands, lips, spirits
Take me over and under and along
Molding me from an unformed mass

Sculpting me in small parts
A thin, closed mouth
Slit, slash, or the other
Small hands, fists forever clenched

Better to break than bend indefinitely
I will always choose
The calamitous, splintering fracture
Over the suggestion of a slow-moving fissure

Rather topple off the precipice
Let wayward winds carry me down
Than cower before the impenetrable
Than make myself small again, unknowable

A blur of features, muted
I can be reassembled from dust

But I cannot become no one
Not again

Now I make myself up with blood,
Drawn from felled forms, streaked across my lips
Wear rattling necklaces of bones and teeth
On strands from a vanquished man's scalp

I leave a trail of bile
Drip, drip, dripping off my lip
I can count time by its persistence
Strange, it almost sounds like

No. No. No.

I've backed away into the earth
Let briar twist around the garden gate
Tearing at the flesh of those who would impose
Abandon all hope, ye who enter here

I don't want to hide
But sometimes, I waver, thinking
Maybe if I burrow deep enough
I can recuse myself

From those hungry, bloodied hands
Frenzied with need
Carving out corners
Of an unwanted smile

(Just smile, honey.)

DAYNA WILKS

YEARS AS MENTEE: 1
GRADE: Senior
HIGH SCHOOL: High School for Medical Professions
BORN: Kingston, Jamaica
LIVES: Brooklyn, NY
PUBLICATIONS AND RECOGNITIONS: Scholastic Art & Writing Award: Honorable Mention

MENTEE'S ANECDOTE: *Girls Write Now, an extensive and exciting program for young aspiring women writers, not only has given me the chance to explore different writing styles but also has helped me overcome my number one fear: letting someone read my work and accepting feedback. My mentor has assisted me in investing time in my work so I can expand on my writing, and she has even taught me how to critique work, whether or not it is my own.*

DANISE MALQUI

YEARS AS MENTOR: 1
OCCUPATION: Writer and personal motivator
BORN: Paterson, NJ
LIVES: Brooklyn, NY

MENTOR'S ANECDOTE: *Dayna has taught me enormously during our year together at Girls Write Now. As all high school seniors are, she is juggling a million and one things that will impact her future in a big way, but she still finds time to write. When I met her she had over sixty pages completed for her fantasy book about the seven deadly sins. Her achievement and commitment humbled me. My proudest moment with Dayna was when she rejected several of my edits and suggestions and trusted herself as a writer. She noted reasons for keeping her writing as is. Her instincts were perfect.*

Work of the Shadows

DAYNA WILKS

"Work of the Shadows" addresses the business of trafficking. Many believe either that it simply doesn't happen or that it only occurs in foreign "undeveloped" countries, but it happens even in the United States.

Dahlia, ten years old, lives with her brothers and sisters in the home of her captives, a couple who purchased her and her siblings from their home country. Her wavy brown hair is always down and her clothes are composed of an oversized t-shirt with leggings covered in dirt. She's in the business of selling smuggled goods her adoptive parents harbor at home to buying patrons on the black market. Patrons of the black market would occasionally stop by to purchase goods that ranged from gold to severed organs and body parts. During her sales in the slums of the city, she only has her mind to talk to and keep her company. If she couldn't make a decent enough amount of $1,048,000, eating would be no more than a distant hope. (Who is she talking to in the monologue? Where is she? What is she doing? And what has just happened? Think of this as a play and you are telling us what the setup is for her monologue. And where is this in the structure of the story?)

Don't look at me. Don't look at me with such sinful orbs you call eyes! I wanted to yell that so bad that it hurt. It hurts staying quiet. It hurts doing such a dirty job. How many of us are out there stuck in situations worse than mine? How many are being used day and night before being locked away in a dark pit to never see the light of day again? I shudder at the thought of that ever being me. I should be grateful, right? The sound of people, who I simply label as suit-cladded scum of the earth (who are they?), clambering about strangely pains my ears and the yelling only makes me feel worse. It was never quiet here; if it wasn't because of the patrons then it would be because of other vendors attempting to gain their attention by any means necessary. I'm sure if the sludge and dirt could speak, they'd be louder than everyone here since they're constantly being stepped on. Hmm, relatable. (What is the place like?) The sound of my own heartbeat even seemed to torture me to the point where there were nights when I'd imagine it slowing down into a steady waltz of One-Two, One-Two.

Hey, there's that girl I saw yesterday! The one with the shiny blond hair and ivory skin! I always thought she was beautiful in comparison to my own slightly tan skin and unkempt brown hair. I still think she's a goddess of some sort. Whenever she comes, she goes to the vendor man who sells what I believe to be severed hearts. (Where is she that she is seeing a girl? And is she pointing out her blond hair and ivory skin because they are different than her own?) She always looks so happy with those two people she calls "Mom" and "Dad." Is that her (bābā){Fa-ther} and (mā){Mother}? I can never help feeling jealous when I watch her strut away with her "mom" and "dad." In my spare time between sales, I find myself thinking about being back home with my brothers and sisters, yet, I left at such a young age that I can hardly remember what it looked like. But even so, I knew that it was nothing here. The sun was the first thing I'd see, then the endless fields of grass, flowers and farmland.

The air was fresh, unpolluted with the stench of trash and blood. (Where is home?) Being happy again and not a slave to a system that cares nothing for me. My eyes began to water at the thought, blurring my vision for a split second just for me to blink them away as a threatening shadow and heavy footsteps approach me (but I thought she was outside looking at the blond girl?). Arming myself with my strongest weapons, a blank face and soulless eyes, I look up, hands outstretched towards the man.

Rise Association

DANISE MALQUI

I wrote this piece while my mentee, Dayna, and I chatted and free wrote about Rise Speak Change. *It's playful and meandering. I loved our freewriting sessions, which reminded me that insight and fun can arise from a few minutes of nonstop writing.*

Rise is a word associated with up, with elevation, with floating. It reminds me of dough rising into bread. It reminds me of fists in the air and those images from the '70s: power revolutions, women with no bras, blacks and Puerto Ricans with natural 'fros.

Rise is also gentle and subtle. The rise of the soul when all the blocks, both from self and others, fall away. Our hearts fly beyond our limited bodies. This is enough to free you and your ancestors, your history, your past, present and future. It can lift up dead kin, you and great great grandkids.

Rise can be small too. That small rise of waking in the morning to brush your teeth. The tiny rise of taking pen and paper and scribbling. Sometimes that's the most important movement needed.

Then, speak and change will come.

But right now I think of music rising. I think of infinity rising. I think of the people rising. I think of the girls writing. The change doesn't matter so much in the present. Maybe the act is all we have right now. And then, we will reap.

SHANAI WILLIAMS

YEARS AS MENTEE: 1
GRADE: Sophomore
HIGH SCHOOL: NYC iSchool
BORN: New York, NY
LIVES: Bronx, NY

MENTEE'S ANECDOTE: *This was my best year of my writing career so far. Brooke showed me a whole new world by listening to me and helping me to find a way to communicate what I wanted through my writing. I'm looking forward to another year with her and Girls Write Now.*

BROOKE OBIE

YEARS AS MENTOR: 2
OCCUPATION: Author, *Book of Addis: Cradled Embers*
BORN: Kokomo, IN
LIVES: New York, NY
PUBLICATIONS AND RECOGNITIONS: *Book of Addis* featured in *Teen Vogue*

MENTOR'S ANECDOTE: *Shanai is just a joyful person. I remember in our first mentoring session at Au Bon Pain, she was in the middle of telling me about her week and she just stopped because Adele was playing over the loudspeaker and she just began to sing and laughed a little before returning to her story. She reminds me to find moments of joy no matter what.*

The Rebirth of Shanai Williams

SHANAI WILLIAMS

Human nature gets it into our minds that familiar and comfortable are best. But there are times where we must give way to a rebirth of our minds in order to get what we want.

Home of seven to a house of two
Once a place of love and joy
They've all moved on and left you

My head was dizzy with anticipation as I approached the blue double doors. It was my first day of freshman year, and I stared at my high school with so much hope. A sense of independence washed over me as well as an undeniable determination to succeed where I had failed before. This was my chance. I longed for a herd of people to call my own. I ascended the steps sure that I'd find at least one person, the person who I'd imagined would click together with me like Lego pieces.

The previous four years had been riddled with the loss of myself. My parents had split, which meant my brother and sisters did too. I was no longer the happy kid in a home of seven. The people who had given me my original sense of where I belonged in the world slowly went their separate ways. I craved the guidance and security I suddenly lacked. What better place to look than a high school full of hormonal teenagers?

When I entered homeroom, my smile bright, teeth reflecting all my ambitions in life, I was met with quiet, blank stares from the white faces staring back. My smile dissolved as I took the nearest seat. I attempted small talk with the three people at my shared table to no avail. I was ignored. I got the message, and kept to myself.

> *But at this*
> *Intersection*
> *of being a Black, Bisexual, Girl*
> *I am unsure*
> *Where*
> *to Rise.*

The wrinkled nose, the scrunched-up face. Here we go again. "*What's 'chopped' mean?*" I'd made friends, but I couldn't carry a conversation without having to explain the slang I was using. I longed for my Bronx peers. The boisterous, confident, care-free mix of black and Hispanic kids. The kids that understood me and kept me laughing, the ones who made me feel at home. Without them I was lost.

"Stop crying!" my mother yelled at me.

How? I couldn't understand how she could possibly think it was that easy. I wasn't angry at her for leaving without putting up a fight. I wasn't angry at my father for making her go. It was the slow progression of the only home I've ever known being broken apart that hurt. My father barely picked up my younger sister anymore, and visits from my older sisters became rare. My older brother moved entirely, not seeing any reason to stay since our mom left. My daddy's job consumed his time but for his two hobbies: sleep and hunting for women. I was shoved into a house full of strangers. And she wanted me to "stop crying."

Where
Do I fit?
Where is
My opening?
Must I create it for
Myself?

"You're too nice," my close friend told me after telling her about another ex who had taken advantage of me. I agreed, but I didn't see how that was really possible. *Isn't being nice a part of being a good person? Aren't I a good a person? So why don't people stay? Is this what I deserve?*

"Uni meaning one. Verse meaning song, you have a part to play in this song so grab that microphone and be brave sing your heart out on life's stage. **You cannot go back and make a brand new beginning. But you can start now and make a brand new . . . ending."**

There, in the words of Prince Ea's motivational video I'd almost passed scrolling through Facebook, I had found the Lego piece I needed. Something clicked in me that night and the tears would not stop falling. My family would never reunite in a single household again. No matter how much my friends tried they would never be able to provide me with the security I sought. My joy wasn't anyone else's responsibility. But just because no one else could give me the things I sought, that didn't mean that I couldn't have them. I still had Myself.

I decided then I would no longer be imprisoned by the impulse to find an easy solution so that I can return to life as usual. I will no longer look to other people to fill the voids in my life. I will no longer base my worth on how other people treat me.

I may never have all the answers and I know I'm going to make mistakes. My pain won't completely dissipate, but it will subside as long as I am actively striving to better myself. I will experience disappointment and pain but I will get through it, because that's how life is. Good times will come, along with the right people who will treat me the way I deserve because I know better than to allow anyone to give me any less.

Home of seven to a home of one
This isn't what you expected
But it's a just platform
To use the knowledge you've collected.

Black Girl Child from the Stars

BROOKE OBIE

I have enjoyed getting to know my mentee Shanai over the 2016–2017 school year. I have been incredibly moved by how cool, joyful, and talented she is and wanted to write a piece that shows how I have seen her rise up and change over the past year.

Joy spills out when her song is on
And everything must pause while she sings.
She throws her head back and you float
On her laugh
And know she's going to be okay.
That there's a cavern she dug
Where she stores up happiness
For the days when the moths come.

She doesn't blame them;
They're only doing what moths do
When they see a light.
When she shook their hand
And left stardust on their palm
They thought her magic meant she wasn't real.
But now through lessons far beyond her years
She's learned the body was made to heal itself.
Wounds clot, scabs stitch, scars are proof.
And now she knows surviving pain doesn't mean
Deserving it;
That strength is not a punishment;
That her questions aren't the problem, they're the point;
That her hair bends and curls and crowns her queen
Because she is enough;
That a Black girl child from the stars
Only belongs in the sky.

NANCY XU

YEARS AS MENTEE: 1

GRADE: Freshman

HIGH SCHOOL: The Spence School

BORN: Akron, OH

LIVES: Queens, NY

PUBLICATIONS AND RECOGNITIONS: Scholastic Art & Writing Award: Honorable Mention

MENTEE'S ANECDOTE: *I never had a lot of confidence in my writing skills before I joined Girls Write Now, and I think it would have stayed that way if I had never met Claire. Every week in our pair sessions, she always brings in interesting writing activities that spark my creativity, and she is always eager to give me a compliment after every piece I write (no matter how bad I secretly think it is). I am very glad I joined the program and I hope that the two of us will continue down our road as writers together.*

CLAIRE PURCELL

YEARS AS MENTOR: 1

OCCUPATION: Freelance Copywriter, Madison Square Garden

BORN: Wolverhampton, England

LIVES: Brooklyn, NY

MENTOR'S ANECDOTE: *I was nervous about becoming a mentor. I was concerned I had been out of my depth, but working with Nancy has been a joy. Over the course of the year, we have spent hours furiously scribbling in coffee shops all over New York, each exploring the limitless possibilities of our imagination. And through all our sessions, Nancy continues to inspire me. She juggles writing with music, athletics, and math competitions—but has always found the time to develop as a writer. She epitomizes the fact that if you are passionate and driven, you are unstoppable—and I cannot wait to see what she does next.*

The Extra Eye

NANCY XU

The current environmental issues will be exacerbated in the near future if nothing is done today. This is my form of rising to speak on an issue that threatens the world.

We were the only ones left.

Our last neighbors, along with their miniature house on short, wobbly stilts, drowned in the hungry waves just a few days ago, after a mild rainstorm.

We watched them struggling to keep their heads and their Nethernam passports above water. We watched them clinging for dear life onto the sturdy stilts that held up our house. We watched them as they floated away in the water, bobbing up and down like a boat lost at sea.

Daddy jumped in after them. He never came back.

I wiped away tears from the corners of my eyes and plunged my hands into the murky gray water. When I was seven, you could see the bottom of the water with the naked eye. Now all that is left to see is floating debris and fish skulls.

"Dawn Mong!" Mommy shrilled. Her voice used to be much more piercing to the ears; now, it sounded like a muted violin. "Take your hands out of there right now!"

I sighed and pulled out my hands. They had become the same color as the ocean, the same murky gray.

"Come back in for lunch!" Mommy yelled again. "I caught a fish the other day."

"But Mommy! That fish has three eyes! We can't eat that."

"What are you talking about? Don't be stupid. It's just a normal fish."

Murky gray clouds floated across the sky and hurried away. Raindrops dripped onto the back of my neck and rolled down my spine. They were ice cold.

Our dwelling is not an exceptional one. Mommy said she and Daddy built a miniature house out of wood that had been passed down by my grandpa, my daddy's daddy. He was a famous environmentalist of the twenty-second century and personally imported materials from the northern parts of South America, a place he called "rain forest." He told my parents that the wood was very precious and that eventually it would come in handy. He told Mommy and Daddy that when the water got high, they would have to take our house apart and rebuild it on top of wooden stilts, but at the time they thought him absurd and laughed it off. Only later, after the water level reached their kneecaps, did they realize their own absurdity.

I sat down at the dinner table and stared at the plate of the three-eyed fish in front of me. The three eyes stared back. A bolt of lightning flashed behind me, illuminating all three eyes into an eerie yellowish glow. "Mommy, I really don't think we can eat this fish—"

"Oh Dawn Mong, don't be so absurd," she interrupted me and passed over a spoon. I took it. "It's simply a different species of fish than those we've been eating. That's all. There's definitely nothing wrong with this fish." She took a fork for herself and plucked out a fish eye. "See? Now it's just a normal fish."

Another bolt of lightning flashed behind me. I felt the

wooden stilts beneath me wobble back and forth in the wind. They seemed ready to give way at any moment.

The two remaining eyes stared back at me as if the fish was scrutinizing its prey. *Eat me if you dare, eat me, eat me*, it taunted. Mommy sliced off the tail of the fish with a plastic knife and took a bite. She cringed at the taste but quickly replaced her disgust with what she perceived to be a pleasant smile. "See? It's not bad at all. It's just a normal fish."

The sound of the raindrops picked up pace. I stabbed at the two remaining eyes of the fish.

"Mom," I said. "If the current situation continues, we will die with or without this three-eyed fish. A three-eyed fish without an eye does not make it a two-eyed fish."

All four stilts collapsed at once under us.

I woke up, finding myself on the floor. Beads of sweat rolled down my neck. *It is only a dream*, I thought. *Nethernam does not exist, and it will never exist. I will personally make sure of it.*

"Wake up, Dawn! You're going to be late for school," Mom shrilled. Her voice was high-pitched, as usual.

"Mom." I stared into her eyes anxiously. "Fish only have two eyes, right?"

"No, honey. *Of course* they have three eyes. Everyone knows that." The edges of her lips curled into a smirk.

I rolled my eyes at her and hurried out the door.

I made a few mental notes to myself:

Mental note #1: Dig out the milk carton in the middle of the garbage bag and move it into the recycling bin.

Mental note #2: Yell at Tom, who dumped it in there in the first place.

Mental note #3: Fish will *never* have three eyes. Not if I have got anything to do with it.

They Told Her

CLAIRE PURCELL

In amidst the political turmoil of the past year, the strength and solidarity of womankind has stood out like a shining beacon. This piece is inspired by fierce women everywhere.

They told her she could not. So she learned to do it better than they ever could.

They told her she sounded shrill. So she learned to speak in measured tones and e-nun-ci-ate so they could understand her points without being offended by her confidence.

They told her not to be so emotional. So she learned to harness her sensitivity and elevate the human spirit in a way that they never would.

They told her, "Sorry, but Roger the Intern really deserved that promotion; yes he has less experience but he really shows great promise." So she took her expertise elsewhere and rose to the top.

They told her, that is a man's job. So she told them that if she ever found a man who was anywhere nearly as competent as she was, she would be sure to let him know that his job was already taken.

They told her, do not worry, nobody expects you to be able to do that. So she rose above their expectations—and her own—to find that she did not have any limits, after all.

They told her, it is not your place. So she searched for her place in the world, and found that it was wherever she damn well pleased.

They told her, you have been warned, you have been given an explanation. So above all else, she persisted.

And after a while, she realized that she did not need to be told. So she forged her own path, pursued her own passions, and stood for her own values.

She rose. She spoke. *She told them.* And she changed the world.

EN YU ZHANG

YEARS AS MENTEE: 1
GRADE: Sophomore
HIGH SCHOOL: Stuyvesant High School
BORN: Hong Kong, SAR
LIVES: Brooklyn, NY

MENTEE'S ANECDOTE: *I am terrible with deadlines and time management, so a portion of our relationship can be summed up as Elizabeth reminding me to send her my writing before meeting up, and about deadlines in general. But it is really fun to just talk with her; I am a closed-off person, an introvert who does not typically venture beyond my set confines, but I get to open myself up a bit, learn more things about the world, talk Trump and politics, complain about school, and write with my awesome mentor. Time just flies when we meet up.*

ELIZABETH KOSTER

YEARS AS MENTOR: 1
OCCUPATION: Creative Writing Teacher, West Brooklyn Community High School
BORN: New York, NY
LIVES: New York, NY
PUBLICATIONS AND RECOGNITIONS: "Modern Love," *New York Times*, August 2014

MENTOR'S ANECDOTE: *En Yu and I share a similar dark, dry sense of humor. We forward each other* Saturday Night Live *videos and pepper political rants into our writing sessions. As a nonfiction writer who can not write fiction to save my life, I am awed by En Yu's ability to create richly realized characters' worlds from her imagination. Also, she taught me how to use Google Docs to edit in real time—I can see what she is writing, as she types, and we can communicate on the document itself—and that is just astounding.*

On Thermodynamics: A Reflection

EN YU ZHANG

This piece explores my work ethic as distilled into the laws and equations of the thermodynamic world.

Second law of thermodynamics: the entropy of an isolated system always increases

∴ Energy must be added to maintain the integrity of the system

Since an isolated system must constantly have an input of energy so as to not fall into disorder, then that system is not truly isolated; the energy must come from another source. However, the idea of a truly isolated system is a beautiful idea. The mind, the consciousness, is the epitome of such a system, contained within one person, seemingly impenetrable but so easily molded by the outside world. And just as the mind is influenced by reality, the perspective of reality is shaped by the mind.

As such, a reclusive person like myself has a more closed-off worldview. At home, I keep myself within as much as possible. Staying confined to that place allows my mind the liberty of not straying beyond my vision of a comfortable world. It is not that I find the outside world to be frightening and stress-inducing, with the challenges of human interaction; I simply am satisfied with such a "low" standard. There was nothing wrong with the hours of solitude I went through every day, nothing wrong with the monotony.

I knew exactly what activities I could do in that room: distract myself with the computer, read a book, take a nap, or do homework. Of course, the last option was only there to trick my mind into thinking that I was on the verge of productivity at any moment. I kept my world under strict control, repeating these activities in orders of my choosing, needing not to think long and hard about anything. As such, I lived in a tranquil, comforting world, just doing whatever I wished, without concerns about future repercussions. Inside my head full of illusions, I thought that I had already fulfilled what I needed to do each day.

The realization came slowly to me, through seeing my peers climb their way up, achieving beyond what I barely even thought necessary. There was the girl, after last year's annual math competition, who studied intensively for this year's, in contrast to myself, who was only reminded of its existence a month before the test, and then still did nothing. There was the girl doubling up in precalc and calculus while being a track star. There was the math team genius who scored a perfect 150 on the math competition. There was the classmate whose eloquence in class I could never hope to emulate. As I directed my eyes beyond my bubble, to expand beyond myself, I saw myself as nothing. I was nothing, just empty space in comparison, whittling my time away in comfort induced by blindness. An isolated system would yield nothing of the sort that they reached.

My isolated system could not be maintained at this point. My sleeping habits were jumbled up, my homework done halfheartedly, my grades great but nothing all too stellar. Everything was becoming disordered, tearing apart at the seams.

Free energy $= \Delta G = \Delta H - T\Delta S$

ΔH = *change in enthalpy*

T = *temperature*

ΔS = *change in entropy*

A reaction is spontaneous, that is, occurs when $\Delta G < 0$.

∴ *Spontaneity is favored by an increase in entropy and a decrease in enthalpy.*

This begs the fundamental question of whether or not I was able to take action. I tried, perhaps bearing the best of intentions, but not the most unbending will. I would have a somewhat productive day, only to spoil it at the end by falling asleep hours too early. Sometimes it was waking up early on a weekend morning to complete one assignment, only to then succumb to the computer, and be released of the trance in the evening.

I am spurred to action when everything undoes itself even further, becomes even more disorderly, and when there seems to be less work. As such, spontaneity is reached, and I get to work. Reverse psychology acts at its finest here; I become increasingly more motivated if the world pushes against me, as if to prove to it that I can do what is seemingly impossible for me.

Then other days, when I seem to have more of my world

under control, perhaps after a productive yesterday, the days I have difficult assignments I want to avoid, then I regress;

there is no spontaneity then.

There is no change.

Such is the continuation of the cycle.

Scaling the Walls

ELIZABETH KOSTER

This piece explores my relationship to the changing political climate.

"If you ever need an abortion," my mother told me, taking my hand and gripping it tightly, "tell me, and I'll get you one." She stared at me hard. "I mean it," she said. "If it's illegal here, we'll fly to London."

I was sixteen, and the Bush administration was toying with the idea of making abortion illegal again. But I did not know why she was acting so intense.

"Okay," I assured her. I still remember the pleading look in her eyes.

Years after my mother died, in my early thirties, I would find a medical questionnaire she had answered:

Circle if you have ever had: Appendicitis   Tonsillitis Abortion

She circled "Abortion" and scribbled "1960."

I stared at the paper. She had been twenty. I had not known. And who would the father have been?

Brenda, her friend, told me recently that my mother had to travel to the Dominican Republic to get an abortion. Only, when she returned to the States, she started bleeding on the street. Brenda took her to the hospital, and said the nurses "treated her like she was a murderer."

It would be thirteen years until *Roe v. Wade.*

Years of coat hanger abortions and backroom botched operations.

My mother was a publishing executive in the early 1970s—a time when women didn't typically hold such positions. She'd had to fight for this. She faced resistance from her male colleagues to gain paperback rights to Erica Jong's *Fear of Flying,* which would become an iconic feminist novel. "If you don't publish this book," my mother had said, "then I quit!"

Were she alive today, she would be appalled by the new White House administration.

At the Women's March in Washington, D.C., I marched with parents and children who chanted with the crowd.

"I can't believe I'm still protesting this shit," one older woman had written.

Neither can I, I thought. Neither can I.

I marched, with my mother's presence by my side.

RISE SPEAK CHANGE

PROMPTS AND WRITING EXERCISES
FOR INDIVIDUALS AND GROUPS

At Girls Write Now, we provide a platform for the voices of our community. Mentors and mentees explore the power of words in different forms, developing strong skills and bonds in the process. In the monthly workshops that frame our annual program and curriculum, we begin the process of sharing—and listening—before bringing our work to the world. As an intergenerational community of women with diverse backgrounds, identities, and beliefs, we collaborate on genres like travel writing, family memoir, found poetry, one-woman show, and short story. Through a communal force more powerful than any one of us alone, we take creative risks and become artists, activists, and friends who choose to rise, speak, and change together.

Use the prompts on the following pages to engage in advocating your own voice to *Rise Speak Change* with the Girls Write Now community and beyond.

—EMILY YOST, Senior Program Coordinator

JOURNALISM: TRAVEL WRITING

In these exercises you will identify and describe places you have traveled. You can use these depictions to write a review or recommendation; both are types of travel journalism.

PART ONE: Travel Writing Brainstorm
Make a list of the places you have traveled. We would suggest listing your neighborhood and the neighborhoods around your home, cities, states, and countries you have visited. After you complete your list, circle your top choice from each category.

PART TWO: Defining Destinations
Use the five senses—sight, sound, smell, taste, and touch/feel—to describe the three top choices from your travel writing brainstorm list.

PART THREE: Travel Writing: Reviews and Recommendations
Write a review or recommendation of a location for someone to visit. A recommendation should be a positive commentary that expresses the unique importance for the reader to visit that place. A review should be a critical analysis of a location that includes both pros and cons to help the reader make a decision. Be sure to include food to eat, sights/landmarks to visit, and tips for travel!

RECOMMENDED READING:

"36 Hours in . . ." by *The New York Times*
"BuzzFeed Travel" by *BuzzFeed*
Under the Tuscan Sun by Frances Mayes
See Aliyah Felix's piece "That Special Charm"
    for an example of local travel writing.

MEMOIR: FAMILY MEMOIR

In these exercises, you will examine the characters that are the real people in your own families to create a memoir piece. There should also be an overall theme woven into your family memoir that portrays a personal lesson you've learned.

PART ONE: Family Prompts
- What are the traits of your family members that make them unique?
- What are some traditions that you celebrate with your family?
- What are some virtues that you have learned from your family or have been passed down to you?

PART TWO: Thematic Prompts
Common themes in memoirs are forgiveness, fairness, identity, and personal growth. Which of the above themes appeals to you the most? Once you choose a theme, list a few memories of family moments that complement your motif.

PART THREE: Vignette Writing
A vignette is a short scene that focuses on one specific moment or character. Using the unique characters of your family members and your chosen theme, write a detailed scene of a memory you have that expresses a personal lesson you have learned.

RECOMMENDED READING:

Fun Home: A Family Tragicomic by Alison Bechdel
Where Am I Now: True Stories of Girlhood
  and Accidental Fame by Mara Wilson
Men We Reaped: A Memoir by Jesmyn Ward
See Kayla Glemaud's "Grilled Cheese" for
  use of voice in a memoir.

Found poetry is a type of poetry where the author repurposes other words and images to create a new poem. We suggest using magazine or newspaper articles to create erasure poems or collages! You can also use the exercise below to create a word bank of your own vocabulary to craft a found poem.

PART ONE:
List ten words that describe your present environment; classroom, desk, bedroom, kitchen, etc.

PART TWO:
List ten words that describe how you are currently feeling.

PART THREE:
Looking at your lists, use your new word bank of vocabulary to create a four-line poem. The words or phrases do not have to make sense—explore and see what you come up with!

RECOMMENDED READING:

Milk and Honey by Rupi Kaur
There Are More Beautiful Things Than Beyoncé
    by Morgan Parker
"Black Girl Magic" by Mahogany L. Browne
See Winkie Ma's "Welcome to Madame Zhu's;
    In the Words of Mr. Trump" for an example of a
    descriptive poem.

FICTION: SHORT STORY

In these exercises, you will create a piece of short fiction by developing a well-rounded character and sensory scene that will be used to tell a story.

PART ONE: Character Prompts
Think about a person you recently saw but have never spoken to. For example, someone on the subway or who you pass in the hallway or on campus often. Use this person as inspiration and answer the following questions to create a sketch of a fictional character for your short story.
- What does this person look like?
- What is their style?
- What are their likes?
- What are their dislikes?
- What are their goals and dreams?

PART TWO: Scenario Prompts
Get to know your character more by placing them in different scenes! Figure out how your character would react to new situations by writing them into at least four of the scenes below.
1. Your character is about to leave for their first job interview but can't find their car keys. Where do they search first? How do they get to the interview?
2. Your character is planning their ideal birthday celebration. Where is it? Who is invited? Why do they like the thing they have chosen to do?
3. Your character has to confess something to their sister. What are they confessing? Why has it taken them so long to talk to their sister about this?
4. Your character has to redecorate their living room. What

things do they choose to add? Why are these objects important to them?

5. Your character is on a breakfast date. What do they order for breakfast? Where are they? Who is their date?

6. Your character is twenty-five years old and just discovered that they have an identical twin! How do they react to their twin the first time they meet? How are they different or similar to their twin?

7. Your character just received an envelope in the mail that will change their life forever. What information is in the envelope? How do they react?

PART THREE: Revision (Partner Exercise)

It's important to include revising and editing in your storytelling process. Read over your scenarios and list three "glows" and three "grows." "Glows" are the sections of the piece that you enjoy and want to keep. "Grows" are sections of the piece that you want to change or edit. Find a partner to read your scenarios and ask them to evaluate your work as well!

RECOMMENDED READING:

We Love You, Charlie Freeman by Kaitlyn Greenidge
Re Jane by Patricia Park
Juliet Takes a Breath by Gabby Rivera
See Madiha Alam's "Closure" for an example
   of a short story.

ABOUT GIRLS WRITE NOW

For nearly twenty years, **Girls Write Now** has been a leader in the arts education space as the first writing and mentoring organization for girls. We match teen girls with women professional writers and digital media makers as their personal mentors. Our mentees—over 95 percent girls of color and 90 percent high need—are published in outlets including *The New York Times*, *Newsweek*, and *BuzzFeed*, perform at Lincoln Center and the United Nations, and earn hundreds of Scholastic Art & Writing Awards. 100 percent of Girls Write Now seniors go on to college.

Girls Write Now has been distinguished three times by the White House as one of the nation's top youth programs and twice by the Nonprofit Excellence Awards as one of New York's top ten nonprofits. Reaching thousands of girls, the organization is a founding partner of the STARS Citywide Girls Initiative. Girls Write Now has received the Youth INC Innovators Award, NBCUniversal's 21st Century Solutions prize for social innovation through media arts, and the Diane von Furstenberg (DVF) People's Choice nomination.

Our annual anthology has received the Outstanding Book of the Year award by the Independent Publisher Book Awards, and has earned honors from the International Book Awards, The New York Book Festival, the National Indie Excellence Awards, and the Next Generation Indie Book Awards. The anthology has also received Honorable Mention from the San Francisco Book Festival and the Paris Book Festival.

LITERARY PARTNERS

Alliance for Young Artists & Writers

Amy Morrill Charitable Trust

AOL #BUILTBYGIRLS

AOL Cambio Huffington Post

Atlantic Philanthropies

Barnard College

Barnes & Noble

Bay & Paul Foundations

BBDO

Blanchette Hooker Rockefeller Fund

Book Group

Book Riot

Brookby Foundation

Bustle

Charles Lawrence Keith & Clara S. Miller Foundation

Children's Book Council

Chime for Change

Columbia University Artists/ Teachers Program

Constantine Family Charitable Fund

Etruscan Press

Feminist Press

Flavorpill

Fletcher & Co

F(r)iction

Fusion

General Society of Mechanics and Tradesmen of the City of New York

Hammer Family Charitable Foundation

HarperCollins

HBO

H.I.P. Lit

Hive NYC Learning Network

Houghton Mifflin Harcourt

Hyde & Watson Foundation

Impact Investing Foundation

Independent Publisher

Jenjo Foundation

John Wiley & Sons

Kelly Writers House, University of
    Pennsylvania

Knopf

Lamprophonic

Lenny Letter

Lotos Foundation

MAKERS

Mattel

McNally Jackson Books

National Book Foundation

Newmark Grubb Knight Frank

New-York Historical Society

New York Shakespeare Festival

New York Women in Communica-
    tions

New York Women's Foundation

News Corp

Newsweek

One Teen Story

Open Road Integrated Media

Open Society Foundations

Outbrain

PaperGirl Collection

Parsons The New School for Design

Patrina Foundation

Pen + Brush

Penguin Random House

PIMCO Foundation

Poetry Society

Poets & Writers

PR News

RBC

Reso Foundation

Riverhead Books

Rona Jaffe Foundation

Schwartz & Wade

She Knows

She Writes Press

Sills Family Foundation

Simon & Schuster

South Wind Foundation

Storch Amini & Munves PC

StoryBundle

Student Science News

Tin House

VIDA: Women in Literary Arts

Wall Street Journal

Women's eNews/Teen Voices

Women's Media Center Live

Workman Publishing

Writers House

YesYes Books

Young to Publishing Group

Youth INC

GIRLS WRITE NOW 2017

STAFF

Maya Nussbaum,
Founder & Executive Director

Tracy Steele,
Director of Operations

Maria Campo,
Director of Programs & Outreach

Emily Wurgaft,
Director of Development

Naomi Solomon,
College Bound Program Manager

Emily Yost,
Senior Program Coordinator

Isabel Abrams,
Senior Program Coordinator

Sierra Ritz,
Program Coordinator

Molly MacDermot,
Senior Communications Advisor & Editor

Caitlyn Pang,
Special Assistant to the Executive Director

Sandra Pons,
Senior Development Coordinator

INTERNS

Nikila Cranage

Erica Galluscio

Julia Lubey

Nina Luo

Jessica Merino

Melina Morris

BOARD OF DIRECTORS

Gloria Jacobs,
Board Chair

Ellen Sweet, *Vice Chair*

Erica Mui, *Treasurer*

Elaine Stuart-Shah,
Board Development Chair

Marci Alboher

Ellen Archer
Galina Espinoza
Michelle Levin
Karen Bishop Morris
Maya Nussbaum
Laura Scileppi

YOUTH BOARD
Tuhfa Begum
Romaissaa Benzizoune
Arnell Calderon
Nyasiah Colón
Chanelle Ferguson
Teamaré Gaston
Rahat Huda
Caroline Lin
Tasha McCalla
Mikey Mercedes
Nahima Uddin
Sharon Young
Luljeta Zenka

CRAFT TALK SPEAKERS
Jennifer Baker
Mahogany Browne
Annie Daly
Sarah Ellison
Tavi Gevinson
Kaitlyn Greenidge
Hallie Haas
Rupi Kaur
Sarah Kay
Jamilah King
Heather Kristin
Patricia Park
Morgan Parker
Bonnie Pipkin
Amy Richards
Maureen Sherry
Mara Wilson

CHAPTERS READING SERIES KEYNOTE SPEAKERS
Hala Alyan
Emma Cline
Karina Glaser
Emma Straub

ANTHOLOGY SUPPORTERS

We are grateful to the countless institutions and individuals who have supported our work through their generous contributions. Visit our website at www.girlswritenow.org to view the extended list.

Girls Write Now would like to thank Random House—and their partners at Scribe and Sterling Pierce—for their help producing this year's anthology, as part of their Random Acts of Kindness initiative.

Girls Write Now would like to thank Amazon Literary Partnership, which provided the charitable contribution that made possible this year's anthology.

The anthology is supported, in part, by public funds from the National Endowment for the Arts; the New York State Council on the Arts, a State Agency; and the New York City Department of Cultural Affairs, in partnership with the City Council, the Manhattan Borough President's Office, and STARS Citywide Girls Initiative.